Interfaith Encounters
in America

Interfaith Encounters in America

KATE McCARTHY

RUTGERS UNIVERSITY PRESS

NEW BRUNSWICK, NEW JERSEY, AND LONDON

LIBRARY OF CONGRESS CATALOGING-IN-PUBLICATION DATA

McCarthy, Kate, 1962–
   Interfaith encounters in America / Kate McCarthy.
     p. cm.
   Includes bibliographical references and index.
   ISBN-13: 978–0–8135–4029–0 (hardcover : alk. paper)
   ISBN-13: 978–0–8135–4030–6 (pbk. : alk. paper)
   1. United States—Religion—1960– I. Title.
   BL2525.M393 2007
   201.'50973—dc22   2006021863

A British Cataloguing-in-Publication record is available
for the British Library.

Manufactured in the United States of America

CONTENTS

ACKNOWLEDGMENTS

This book would still be a collection of clippings, overdue library books, and notes scribbled on cocktail napkins if it weren't for the extraordinary support of my colleagues, friends, and family.

For research assistance I am grateful to Arin Cole and especially Rebecca Anker, who also transcribed and coded interviews and helped me through the editorial process. Stephanie Hamel gave me valuable insight into using grounded theory to get the most from interview data.

I am lucky to work in what must be the most collegial department in the history of academia. My colleagues in the Department of Religious Studies at California State University, Chico gave me wise feedback on drafts, picked up my slack in departmental duties, and provided a warm and supportive intellectual community. I am also grateful to California State University, Chico for generously supporting this project through grants and release time.

To those who took time to talk to a stranger with a tape recorder about their interfaith experiences, I want to express my deep thanks and hope that, by way of small repayment, I have told their stories well.

Adi Hovav at Rutgers University Press has been a generous and insightful editor, offering helpful feedback throughout the writing process and gracious accommodation of my sundry delays.

My friends Elizabeth Renfro, Carol Burr, Lisa Emmerich, and Lori Beth Way created a circle of support that made anything seem possible, and always called a meeting just in time. Piper Bravo is the best friend every woman wishes she had—back-up mother to my children, bearer of emergency chocolate, sister of my heart. Without her, things would surely have fallen apart.

For my children, Duncan and Lilly, this work has been measured in lack—tuck-ins deferred, sick days spent on the floor of my office, pizzas passing as dinner, and never enough time to do nothing. Fortunately, their father is the best mother in the world. I dedicate this to you, Rich, though it has no value next to what you've given me: guilt-free time, a keen editorial eye, unutterable kindness, and the daily joy of irreducible otherness.

Interfaith Encounters
in America

Introduction

The volume of American conversations about religion has perhaps never been higher. Both the frequency and the stridency of references to religion in national discourse—from talk radio to popular films to media analyses—have been turned up high. Terrorist attacks keep us fixed on an abhorrent version of militant Islam. *The Passion of the Christ* and *The Da Vinci Code* make blockbuster material (and controversy) of the origins of Christianity. The best-selling *Left Behind* novels do the same for the apocalyptic visions at the other end of the New Testament. The 2004 presidential election, we are told, was decided by religiously driven moral values. A majority of Americans are reported to believe that religious differences are the biggest obstacle to world peace. But beneath all this noise are quieter conversations about what it means to be religious in America today—conversations among recent immigrants about how to adapt their practices to life in a new land; conversations among young people finding new meaning in religions rejected by their parents; conversations among the religiously unaffiliated about eclectic new spiritualities encountered in magazines, book groups, or online.

History tells us that this is nothing new. Americans have been talking about religion since the first European settlers arrived in the New World, and the discussion has always occurred at the strange intersection of freedom and passion. The Puritans who came to America seeking religious freedom had to reconcile their intense religious commitment both with the presence of non-Christian natives and almost immediate internal religious dissent. The framers of the Constitution built in the protection of a religious diversity that would soon outstrip their imaginations. What it means to be religious in America, then, has never been a given but rather something to think and talk about, to consciously construct, and to negotiate with others who have an equal stake in the society but may see things very differently.

Surveys consistently show that Americans are among the most religiously committed citizens of all industrialized societies, somehow dodging the forces of secularization that have transformed Japan and western Europe (Pew Research Center 2002). But this religiousness is not monolithic. The United States is surely not the only society to include multiple religious traditions, and Diana Eck's (2001) assertion that it is now "the world's most religiously diverse nation" may obscure the ongoing overwhelming dominance of Christianity in that mix, but it is true that in the United States religious diversity is vast, and somehow more meaning-laden than it seems to be elsewhere. Perhaps it is because freedom of religious expression and the prohibition against a state religion are enshrined in the country's most important document. Perhaps it is the power of the American unity-in-diversity myth that makes the mix of American identities not just a social fact but the stuff of children's pageants and holiday parades. Perhaps it is the role of religion in establishing the nation's unique sense of purpose. Whatever the reason, when Americans talk about differences of religion, they are not just discussing alternative visions of the afterlife or comparing ritual practices, but are talking about what it means to be American.

In recent years, of course, those discussions have become extremely contentious. There is a culture war underway, we are told, and we'd best get clear about which side we are on. We are all now either red state or blue state, pro-choice or pro-family, Fox News or *Democracy Now!*, yellow ribbons or peace signs. While these two sides have a great deal to say *about* each other, they seem to do very little talking *with* each other. It is in that context that I have been drawn to investigate American interfaith conversations, the mostly quiet, mostly unrecognized efforts of Christians, Jews, Muslims, Buddhists, Hindus, Sikhs, and others to understand and collaborate with each other in the shaping of their identities and their communities. In these conversations, American commitments to religious particularity and to the values of a pluralistic society—commitments typically kept separate and often viewed as inimical to each other—are laid on the table together, with interesting results. Might some of what has been learned by participants in these exchanges across religious lines be of use in speaking about and across what divides us as citizens?

In order to address that possibility, this book investigates interfaith encounters in five sites of American experience. Chapter one offers an overview of the most elite of these encounters, the intellectual exchanges among scholars of philosophy, religion, and theology, current participants in a conversation that has been going on for over a century about how to make intellectual sense of conflicting claims about what matters most. Subsequent chapters track the relevance and applicability of these ideas "on the ground," in different settings where real people of different religious identities come together—intentionally—for some shared purpose: national interfaith public policy initiatives (chapter two), local interfaith councils (chapter three), interfaith families (chapter four), and online interfaith discussion groups (chapter five). This is not, then, a study in religious conflict, though each of these encounters has its moments of tension. It is also not an ethnographic study of American religious communities, though I hope it will provide some insight into the lived religious experience of a variety of Americans. It is rather a study of intersections— between people of different religions, between public life and private faith, between theoretical constructs and lived reality. In these intersections, a small but significant segment of the American population is raising important questions—and offering a few answers—as to how we might live with our deepest differences, and in the process they are also making space for *being religious* in new and distinctly American ways.

Diversity and Pluralism in American Religion

We learn in grammar class that "plural" means "more than one." In matters of religion, though, a more complex understanding of pluralism is needed. Most scholars today distinguish between diversity, the simple fact of social difference, and pluralism, which is taken to refer to some kind of affirmative attitude toward that diversity. As we'll see in chapter one, pluralism can also refer technically to a set of theological positions regarding religious difference, salvation, and the nature of religious truth. The United States has always been a place of religious diversity, even long before the country had that name, when countless indigenous communities maintained their own complex belief and ceremonial systems. European settlers brought their own complex and conflicting religious worldviews as they sought to establish themselves in the New World, and each new wave of immigration has added to the mix. As a national rhetoric about religious and other forms of difference developed, the word "pluralism" has taken on complex meanings.

William Hutchison's 2003 study, *Religious Pluralism in America*, helpfully tracks the "contentious history" of this ideal at the heart of national self-understanding, drawing not only on traditional historical sources but also on the stuff of popular culture—cartoons, secular and sacred music, architecture, fiction, etc.—in which the complexity of attitudes toward religious difference is displayed. What Hutchison demonstrates vividly is that while Americans have always claimed allegiance to the ideal of religious pluralism, the *meaning* of pluralism has shifted over the centuries. From the revolutionary period through the nineteenth century, he argues, pluralism took the rather limited form of *toleration*, the willingness to permit different groups to live free of legal and social persecution, but largely as outsiders to the formal and informal structures of social power. Such tolerance is typical when one group enjoys such overwhelming majority, and when the minority groups offer no significant threat to the freedom and prosperity of the dominant.

A new understanding of pluralism developed in the twentieth century—driven powerfully, Hutchison documents, by the effects of interfaith military experiences in World War II and the pressure to create a unified American spiritual bulwark against atheist communism and fascism By midcentury the prevailing sense of pluralism was one of *inclusion*, in which non-Protestant groups (that is, Catholics and Jews) were at least formally included in the new reigning understanding of the American religious identity as "Judeo-Christian." In this period, the Protestant establishment expanded to become a tripartite mainstream, in a model made famous by sociologist Will Herberg's 1955 *Protestant-Catholic-Jew* (196–218). It is now easy to see the limitations on the inclusiveness of this arrangement, however effective it was in marshaling diverse religious constituencies for a common political agenda. Hutchison points to the design of the Air Force Academy Chapel in Colorado Springs, completed in 1962, as a symbol of this inadequacy. At the cutting edge of interfaith architecture for its time, the chapel nonetheless makes an important statement in the fact that the worship spaces set aside for Jews and Catholics account, together, for only 20 percent of the chapel's space, and are subterranean (209–213). Looking at images of this chapel, I recalled my own experience at the "interfaith" church on the campus of the liberal arts college I attended in the early 1980s. As a Catholic, I attended Mass in a small carpeted room in the basement, beneath the soaring nineteenth-century Protestant space above. But for me, at least, the iconography upstairs was familiar. The "tripartite settlement" (Wuthnow 2005, 30) was most problematic for Jews, who were savvy to the ambiguity of being "included" in a religious system, something called "Judeo-Christianity," that effectively represented Jews as one more Christian denomination (Wuthnow 2005, 32). The frequency with which I hear otherwise culturally literate undergraduates refer to Jewish "churches" attests to the persistence of this effect.

Finally, since the 1960s, Hutchison observes Americans groping toward a new, nonassimilative model of pluralism, one driven by the effects of liberalized immigration policies and the civil rights and other empowerment movements of the 1960s and 1970s. Hutchison calls this new approach, not yet fully realized and powerfully resisted, a "pluralism of participation," in the sense that it implies "a mandate for individuals and groups (including, quite importantly, ethnic and racial groups) to share responsibility for the forming and implementing of the society's agenda" (7). In this kind of pluralism, particular identities are not compromised for the sake of inclusion in an established order; that order itself becomes something to be assembled through conscious processes of negotiation.

This sense of pluralism as a national virtue, at least in the abstract, has evolved in the context of dramatically changing demographics. It is important to have a sense of those demographics in order to make sense of the interfaith encounters reported here, but it is frustratingly difficult to offer statistical reports on the American religious identity. Official census surveys don't include religion, and different religious communities have vastly different ways of measuring affiliation. Must you be a registered member of a religious institution? Have participated in at least one gathering? Do children count? What if a religion is an important part of your cultural identity but you don't ascribe to most of its beliefs? In the face of such complexity, the most reliable religious data is self-reported; that is, the best description of a person's religious identity is the one used by that person.

Of course, allowing people to identify their own religious affiliation permits great variety. Among the most recent comprehensive surveys is the American Religious Identification Survey (ARIS), conducted in 2001 by researchers at the City University of New York (Mayer and Kosmin 2001), which proceeded from the simple question, asked of over 50,000 people, "What is your religion, if any?" Responses to this opening question generated over 100 different responses, which the ARIS researchers then sorted into 65 categories. One of the most dramatic findings of the survey was the rapid growth of the "no religion" groups, which include atheists, agnostics, humanists, and those identifying themselves as "secular." Representing only 8 percent of the population in 1990, this group made up 14 percent in the 2001 survey. Of the huge majority who still identify with a religion, the vast majority, over three quarters of the total U.S. population, is Christian. Where, then, is all this celebrated diversity? First, though the fact is often overlooked, it is *within* the Christian population. Fully 35 of the 65 total religious groups in the ARIS survey are Christian, including— along with Catholics, mainline Protestants, and Evangelicals—Jehovah's Witnesses, Mormons, Quakers, Pentecostals, Christian Scientists, and the Salvation Army. Surely there is as much diversity among these groups, especially when ethnic and regional variety is considered, as there is among, say, Presbyterians and (non-Christian) Unitarians.

But non-Christians, while still only a small minority, have significantly redefined religion in America in the past two generations. The ARIS survey puts non-Christian religious affiliation at just 4 percent; other recent studies push it to 11 percent (Barna 2004) and 13 percent (Wuthnow 2005). Whatever the actual number, it represents a dramatic increase in a very short period of time. Most of the growth in non-Christian religions can be accounted for by the changing ethnic makeup of the United States since the McCarran-Walter Act of 1952 removed the ban on Asian immigration, and the Immigration and Citizenship Act of 1965 that abolished the immigration quota system. In the decades that followed, the Hindu

and Buddhist populations swelled from several thousand each to approximately a million each as Indian, Chinese, Japanese, Vietnamese, Thai,
Indonesian, and other immigrant communities have implanted their traditions in American communities. Even more dramatically, Islam is now
one of the fastest-growing religions in the United States, more than doubling its population in just the period from 1990 to 2001 (ARIS). The
"religious organizations" heading in telephone books across American
cities, no longer limited to churches and the occasional synagogue, now
includes mosques, Hindu temples, Sikh gurdwaras, and Buddhist meditation centers.[1] The religions of these immigrant communities are dramatically restructuring traditional models of "interfaith" efforts, which used
to refer to the work of Catholics, Protestants, and Jews trying to better understand each other. Community-based interfaith projects today might
involve Hmong elders educating neighbors about their shamanic practices, or Sikhs inviting other local religious groups to help celebrate the
opening of a new temple.

How these groups will define their place in the wider American society is an open question, informed not only by the attitudes and actions of
their more established neighbors, but also by the availability of a wider
set of options than were accessible to earlier generations for how to combine ethnic and religious identities with being American. Racial and ethnic empowerment movements of the 1960s and 1970s generated new ways
of thinking about diversity in which American identity could be hyphenated with other markers both as expressions of pride and as protest
against racism and forced assimilation. This approach is clearly compelling
to minority religious groups as well, as evidenced by a recent newspaper
advertisement run by the Council on American Islamic Relations (CAIR)
that features a young woman wearing a headscarf proudly stating, "I am
an American, I am a Muslim" (cited in Takim 2004).

But it is not only immigrants and their children who account for the
new diversity of American religion. Since the 1960s, greater exposure to
nonwestern religions, as well as economic growth and social mobility and a
cultural mood encouraging challenges to tradition and authority (Lippy
1999, 50–51), have revived among U.S.-born Americans the long-standing
national tradition of spiritual exploration and experimentation. Americans,

it seems, have a deep-seated confidence in the therapeutic value of religion, and seek it out widely. As American religious historian Amanda Porterfield argues, this confidence is part of the pragmatic and aesthetic strains in American religion that links the eighteenth-century Great Awakening with the nineteenth-century Transcendentalism of Emerson and Thoreau and with today's unconventional spiritual shoppers. In each of these contexts, "thoughtful reformers applied themselves to the work of sifting through new forms of religious expression in order to lift out and carry forward their most salutary aspects" (Porterfield 2001, 229). For American Baby Boomers and their children, Hinduism, Buddhism, fragments of pre-Christian Paganism, and Native American traditions are all resources in this endeavor. "The expectation that spirituality should result in social and therapeutic benefit is a common one," Porterfield concludes, "and reflects the pragmatic orientation of American religion, as does the willingness on the part of many Americans to try out new forms of religious experience" (231). Porterfield also credits the impact of the feminist movement in this process. By raising awareness of gender as a social construct, deconstructing the patriarchal underpinnings of so much of western religion, and revisioning religious symbols and rituals in women-centered ways, feminism highlighted the constructed nature of all religious identities, "in turn making religion more malleable, more vulnerable, more subject to correction, and more humane than ever before" (167). The insistence that any conceptualization of religious diversity must be accountable not only to the particular identities of religious subgroups, but also to social justice is a legacy of the women's and civil rights movements that is heard in interfaith work today at every level.

What all of this means is that even the religious identities of Americans who have been here for generations no longer fit as neatly as they once did into traditional categories, even if the same boxes are still being checked on survey forms. Studies of American religion over the past generation suggest that our religious ideas and practices are no longer tightly fastened to specific texts and institutions; more and more, Americans espouse religious identities that are individual, eclectic, and dynamic (e.g., Bellah 1986, Hammond 1992, Wuthnow 1998, Cimino and Lattin 1998, Roof 1999). Those of the Baby Boom, "X," and "Y" generations increasingly live their religious lives in what Wade Clark Roof has called a "quest culture." Whether one is an eclectic seeker or a born-again dogmatist, there is emerging a common pattern of American religion as a conscious process of creative personal choice (Roof 1999). Interfaith encounters occur within and are an increasingly important element of this new American religious marketplace.

But this process of learning about each other is not always smooth. The inculturation of new religious minorities is not simply a matter of being welcomed by spiritually curious neighbors, but often involves conflict and controversy as previously unknown peoples and practices come up against both prejudice and authentic concerns about civic unity. It is in the public spaces of school, work, and the military that a society's real openness to minority religious groups gets tested. Diana Eck names just a few of the recent hotspots:

> Can a Sikh wear his turban on a hard-hat job or as part of his uniform in the U.S. army? Can a practitioner of Wicca exercise his or her religion on a Texas army base? Can a Sikh high school student carry the symbolic dagger of Sikh religious initiation to school? Will the Whirlpool Corporation in Nashville find a way for Muslim employees to meet their obligations for prayer? Does a Hindu temple have to look more "Spanish" to meet the planning board standards of Norwalk, California? Will a young Jain, an observant vegetarian, find the contents of the meals in her school cafeteria clearly marked? (Eck 2001, 8)

These questions suggest that the kind of participatory pluralism Hutchison sees struggling to be born will emerge, if it does, not so much out of philosophical and theological discourse, but out of the small negotiations of everyday life in a community.

Religion: The Missing Piece in Diversity Work

What do we bring to such negotiations? How do ordinary Americans think about religious otherness? In other domains of social difference—race, gender, class—a rudimentary knowledge base and working theoretical frameworks have developed over the past two generations to help us understand and appreciate each other, or at least mostly get along. Elementary school children learn something about the experience of African Americans in curricular units built around Martin Luther King Day. The feminist movement has given us a vocabulary for talking about domestic violence, employment discrimination, and gender stereotyping. Long before that, Marxist theorists offered analyses that allowed us to see economic classes in social structural rather than moral terms. None of these efforts is adequate and all face strong ongoing resistance, but the point is that there is a framework in place for conversations about diversity in these domains. Such is not the case, oddly enough, with religion. There is a reason why the activist and academic communities most assertive in promoting an appreciation of diversity in the areas of race, class, and gender have generally not put religious difference on the agenda: for many in these communities, religions themselves are seen as part of the traditional structures of social hierarchy and domination that their efforts seek to critique and dismantle, not as another aspect of cultural diversity to be celebrated.

The language of religious pluralism, then, rather than becoming part of the public conversations about diversity and multiculturalism, remains largely the language of specialists—sociologists who talk about assimilation, secularization, and privatization; theologians who talk about exclusivism, supercessionalism, and universalism; and church-state experts who talk about accommodationism and separationism. Ordinary Americans have little to draw on in assembling an understanding of religious diversity, given the common understanding of the separation of church and state that has left public education almost void of information about religion. As recent flashpoints around evolution and intelligent design theories make clear, a teacher who attempts to address religion—or even issues in which particular religions have a strong stake—in the public classroom enters a minefield. Most are aware of this and steer clear of the topic entirely. The result is that Americans are simultaneously passionate and ignorant about religion. A study of the religious lives of American teenagers recently reported that while these young people are far more devout than one might suspect, with fully 82 percent affiliated with a local congregation and 71 percent feeling "close to God," their actual knowledge about their respective religions' beliefs about this God—let alone the beliefs of religious others—is almost nonexistent (Smith 2005). The researchers found the teens *"incredibly inarticulate"* about religion, most of them simply answering "no" or "not really" or "not that I can think of" when asked if they held any particular religious beliefs (131). When pressed, the teenagers expressed a set of religious ideas that the author characterizes as "Moralistic Therapeutic Deism," an alternative worldview that, thanks to the dominant secular culture, has "colonized" the religions with which the teens claimed to be affiliated. In this religion, God is "something like a combination Divine Butler and Cosmic Therapist" (165), always on call, and infinitely devoted to promoting our self-esteem.

While we may attribute Smith's and Denton's startling findings to the confusions of adolescence, they offer important insight into trends in American religion evident elsewhere as well. For a complex array of reasons, Americans now receive less formal, structured religious education in their own traditions, and none or next to none in public educational settings. This ignorance creates a void that often gets filled by the values and rhetoric of the surrounding culture. It should not be surprising, then, to find that when asked to think about religious difference, Americans of many stripes, not just pluralism-affirming spiritual "seekers," draw upon the language of tolerance, individualism, and equality, often in direct contradiction with the teachings of religious traditions with which they claim affiliation. This gap between religious conviction and approaches to difference has been shown among adults as well. Robert Wuthnow's survey-based study of American attitudes to religious diversity is replete with puzzling statistics like this one: 57 percent of "churchgoing Christians said it was true not only that 'Christianity is the best way to understand God' *but also* that 'All religions are equally good ways of knowing about God'" (2005, 131). He also cites a conservative Christian woman who says of the Jewish friend whom she believes to be damned, "I respect her and what she believes."

Even those with the most restrictive theological positions on religious diversity, then, frequently express a characteristically American tolerance when pressed to define their attitudes toward religious others. But how deep does this tolerance run? Because it is not in most cases borne of substantive knowledge of another's religious beliefs and practices, it is often a thin veneer over a self-reinforcing ignorance. That is, if I don't know much about my coworker's Sikh tradition, but respect him and am wary of offending, I am probably not going to be comfortable asking him about it, thus letting my own religious worldview remain unengaged, leaving assumptions about him in place, and espousing a "tolerance" that therefore means very little.

Interfaith Encounters and New Pluralist Possibilities

However latent, the American impulse to embrace diversity is embedded in the ambiguity of these common responses. As in all contexts of social difference, that impulse is challenged from two sides. On the one hand, the pressure to assimilate all difference for the sake of a common purpose is always a threat to pluralism. Even when the shared identity is framed as inclusive, as in such constructs as Judeo-Christianity, or in the president's insistence on September 14, 2001, that we were sustained by a "unity of every faith and background," it does not take very long to discern that for many, the price of inclusion is the muting of particular identity. On the other hand, the preservation of diverse identities has a centrifugal drive that threatens ultimately to leave us in a state of absolute individualism, where what passes for community is the simple agreement not to offend, or at least not to kill each other. In Richard Wentz's study of the culture of religious pluralism, he puts the central issue this way: "Can Americans exist in a state of 'raw' diversity? Is there a public dimension to their existence that is shared beyond religious and cultural enclaves?" (Wentz 1998, 57). When Americans intentionally come together across lines of religious difference, they may be feeling out an answer to this question, negotiating a way between the options of "raw" diversity and a false, assimilative diversity, testing the possibility that religious difference might be affirmed as a lived reality as much as a rhetorical strategy, and might serve as a resource for real communal, not just individual, meaning-making.

The following chapters investigate that possibility by observing a range of real people, on their own and as part of organizations, as they do the work of interfaith engagement. In exploring this work in contexts as varied as national interfaith political activism and interfaith marriages, I was oriented by a common set of questions. First, who's involved? What kinds of people choose to participate in interfaith exchanges? Are those in progressive religious communities more likely than their conservative counterparts to reach out to religious others? What is the significance of other factors like ethnicity, gender, class, and education in determining who participates, and how? Second, what motivates them? Are interfaith encounters pragmatic, strategic affairs aimed at resolving problems or achieving common ends, or are they more deeply dialogical? Can they do both? How do the different venues of interfaith encounter steer these purposes? Third, what happens in the encounter? How does engaging with those whose beliefs and practices profoundly differ affect the participants in interfaith work? How do the outcomes of these encounters square with participants' expectations? Is anyone converted? Fourth, what is the theology underlying these efforts? That is, how do those involved with religious difference conceptualize that difference? Are they all theological pluralists? Must one be a pluralist to do effective interfaith work? Is theology even relevant to that work? Finally, how do American interfaith activities reflect or challenge emerging patterns in American religion generally and conceptions of religious pluralism specifically? Are they fostering the growth of spiritual individualism and eclecticism, or a redefining of the relationship between individuals and religious institutions? Do they prompt the kind of reflection that might reinvigorate traditional religious affiliations? Is it possible to be "interfaith" as a religious identity? Would anyone want to be?

Those who are talking about these deep differences—whether it is at the family dinner table, in a political coalition, or with strangers online—put themselves at risk in significant ways. Alienation from family members, sanction by religious communities, profound personal religious re-assessments—these can all be the challenging consequences of interfaith exchange. In taking these risks, though, they may be learning something that will be instructive for a society that is sharply divided and not very good at talking constructively across those divides; that possibility alone makes their stories worth telling, and worth listening to.

1

Theories of Religious Difference

The "Experts" Map Interfaith Relations

"The map is not the territory," we learned a long time ago from general semantics. This has certainly become clear to many of us on long hikes when the topographical map and the trail in front of us seem to bear little relation to one another. But we carry our maps just the same. My goal in exploring interfaith encounters in the United States today is to get at the territory itself, the experience of Muslims, Christians, Jews, Hindus, Pagans, Buddhists, Sikhs, and others as they engage one another in various kinds of relationships. Mapping these actual lived relationships is part of the purpose of this book, identifying the hidden and constantly changing features of the terrain that can only be seen while walking through it. For orientation, though, it will be helpful to study the maps that are available already—those that have been developed over the past hundred years or more by people and groups who for a wide range of reasons have sought to chart the relationship between one religious worldview and the wider world in which there are, among other things, other religions.

There are two kinds of acknowledged experts in the field of interfaith relations: leaders of religious institutions who initiate, participate in, and offer rationale for interfaith encounters from within their own traditions; and scholars who attempt—from within, on the edges, or outside of these dialogues—to describe and systematize such encounters and their complex motivations, logics, and tensions in the context of broader social and intellectual issues. Historically, of course, these two roles were often merged. Most conceptualizations of the relations between different religions prior to the middle of the twentieth century were developed by scholars who were also deeply involved in religious, especially Protestant Christian, institutions. Thus the earliest scholarly efforts to understand religious diversity typically took theological and philosophical, rather than sociological, form, with a legacy that has proven remarkably influential.

Historical Roots and Tangled Branches

The late nineteenth century marks the beginning of both the modern interfaith movement and scholarly efforts to understand religious difference, each impelled by that century's version of what is today known as globalization. The 1900s witnessed a dramatic increase in the availability to western theologians of information about other religions, a product of burgeoning colonial and missionary activity. Archaeological expeditions brought back to Europe evidence that placed Christianity in a much broader context, while exotic foreign scriptures became accessible through massive translation projects like F. Max Müller's *Sacred Books of the East* series (1879–1894). In this period the topic of other religions came to be seen for the first time in the west not just as a problem for Christian theology, but as a field of inquiry unto itself, given to more or less objective efforts at the comparative study of religion. But this was in large part a difference in method, not purpose, from previous inquiries. Unlike apologists of earlier eras, nineteenth-century assertions of Christian superiority were based not on the dogmas of Christology but on the quasi-empirical comparison of whole religious complexes—but the unique status of Christianity continued to be affirmed. Many theologians and philosophers who took up the comparative task were able to find in these evidences the basis for developmental or evolutionary schemes that account for all religious traditions but place Christianity at the apex.

Once opened though, the floodgates of information about the historical and contemporary religious world could not be closed, and by the end of the century data from the "science" of comparative religion were quickly outrunning all efforts to channel them to christocentric ends. This realization is the enduring legacy of the work of German theologian, philosopher, and sociologist Ernst Troeltsch. Troeltsch stated in an essay written shortly before his death in 1923 that his entire career had revolved around the apparent irreconcilability of historical investigation and religious commitment (55). When examined critically, Troeltsch discovered, history revealed neither a common unifying essence of all religions nor an "upward trend toward Christianity" (43). For Troeltsch, the realization of Christianity's non-absoluteness in any empirical sense was a profound crisis. He finally concluded that this religion "is final and unconditional for us, because we have nothing else, and because in what we have we can recognize the accents of the divine" (55). It is this poignantly circumscribed "absoluteness" that current theological reckonings with religious pluralism inherit as their point of departure. What Troeltsch could not have foreseen was the degree to which the "we" he refers to, that of modern European and North American society, would transmute itself through interaction with other cultures and their religions, and thus that it would cease to be true that "we have nothing else."

Non-Christians worldwide, of course, have experienced the reality of religious diversity for at least as long as Christians, and have often borne the brunt of assumptions of Christian absoluteness coupled with western economic and political power. Because of this power imbalance, and because religious diversity is such a vexing problem for a religion like Christianity, which understands its worldview to be uniquely true and uniquely able to offer salvation, critical reflection on religious pluralism and initiatives for responding to it have been, even in their most irenic forms, largely western, Christian enterprises. They have also, therefore, been deeply steeped in a colonialist, missionary, and patriarchal history.

A single event, the World's Parliament of Religions held in Chicago in 1893, is now often identified as the starting point of the modern interfaith movement.[1] The parliament, situated in the colonial context of the World's Columbian Exposition, typifies the nineteenth-century legacy even as it initiated the next century's explosion of interfaith activity. This spectacular gathering, which drew thousands of participants and official representatives from a dozen world religions, was founded on late-nineteenth-century optimism about human progress and confidence in the possibility of universal human "brotherhood." In spite of resistance from many Christian churches, including the Church of England and the Presbyterian Church in the U.S.A., the parliament's organizers insisted that the event would present Christianity as one among many faiths, in all of which God was understood to be deeply involved. After all, as the chair of the parliament's general committee John Henry Barrows asked, "Why should not Christians be glad to learn what God has wrought through Buddha and Zoroaster—through the sage of China, and the prophets of India and the prophet of Islam?" (1893, 74). The participation of non-Christians at the parliament, especially those from Asia, was pronounced and provocative. Hindus, especially, made a major impact, including Swami Vivekananda, who stayed on after the parliament, eventually founding the Vedanta Society and, after returning to India, the Ramakrishna Mission Association.

But it was also clear that the supremacy of Christianity and Christian control of the interfaith encounter were organizing principles of the gathering. Fully 78 percent of the 194 papers presented at the parliament were delivered by Christians, and 73 percent of the Christian participants were from the United States (Braybrooke 1992, 27). These Christians were overwhelmingly members of liberal Protestant denominations; Catholic participation was limited, and contributed, in the following years, to the growing divisions between liberal and conservative Catholics in America (29). While organizers made clear that explicit efforts to convert would not be welcomed, their addresses and later reflections made clear their assumption that the global forum would, in the spirit of open exchange, allow the inherent superiority of Christianity to emerge. What's more, the situation of the parliament in the larger Columbian exposition, whose purpose was to display and celebrate 500 years of western ascendancy, underlined the limits of the parliament's openness to non-Christian traditions. Indeed, this context framed religious pluralism itself—collated and displayed as a beautiful and unthreatening spectacle by the American Christian organizers—as one more brilliant achievement of western civilization. Still, the significance cannot be overlooked of the very fact of the parliament, the bringing together of religious leaders and ideas previously unknown in the west under a rubric in which Christianity was identified, at least formally, as one among many. And like much of the nineteenth century's historical-critical investigations of religion, the gap between the parliament's intentions and outcomes is wide. Relationships established, information shared, and conversations on the issue of religious pluralism begun at the parliament generated an interfaith movement whose size, diversity, and vibrancy has grown apace.

I dwell on these complex roots of the modern interfaith movement to highlight two specific points: First, encounters between participants in one religious tradition and those of another are always situated in larger social contexts in which asymmetries of power and underlying theological assumptions act as powerful regulators. Second, however, neither the stated intentions of interfaith encounters nor these subtextual forces ever exercise complete control over the interfaith event. Interfaith encounters are always encounters between people, and therefore unpredictable. When the religious other is met in a setting at least minimally conducive to open and noncoercive exchange, the religious subject is necessarily transformed, requiring the theorist to make new maps of the relationship.

The Modern Interfaith Movement: Participants and Purposes

The 1893 World's Parliament of Religions in many ways established a normative model for interreligious encounters in the modern era—that of formal encounters between clergy and scholars of diverse religions, in a spirit of openness and tolerance, with the goals of promoting mutual understanding and enrichment, not conversion. Today, the "interfaith movement" is an enormous conceptual tent under which vastly different activities occur. It flourishes, as Kusumita Pedersen, a longtime participant in interfaith work, argues, wherever several catalyzing factors are present: a multireligious population, interreligious tensions or conflicts, and active scholarly pursuit of comparative religion and interfaith questions (Pedersen 2005, 13–14). The movement appears to be most robust in Canada and the United States. It is important to note here that this movement, built on the premise of the equal dignity of all religions and the value of open exchange, is a product of modernity, and could "only develop in a free, open and democratic society where traditional hierarchies and leadership based on ascription are no longer the norm" (U. King 1998, 45). Challenges to modernity regarding its assumption of universal principles (progress, reason, objectivity) are thus also challenges to much of the rhetoric and structure of formal interfaith dialogue.

Structures for interfaith encounter include religious institutions with dedicated offices for interfaith matters, like the Vatican Secretariat for

Non-Christians and the World Council of Churches Sub-Unit on Dialogue, as well as independent organizations that exist to bring multiple religions into dialogue. These include the World Council of Faiths, the Global Ethics and Religion Forum, the North American Interfaith Network, and the ongoing Parliament of the World's Religions. The activities of organizations like these, both independent and religiously affiliated, typically include organizing (usually large-scale) interfaith events—conferences, symposia, days of prayer—and mobilizing religious communities for action on issues like world peace and environmental stewardship.

Another set of participants in the interfaith movement are university-affiliated organizations dedicated to putting scholarly resources in the service of interfaith understanding. These include groups like the Global Dialogue Institute, founded by Temple University's Leonard Swidler and Ashok Gangadeen of Haverford College. The Global Dialogue Institute (www.global-dialogue.com) organizes international interfaith encounters between scholarly representatives of diverse religions, and facilitates reflection on interfaith and intercultural issues by social and business organizations. One of the most visible products of the Global Dialogue Institute is the "Dialogue Decalogue," a set of rules for successful interfaith encounter developed by Leonard Swidler in 1983 and now widely used by interfaith groups. Swidler's definition of dialogue in this document as "a conversation on a common subject between two or more persons with differing views, the primary purpose of which is for each participant to learn from the other so that s/he can change and grow" (Swidler 1983) is by now normative in the interfaith movement.

A very different approach to religious diversity is taken by another academic initiative, Harvard University's Pluralism Project, directed by Diana Eck. If the Global Dialogue Institute represents high-level theorizing about how and why those of different religious and cultural perspectives ought to come together, the Pluralism Project represents a more bottom-up model, where the mission is to help Americans "engage with the realities of religious diversity" in their communities by offering detailed reporting and analysis of the "changing contours of American religious demography" (Eck et al. 2005). The Pluralism Project sponsors in-depth studies of religiously diverse cities and towns, as well as of individual faith communities, with a particular focus on those of newly arrived immigrants. A well-known product of the Pluralism Project is its CD-ROM, "On Common Ground: World Religions in America," which brings together much of the Pluralism Project's research in a format suitable for high school and university teaching. The range of academic studies of interfaith relations is suggested not only by the vast number of books published by philosophers, theologians, and sociologists of religion, but also by the variety of scholarly journals devoted to the subject, including *Studies in Interreligious Dialogue*, *The Journal of Ecumenical Studies*, and *Studies in Comparative Religion*, as well as those focused on bilateral relations, like *Islam and Christian-Muslim Relations* and *Buddhist-Christian Studies*.

Several theorists have recently developed helpful typologies for understanding these broad-ranging interfaith efforts in terms of their different purposes. Kusumita Pedersen organizes these projects according to three distinct motives: dialogues aimed at helping different religious groups live together more harmoniously; those focused on solving a shared community problem, like poverty, violence, or racism; and those that search for religious truth in a pluralistic context (Pedersen 2005). Mark Heim uses the Hindu concepts of *jnana* (knowledge), *bhakti* (devotion), and *karma* (action) to distinguish the dialogue of doctrine, the dialogue of spiritualities, and the dialogue of social reformation, respectively (Heim 1995, 99–100). Paul Ingram sorts interfaith dialogue into another three-part scheme: "conceptual," "interior," and "socially engaged" (Ingram 2001).

The language differs, but the categories seem to coalesce quite neatly. When people of different faith traditions come together constructively, they generally do so for one of these three purposes (or a combination of them). For the first group, the work is very practical: religious identities often provoke social conflict, yet their practitioners see in their traditions profound resources for social healing. Dialogue with religious others, then, is understood as a practice dedicated to sharing those resources and training them on local and global problems. Interfaith coalitions have been active and effective in peacemaking, addressing the environmental crisis, and critiquing economic systems that engender poverty. At the local level, they might lead, as they have in my home town, to the establishment of task forces on racism and partnerships for meeting the needs of the community's homeless. Or they might aim for a wider impact, like the Network of Spiritual Progressives (NSP), "an interfaith movement welcoming to 'spiritual but not religious' secular people as well." A project of the Rabbi Michael Lerner and the Tikkun community, the NSP has established an online community as well as local chapters across the country, and held national conferences in Berkeley (2005) and Washington, D.C. (2006) in an effort to mobilize religious forces to challenge "the misuse of religion, God and spirit by the Religious Right," as well as to prompt the "liberal culture" to rethink its tendency to dismiss religious perspectives (Network of Spiritual Progressives 2006). In the process, these karmic or socially engaged dialogues prompt interesting and sometimes contentious comparisons of different religions' social values. The challenge of crafting common positions on pressing global issues is revealed, for instance, in the contentious discussions that have followed the release of Hans Kung's "Towards a Global Ethic: An Initial Declaration" at the end of the 1993 Parliament of the World's Religions. Critics have raised challenges to the document regarding its assumptions of similarity across religious lines, its implicit western bias, as well as larger concerns about the universal applicability of the language of human rights (see for instance S. King 1998). Feminist critics of the document have specifically charged it with failing to account for the degree to which religions are themselves complicit in the oppression of women, an area that the Declaration targets as one of the primary directives of interfaith ethical efforts. "The directive is phrased," feminist theologian Ursula King writes, "as if the religions already had the answer to the exploitation of women, whereas religions themselves are part of the problem and cause of this oppressive state of affairs" (U. King 1998, 51).

The second mode of dialogue these schemes describe focuses on the spiritual life of practitioners and their interior transformations. Roman Catholic and Buddhist exploration of the points of contact between contemplative prayer and meditation, as pioneered by the encounter between Thomas Merton and D. T. Suzuki in the 1960s, is perhaps the paradigmatic instance of this type of dialogue, but it takes other forms as well. Mark Heim, a Christian deeply steeped in Indian religious traditions, writes: "Whether the practice is yogic, meditational, or cultic, this dialogue looks to the inner world, the 'cave of the heart' where direct experience replaces concepts. Not study, but participation is the avenue of encounter. This is a dialogue of mutual spiritual discipline. In it, Christians and Hindus engage in each other's practice, seeking a common core of mystical experience" (1995, 100). This type of dialogue, centered on individual religious experience, involves the most profound border-crossing between traditions, as an adherent of one tradition moves into the heart of another by taking on its spiritual disciplines. This approach is illustrated in the work of Monastic Interreligious Dialogue, a group of Roman Catholic monks and nuns "committed to fostering interreligious and intermonastic dialogue at the level of spiritual practice and experience between North American Catholic monastic women and men and contemplative practitioners of diverse religious traditions" (Monastic Interreligious Dialogue 2005). Catholics and Buddhists have also come together to share their contemplative traditions at gatherings from California to New York, where monks and nuns from neighboring monasteries—one Franciscan, one Buddhist—recently met for a weekend of shared meals, conversations, and rituals (Lefevere 2003, 10).

But it is the third type of dialogue, *jnanic* or conceptual or truth-seeking, that tends, not surprisingly, to be taken up by academics, and that will be the focus of the remainder of this chapter. The two kinds of scholarly initiatives sketched above—represented by the Global Dialogue Institute and the Pluralism Project—illustrate some of the diversity of academic approaches to interfaith issues, especially in the United States. On the one hand, there is a great need simply to inventory the diversity of American religious experience. Work like that of the Pluralism Project approaches religious difference primarily as a phenomenon of the social experience of ordinary people that must be explored as it is occurring "on the ground" to be understood. And as Dwight Hopkins has observed, its perspective reverses traditional modes of thinking about religious difference; its primary focus is on non-Christian religions from outside the west and their impact on an ostensibly Christian culture (Hopkins 2001, 8). On the other hand, organizations like the Global Dialogue Institute put scholarly representatives of the religions at the forefront, organizing encounters among them and promoting their analytic efforts. From these two different efforts, two sets of maps are emerging—those that help us to see religious diversity in America, to come to understand, for instance, that there are now more Muslims in the United States than Episcopalians or Presbyterians (Eck 2001, 2); and those that help us make sense of it in religious and philosophical terms.

The remainder of this book takes up the former of these tasks, exploring the ways in which people of different faith identities actually engage one another in various modes and contexts. As they do, they find themselves reckoning with very difficult questions of meaning and identity for which the latter set of maps may prove useful. Once we come to see and understand something about the religious other in our neighborhood, community, or even our family, what do we do with that difference? How do we hold together respect and appreciation for the other with commitment to our own faith traditions? Do we believe the other to be worthy of respect but nonetheless ultimately spiritually deficient, or simply wrong? Do we try to persuade the other to see things our way? Do we affirm the equal validity of all religious paths, and if so, then why adopt or maintain the ideas and disciplines of one over another? Or do we simply live in relationship, bracketing such questions in favor of simply getting along? Scholarly reflection on these questions is deep and wide, and at a very interesting point in its development.

What's True? Who Can Be Saved?
Diversity's Hard Questions

For at least a century, at countless conferences, symposia, parliaments, and councils, representatives of the elite strata of different religious communities—scholars and institutional religious leaders—have come together to talk about the philosophical and theological ideas of their religious worldviews, exchanging views on such topics as the nature of ultimate reality, human nature and destiny, the problem of suffering and evil, and religious epistemology. The goal of such exchanges is not always explicit, and often vague; phrases like "mutual understanding and enrichment" tend to fill in the subtitles.

Often implicit in such encounters, though, is the legacy of nineteenth-century efforts at making sense of religious difference. While comparative religion came to be seen in that period as a field of study unto itself, distinct from earlier, faith-based apologetics, it is critical to remember that the initiative for that new and ostensibly objective project came from the powerful Christian west, informed by its cultural assumptions, its theological and philosophical categories, and its particular understanding of the purpose and rules of engagement with religious others. Thus at the same time that generally open and liberal disposition of academics has prompted attitudes of tolerance and celebrations of diversity in the encounter with religious others, the potential of that spirit has often been limited by the unexamined preeminence of Christian ways of thinking about religion. Specifically, intellectual reckoning with religious difference has focused on the problems of conflicting truth claims (Whose beliefs are true? How can we know?), and questions of salvation (Who can be saved? By what power?). These are problems obviously at the forefront for those whose spiritual life centers on particular claims about the uniquely salvific significance of a single historical figure as a manifestation of the divine, but perhaps not central to the reflections on religious difference that might emerge indigenously from, say, a Buddhist, Pagan, or Native American context.

And so the prevailing scholarly ways of thinking about religions comparatively, what have come to be known (in a phrase that further belies their western pedigree) as theologies of religion, have been framed by the meta-question of the truth status and salvific efficacy of these different traditions. All this is to say that what we generically term interfaith dialogue often tends, in theory and practice, to be a dialogue between Christianity, or Christian ways of thinking, and other religious ideas and practices. In the United States, where over three-quarters of the population still identify as Christian, this framing of the issue is perhaps not inappropriate. Increasingly, however, this is an aspect of interfaith dialogue prompting unfavorable attention from critics and self-awareness among participants.

Two decades ago, the trajectory of these theologies of religious pluralism seemed clear. When Alan Race put forth the typology of "exclusivism," "inclusivism," and "pluralism" in his 1982 *Christians and Religious Pluralism*, it seemed to bring clarity to decades, if not centuries, of ecclesial and intellectual assessments of religious difference, and quickly became the prevailing intellectual framework for understanding this issue, rehearsed in countless academic treatments. If we identify these positions in terms of their responses to two questions—(1) where does religious truth lie, and how can we know?, and (2) who can be saved, and by what?—they fall out something like this.[2]

Exclusivism is the view that there is a disjunction between one's own religious worldview and all others, that one revelation is true and others false, and that salvation requires explicit affirmation of the truths of—if not institutional affiliation with—one particular religious tradition. While it dominated for much of Christian history, exclusivism is not widely held as the official position of the mainstream Christian churches in America, though it remains prominent in much of popular Christianity, and is affirmed by some conservative denominations, including the powerful Southern Baptist Convention in the United States. Forms of exclusivism can be found among non-Christian groups, wherever one hears the claim to the uniqueness of one religious vision and the inadequacy of all other paths, but given the unique role of truth claims in Christianity, exclusivism is articulated most fully and systematically, if not formally, in Christian contexts.[3]

Inclusivism refers to the position that significant religious truth can be found in multiple religions, though that truth is perfected or fulfilled in one's own. Paul Griffiths distinguishes "open" and "closed" versions of this view, based on whether or not "it affirms the possibility that some alien religion may teach truths not already explicitly taught by the home religion" (Griffiths 2001, xv). On the question of salvation, inclusivists take the position that salvation is available to the religious other, through the pervasive efficacy of the divine as understood by the inclusivist's own religion. In its Christian form as developed by Karl Rahner, who was the primary architect of Vatican II's position on the issue as expressed in *Nostra Aetate* (1965), this view asserts that non-Christians can be saved because of the inclusive power of what God has done through Jesus Christ. Or, as an Evangelical colleague of mine once put it, "Buddhists might get into heaven, but there's a cross over the door." Rahner developed the notion of "anonymous Christians" to refer to those non-Christians who, by living in right relation to God and neighbor within the structures of their own religious paths, are as worthy of entry into the (Christian) Kingdom as the most devout Christian, though they may know nothing of Christianity at all. Most inclusivists do not reject the aim of conversion, though, for while not absolutely necessary to salvation, knowledge of and affiliation with the home religion is seen as preferable, for it is there that revelation is clearest and/or most complete. In the Catholic case, this view has become more pronounced since the papacy of John Paul II, and is expressed forcefully in the 2000 declaration *Dominus Iesus*.

While inclusivism is certainly well suited to a religion like Christianity with a universal message and often associated with colonialist designs, inclusivism can also be seen in other traditions. Islam, for instance, understands itself as the fulfillment or completion of the other monotheistic "religions of the book," and is therefore inclusivist in a sequentialist sense. That is, Islam completes and fulfills the partial revelations of God in Judaism and Christianity. One could also hear inclusivism in the Buddhist doctrine of "skillful means," which maintains that ultimate truth must be communicated in ways that are appropriate to the capacities of the individual, and therefore that penultimate, non-Buddhist conceptions might usefully lead others to the ultimate truth of Buddhist insights.

Finally, *pluralism* refers to a position, developed by philosophers and theologians beginning in the 1970s (with roots, they would argue, that are solidly historical and even biblical), that holds that no one religious tradition can be said to have unique access to religious truth, and that all religions are potentially equally valid paths to salvation.[4] For Christian pluralists, the uniqueness of Jesus is circumscribed to refer to a kind of distinctiveness rather than finality or unsurpassability. For some, the shift to a pluralist position is motivated by ethical and dialogical concerns; these include Leonard Swidler, Paul F. Knitter, and Rosemary Radford Ruether, among others. For these theologians, the historical legacy of triumphalist claims to knowledge of absolute truth in the forms of Christian anti-Semitism, the patriarchal subjugation of women, and religious imperialism calls exclusivism and inclusivism into radical question, while the imperative of interfaith and intercultural dialogue prompts ever more open attitudes toward the other and modesty in one's own religious claims. Others come to the pluralist position via what Paul Knitter has called the "religious-mystical bridge" (2002, 125–134). For these thinkers, who include many Asian theologians, most prominently Raimon Panikkar, an Indian Catholic, it is the mystical experience of encounter with a divine presence that prompts the affirmation of multiple ways to God. If the primary quality of God revealed by intense religious experience is God's infinity, and therefore final unknowability, then there is no basis on which to affirm exclusive truths. What's more, engagement with mystical practitioners of other traditions often reveals common experiences suggestive of an underlying unity to that unknowable divine reality. As Knitter puts it, "The deeper one descends into one's own religious well, the more one will realize the one underground river that nourishes them all" (2002, 126).

But it is with the work of British philosopher of religion John Hick that the "pluralist hypothesis" in religion is most closely associated. As a philosopher and theologian, Hick's work has revolved around a problem comparable to that faced by Ernst Troeltsch nearly a century ago. As Troeltsch struggled with the problem of reconciling Christian commitment with historical investigation, so Hick has expressed the challenge to his own faith commitments of philosophical questions raised by the apparent diversity of revelations. In 1968, in his *The Center of Christianity*, Hick called for a "Copernican revolution" in which the faiths of the universe of faiths come to be seen as revolving, not around a Christological center, as the inclusivist models suggest, but rather around God or the ultimately Real. Different religions, then, are to be understood as "different ways of experiencing, conceiving, and living in right relation to an ultimate reality which transcends all our varied visions of it" (Hick 1989, 235–236). For Hick, this ultimate reality is one; he is no metaphysical pluralist. But using Kantian terms he insists that the Real *an sich*, or in itself, is unknowable. What we have in our various religions are pictures, or divine *personae* (for those traditions that understand God in personal terms) and *impersonae* (for those traditions that experience the sacred in nonpersonal terms), which truly reveal but never fully contain the divine mystery (1989, 248; 1990, 190–191; 1993, 164–179).

Pluralist positions in theologies of religion may be further subdivided into those, like Hick's, that I have termed "convergent," and those, like Panikkar's, that are "non-convergent" (McCarthy 1998, 92–94). The difference here is whether or not the ultimate reality to which practitioners of various religions seek to orient themselves is itself understood to be singular or plural. For Hick, religious pluralism is a reflection of the diversity of human histories, cultures, and imaginations; for Panikkar, pluralism is part of the very structure of the divine. Because, from his

mystical perspective, humans, the divine, and the cosmos exist in insepa-
rable interpenetration (what Panikkar terms a "cosmotheandric experience"), the diversity of human experience implies the diversity of the
divine itself. With reference to Hick's metaphor of many paths of the
same mountain, Panikkar states, "It is not simply that there are different
ways leading to the peak, but that the summit itself would collapse if all
the paths disappeared. The peak is in a certain sense the result of the
slopes leading to it. . . . It is not that this reality has many names as if
there were a reality outside the name. The reality is the many names and
each name is a new aspect" (Panikkar 1981, 24, 29).

While developed primarily by western thinkers drawing on western
intellectual categories, pluralism as a perspective on religious diversity
can certainly be found in non-Christian settings as well. Hindu intellectu-
als, including Swami Vivekananda at the 1893 World's Parliament of Religions, have for over a century offered Hinduism as a model of religious
tolerance, open to the sacred stories, figures, and practices of all religions. Philosophical Hinduism's account of the Infinite as an unknowable
reality approachable through multiple routes, heard also in the work of
both Gandhi and Radhakrishnan, makes easy connections with Hick's
pluralist moves. Pluralist thinking is less evident in the other monotheistic religions, in which traditional language about the oneness of God
and the singularity of the path to God would require more thoroughgoing
reinterpretation. Interestingly, though, it can be heard in the writings of
feminists of these traditions, who are deeply sensitized to the oppressive
power of theologies that clearly define orthodoxy and punish otherness.
For example, Judith Plaskow, a prominent Jewish feminist theologian,
takes a pluralist position in her call for a Jewish rejection of conceptions
of *chosenness* in favor of *distinctiveness* (1990, 105) that parallels Christian
repudiation of claims to the uniqueness of Christ—both in light of the
ways in which such exceptionalist claims have, historically, been used to
legitimate the oppression of others.

Pluralism and Its Discontents

Perspectives on how to make sense of the religious diversity that is more
and more prominent in American consciousness are thus varied, complex,

and often highly nuanced. But in addition to helping organize the various positions on the issue, the exclusivism-inclusivism-pluralism typology also seemed in theological circles over the past several decades to offer a subtly normative framework. That is, what was presented as an organizing typology appeared to serve as an evolutionary scheme of inexorable progress. (It's worth noting that the positions are almost always represented in this order—pluralists tend to get the last word.) In much of the academic theological reflection on religious pluralism throughout the 1980s and into the 90s, exclusivists were admired for their piety, inclusivists for their intellectual agility, but for those who were serious about improving interfaith relations, atoning for centuries of christological arrogance, and staying at the leading edge of philosophical discourse on religious difference, some form of the pluralist position seemed the only plausible option.

But a funny thing happened on the way to universal affirmation of pluralism: some very smart, open-minded scholars deeply involved in interfaith dialogue began to raise very impressive objections. The most potent of these challenges is the assertion made by a number of philosophers and theologians that pluralism, as represented paradigmatically by John Hick, is not really pluralistic at all, but rests on unsustainable metaphysical dogmas. A closer look at Hick's model is needed to fully grasp this surprising critique. Hick has argued that the object of all religious seeking is a noumenal Real, known and responded to in varying ways across the world's religions, all of which must be acknowledged as potentially equal in truth and salvific value. Aware that he cannot ascribe descriptive characteristics to this Real without privileging his own Christian perspective, Hick presents this Real *an sich* as a hypothesis, correlating with but not described by religious philosophers as the unknowable divine reality beyond all language and form: *nirguna* Brahman, the unnamable Tao, God beyond God. The various paths toward that noumenal reality are also unified, in Hick's view, in their common agenda of reorienting the practitioner from a worldview that is self-centered to one that is Other-centered (Hick 1981, 452–453; 1993, 17–32). The pluralist hypothesis, as Hick's move is known, has offered philosophical support for other pluralist theologies of religion, including those, like Knitter's, that locate the commonality of different religions not in the psychological

shift from self to Other, but in the ethical mandate to liberate the oppressed.

Charges against pluralist theologies have emerged not only from exclusivist thinkers who reject its departure from orthodox positions, what
Hick has called "parochial egotism" (Hick cited in Heim 1995, 23), but
also from those who want a more solid foundation for comparative theological efforts. Simply put, these challenges ask Hick and other pluralists,
"How can you know?" Given that it is impossible to get outside one's own
cultural and religious frame of reference, where could one possibly stand
to make such god's-eye-view claims about all human religiousness? James
Fredericks, among others, insists that what Hick has developed is not really pluralism at all, but a quasi-inclusivism that rests not on a hypothesis, since there are no conditions under which it might be proved false,
but on an assertion with no greater claim to veracity than any other con-
ditioned statement of human belief (Fredericks 1999, 104–11). Or, as Mark
Heim puts it: "His thesis is distinctively a meta-theory of religion, like
those derived from Freud or Marx. Its plausibility depends on the claim to
transcend the frame of reference of the religions, to speak not from
among them but from above them" (30). In other words, Hick's claim of
diverse but equally valid paths to a single Reality stands on no more solid
ground than those of specific religious traditions asserting the truth of
their own worldviews.

Feminist scholars of religion have issued a similarly critical response
to theologies of pluralism, and indeed to the very legitimacy of such typologies. Like much androcentric theorizing about religion, feminists
argue, concepts like "pluralism" appear to stand outside of historical experience as universally applicable categories, inattentive to the lived reality of those who may in fact experience their religious lives much
differently. Ursula King refers to the "violence of abstraction" committed
by such schemes, which render invisible the complexity and ambiguity of
much—especially women's—religious experience. "These three categories
of exclusivism, inclusivism and pluralism appear much too narrow, static
and insufficiently differentiated to capture the organic, fluid, and dynamic reality of religion at a personal and social level. Nor do they in any
way allude to the subtleties and existential commitment of faith" (U. King
1998, 46–47). Thus while they tend to privilege Christian concerns about

religious truth claims and salvation, concepts like exclusivism, inclusivism, and pluralism may also privilege abstract ways of thinking about religion and religious difference that do not correspond usefully with those—especially women—whose spiritual experience may take more concrete, embodied, and less categorizable forms.

In addition to its epistemological vulnerability, though, these critics also insist that pluralism is not actually conducive to real endorsement of religious difference, or even good dialogue. The specific truth claims made by religious people—that Mohammed is the final prophet of God, that Amida Buddha's vow is efficacious—require such radical, "demythologizing" reinterpretation to fit the pluralist position that when believers actually make these claims they must be reckoned as fundamentally mistaken (Heim 34).[5] When a hypothesized commonality is the basis for interfaith encounter, differences are understood to make no difference, and therefore are really not worth talking about, dooming the comparative and dialogical enterprises. What's more, Paul Griffiths argues, Hick's hypothesis not only requires reinterpretation of traditional claims, its substantive understanding of the common salvific aim of all religions means that it must also be very selective in what it recognizes as religion. In speaking of newer or "lesser" traditions where the transformation from self-centeredness to Reality-centeredness might not be readily apparent, Hick opts for an agnostic view in anticipation of further data, but he says nothing, Griffiths charges, about the already available data concerning such marginal religions as Heaven's Gate, the UFO-based religious group known for its mass suicide in 1997. The inability to offer more explicit assessments of religious soteriologies points for Griffiths to a central weakness of pluralist views of salvation: "[S]uch responses can maintain themselves only by using a narrow understanding of religion. They can, that is, be plausible only if they limit the religions they consider to those whose substantive teachings about the proper end of human life are significantly like theirs" (2001, 147). Fredericks levels a similar charge against Knitter's liberationist reading of the common salvific thrust of religions: "His deeply held Christian commitments to social activism have placed him on what is turning out to be a collision course with those who want to maintain that all religions are variant expressions of the same transcendent reality" (1999, 143). What happens, we must ask Knitter, when a truly religious perspective shows no evidence of parallel social commitments?

Current attention to religiously motivated terrorism brings this issue into sharp relief. A Pakistani Muslim relief worker recently reported on her four years of interviewing the most radical segments of the Palestinian resistance movement about the backgrounds and beliefs of suicide bombers (http://www.timesonline.co.uk/article/0,7–1692606,00.html). Her conclusion: they are deeply religious. This issues a profound challenge to theorists of religious difference. If scholars are to dismiss the faith of suicide bombers as distortions of "true Islam," or of those who bomb abortion clinics as misrepresentations of "true Christianity," produced only by social upheavals and injustices, they can be of little service in the effort to understand, engage, and thereby defuse such impulses. Historians of religion learned generations ago to be wary of essentialized understandings of what are in reality complex and evolving historical systems. College curricula now aim to foreground for students the internal diversity of what might more properly be called Hinduisms, or Christianities, or Buddhisms. Pluralists, it seems, are late-comers to this insight, perhaps due in part, ironically, to their overwhelmingly Christian foundations and consequent overriding concern to put a tolerant face on encounters with religious others. These critics of the pluralist position challenge them to find a basis for interfaith engagement that is not so safely pre-selective.

Finally, the presumed preeminence of pluralism as the foundation for successful interfaith dialogue is also challenged by the ironic charge that its effort to grant all religions equal status in fact represents a new form of western Christian arrogance. John Azumah, a Christian expert on Islam in Africa, asks pointedly, "Is it any less arrogant to assume the right to include others in God's plan of salvation than it is to exclude them? Both these attitudes are signs of Christians arrogating to themselves the role of visa officials in the consulate of heaven here on earth." He goes on to note that non-Christians may not receive such generous assessments of their traditions so generously: "Indeed, many members of other religious traditions see the Christian pontification on the value of their religious traditions as at best presumptuous and at worst offensive" (Azumah 2002, 271).

So the rock and hard place between which comparativists who would be pluralists find themselves today is, on the one hand, letting the other in the comparative project remain truly other so as to make comparison authentic, substantive, and fair; and, on the other hand, finding a way to articulate the connections and mutual regard that make comparison worthwhile. In response to this challenge, some theologians and philosophers are developing alternative approaches that aim either to revivify inclusivism in more sophisticated forms, or reconceive pluralism in more radical ways. Paul Griffiths' solution as a Christian theologian is to reject pluralism for an "open inclusivist" view of religious truth (2001, 60–64), and a form of exclusivism on the question of salvation that uses a "deliberately relaxed" understanding of what it means to belong to Christianity (164). In this view, Christians can learn religiously significant truths from non-Christians, but there is no necessity to argue for the equal salvific validity of all religions. Heim (1995) develops what he sees as a more fully pluralist option that makes no effort to articulate the convergence of religious traditions as a means of legitimating them, but rather sees various religions as having truly plural ends, and therefore requiring truly different paths, each of which are valid and each of which require a kind of absolute commitment. As these proposals grow in number, complexity, and nuance, the exclusivism-inclusivism-pluralism typology itself may well go the way of flat-earth maps. Alternative typologies are already emerging; Paul Knitter's textbook on theologies of pluralism (2002), for instance, replaces the old three-part typology with a four-part schema of replacement, fulfillment, mutuality, and acceptance. While still no doubt missing much of the nuance of the positions of individual thinkers and organizations, this model, especially by distinguishing mutuality (comparable to pluralism in the old typology) from acceptance, makes room for positions like Heim's and Griffiths' that appear to take difference more seriously and view the goals of dialogue more modestly.

Globalization and Pluralism

The challenge to the experts' maps of interfaith relations addressed by Griffiths, Heim, and others is complicated by the social contexts in which interfaith encounters now occur; these must be attended to before we can assess the congruence of the theory and practice of interfaith encounters. Thanks to technology and population movements, the multireligious character of the world has become a lived reality for millions. Paradoxically, in the way it brings people of different religious identities together, globalization has given rise to both new modes of pluralistic thinking and intensified exclusivism. In a recent paper on religion and globalization, Donald Swearer quotes Anthony Giddens' characterization of one of globalization's basic tensions:

> The battleground of the twenty-first century will pit fundamentalism against cosmopolitan tolerance. In a globalising world where information and images are routinely transmitted across the globe, we are all regularly in contact with others who think differently, and live differently, from ourselves. Cosmopolitans welcome and embrace this cultural [and religious] complexity. Fundamentalists find it disturbing and dangerous. Whether in the areas of religion, ethnic identity or nationalism, they take refuge in renewed and purified traditions—and quite often, violence. (Giddens, cited in Swearer 2003)[6]

It is vital, given this development, that academic interfaith work articulate analyses that can account for both of these modes of interreligious encounter, rather than assuming (as we seem to have for some time) that the cosmopolitan option is the inevitable destiny of religious people.

That cosmopolitan option itself begins to look different when we view it not from the perspective of the postmodern west, but from globalization's underside. Wesley Ariarajah has highlighted three overlapping concerns motivating strong religious resistance to globalization. First, echoing the critique of pluralist theologies of religion raised by some of the scholars noted above, many people in traditional religious communities sense that global forces are a threat to their religious particularity. "Global forces, especially those of the economic variety, have problems dealing with great diversity and they always try to 'standardize' peoples' tastes, preferences and needs so that they can be catered to en mass. 'Standardization' and leveling down of many aspects of global life is experienced as a threat to religious diversity as well. This is further aggravated by the fact that those who hold the strings of power within the process of glob-alization come from predominantly one religious and cultural milieu." (Ariarajah 2003, 7)

Ariarajah's second concern is that of values: The cultural penetra-tion facilitated by global free trade constitutes "a subtle attack on the plurality of value systems through the use of the mass media, controlled by those who hold a particular set of values" (7). And it is not so much the dominance of Christian values that Ariarajah fears in this context, but that of globalization's real religion—consumerism. So pervasive is the marketplace model of individual preference and uninhibited choice that religion might come to be seen as one more lifestyle selection. There is a powerful tendency for celebrations of pluralism in a globalized world to devolve into the "McDonaldization" of religious difference. An ap-proach to pluralism like that of John Hick, that begins with the premise that all religions are forms of a generic faith, has a tendency, as many critics have noted (Surin 1990; Griffiths 2001, 84–88; Heim 1995, 110), to erase differences in a way that serves the interests of the culturally and economically dominant. "Insistence that religions are all simply 'forms of faith' is the perfect correlative of a global consumer culture, which subverts any alternative structures but welcomes the 'franchise' men-tality. Religious faith, like brands of detergent, becomes a choice with no structural implications, but only personal, expressive ones" (Heim 1995, 58).

Finally, Ariarajah argues that globalization is often experienced as an assault on identities—gender, family, tribe, language, etc. Many of these have been effectively undermined by globalization; religion then can ap-pear as the only identity offering a solid sense of distinctive belonging. "An attempt to disparage or subvert it is experienced as a threat to the very last straw of identity one holds on to" (8). Hence the logic of funda-mentalisms. Hence also the need for a theology of religions that works as an advocate for distinctive, unhomogenized religious difference. It is in this odd place where postmodern theologies of pluralism and premodern forces of religious orthodoxy might have something to say to each other in the common effort to resist what Paul Griffiths has called the "con-sumerist construal of religious assents" (Griffiths 2001, 88).

Making Better Maps

As anyone who has compared the world map developed by Arno Peters in 1967 with the traditional Mercator projection map knows, maps are normative, not just descriptive. For as much as they help us to perceive a given landscape in a larger perspective and to see things we couldn't previously see, maps also render other things invisible. What the mapmaker hasn't seen or heard of is not recorded, and so is not looked for by those who follow his map. More important, the way geographical features are represented, even how they are named, will go a long way in defining the experience of those using the map. Nineteenth-century globalization necessitated new conceptual maps of the interreligious landscape, in which Christianity's place would shift dramatically. Today, the primary scheme for conceptualizing religious difference that emerged out of that era—the typology of exclusivism-inclusivism-pluralism and its implicit assumptions about the ascendancy of pluralism—is itself undergoing major revision, in response both to a new global situation, and to the increasing complexity of religious experience within it. Sociologists like Robert Wuthnow (2005), for instance, are drawing attention to the complex array of social factors that, perhaps even more than theological convictions, lead people to different affirmations about religious others. While the discussion is still quite contentious, there does seem to be an emerging consensus on three themes that may come to define the contours of twenty-first-century conceptualizations of religious difference.[7]

Dialogue First, Theory Later

The first of these emerging themes concerns the process by which theologies of religion are developed. Due in part to the influence of liberation theologies that came to prominence in academic circles in the 1970s and 1980s, there is a growing push to reverse the order of theory and practice in the doing of theology. Instead of viewing engaged religious commitment as the product of theological reflection deduced from extrahistorical sources, liberation theologies reorient the process to begin with our experience of our faith in the conflictual social world and seek to develop theologies adequate to that experience.[8] For liberation theologians, the primary experience out of which meaning is to be made, and in light of which all theological reflection must be understood, is the struggle of the oppressed—the poor, women, people of color, sexual minorities—for liberation.

Without drawing on liberationist sources explicitly, a number of scholars have for the past decade or so been quietly developing a model of "comparative theology" that uses this foundational methodological insight to find a path out of pluralism's cul de sac (e.g., Clooney 2003; Fredericks 1999, 2004).[9] For these theologians, though, the primary experiential source of theological meaning is not the struggle for social justice, but the dialogical encounter. Rather than first working out a theology of religions adequate to our pluralistic context, comparative theology argues for beginning with the dialogue itself, engaging the religious other so as to deepen one's experience of one's own tradition. This model is fully articulated by Catholic theologian James Fredericks, who contrasts it with theologies of religion:

"Unlike theologies of religions, comparative theology does not start with a grand theory of religion in general that claims to account for all religions. . . . [It] does not look for some abstract lowest common denominator or essence that all religions, including Christianity, share. Instead of theories about religion in general, comparative theologians are interested in studying other religions on their own terms and then exploring their own Christian faith using what they have learned about the other religions" (167–168). Francis Clooney, another Catholic theologian working in comparative theology, insists that it is simply no longer tenable for theologies of religious difference to be developed apart from the dialogical encounter itself. "It will no longer be plausible to imagine that Christians among themselves will be able to decide, in serene isolation, the value of other religions" (Clooney 2003, 321). Clooney develops his Christian theology in the context of a deep and long engagement with Hindu texts and communities. He writes, "If a Christian reads a Hindu verse and ponders it according to traditions of Hindu learning, this eventually has an effect—salutary, I suggest—on how he or she thinks and reads, contemplates and encounters Jesus of Nazareth, who even today wishes to encounter us" (2002, 57).

Clooney's and Fredericks's is a Catholic position, but it models a praxis-based approach to the comparative task well suited to those of any (and no) religious perspective who want to engage religious others as others, yet in meaningful connection with their own experience and understanding. As I have argued elsewhere, the rush to consensus for which projects like the Global Ethic have been criticized can be avoided "if participants can shift from anxiety about the premises to trust in the process of interfaith encounter" (McCarthy 1998, 11). In defending the exclusivist-inclusivist-pluralist typology, its original author, Alan Race, makes a similar shift in calling attention to dialogue itself as the proper end of interfaith work, not as a means to something else, since dialogue reflects the ultimately pluralist nature of reality (Race 2001).

Respect for Irreducible Otherness

A second theme on which pluralists and their critics alike seem to agree is the need to preserve the otherness—the real difference—of the religious ideas, practices, and people with whom we might engage, rather than seeing them through the filters of our own predefined categories. As Clooney puts it, "The other—which is always multiple and varied and irreducible to any single template—must be respected as such, and not reduced to a merely exotic, slightly altered version of oneself" (Clooney 2003, 323). This commitment is not made simply as a gesture of respect for those of a different religion, but often as the consequence of a specific theological commitment—belief in the radical otherness of God. Summarizing this argument, which he sees as a component of the "acceptance" model, Paul Knitter writes:

> In the other religions (but not only in them), God keeps reminding us of the divine otherness, of the divine "more" that is always more than we can ever know, even more than we can ever imagine or expect. So it is precisely in the finite other that the Transcendent Other of God keeps entering our lives, keeps showing itself to us in the very act in which it evades us. . . . God is being other in the otherness of the religions. Therefore, to reduce the otherness—that means the real diversity—of the religions to some kind of higher or final unity is to reduce the otherness of God to what we can know and possess. But that's another word for idolatry. (2002, 221)

It is important to note in this view that the acceptance of the other as other is driven by a logic interior to the theologian's own tradition, not by an exterior commitment to modern, presumably universal, notions of fairness, tolerance, or equality. Several Catholic theologians are similarly drawing on the doctrine of the Trinity as a foundation for accepting real religious difference and irreducible otherness. Pressing inclusivism in new directions, theologians like Jacques Depuis (2002) and Gavin D'Costa (2000) suggest that the interconnectedness of the three persons of God implies both that nothing is outside of God's work in Christ, and thus that Christians need not sacrifice any of their universal claims, and also that God cannot be contained by the revelation in Christ, that dialogue with the other is therefore required in order to know more of God's fullness. What is preserved in these moves, of course, is not only the distinctiveness of the dialogue partner, but of the "home" tradition as well.

While it will never be possible to remove the interpretive lenses formed by our cultures, experiences, and beliefs, contemporary pluralist scholars are at pains to make those lenses a conscious part of their interactions, rather than to assume that their particular views are universal ones. This is the fundamental challenge of the postmodern shift in intellectual life: how to connect with the other without consuming the other. Theologies of pluralism seem to be reaching, in their various ways, for modes of comparatively analyzing diverse religious traditions that, in Mark Heim's words, "move beyond enlightenment assumptions and yet stop short of the totally relativistic types of postmodernism" (1995, 213).

Including the Unincluded

A critical component of attentiveness to the otherness of different religious traditions that is also receiving increasing consideration is attentiveness to the others within the religions, that is, those whom religious traditions have marginalized within their own social and theological systems. Official dialogical encounters organized by religious and academic institutions tend to be marked, as Ursula King has noted, by the near complete absence of women. "Proof for this is found in every single book on interfaith dialogue, religious pluralism, the theology of religions, or the 'wider ecumenism' of global interreligious encounter" (1998, 42). One could certainly add that poor and minority practitioners of various traditions are equally unrepresented.

There are two important consequences to the elite male dominance of interfaith events. First, it means that issues of specific relevance to nondominant groups will not tend to find a significant place on the dialogical agenda. I recall a painful interfaith session in 1988 at a conference on liberation theology at which a Pakistani Christian woman stood up in anger after a ninety-minute "dialogue" between Muslim and Christian men about their traditions' perspectives on poverty and oppression. Her voice shaking in anger, she demanded to know how a conversation like this could go on for so long without a single reference to the plight of women. Awkward silence followed, but no answers. The potential of interfaith work to address global issues of injustice along the lines suggested by the "socially engaged" or "karmic" model of dialogue is not likely to be realized, more and more participants are coming to understand, if those who suffer these injustices are not made part of the conversation. Feminists invested in interfaith work stress, conversely, the benefit to be gained from women's full participation, not only for the dialogue, but for the religions themselves: "If more women became prominent and visible in such dialogue, this in turn might help to transform the oppressive patriarchal structures of religions and produce more compelling, more just and inclusive, but also more gender-aware religious worlds which would be more life-sustaining and life-enhancing for all peoples and the earth" (U. King 1998, 52).

A second issue raised by elite male dominance of interfaith exchanges is the profound question of who speaks for the religions. Most religions, as Pedersen argues, are "polycentric" rather than centralized in their authority structures, so it is difficult to determine who rightfully represents the traditions. "Further, which are the institutions and communities that will be looked upon as in their turn representing a 'whole' religion? Indeed, what counts as 'a religion'—and who is to decide?" (Pedersen 2005, 16). While women hardly represent a subtradition in most religions in terms of numbers, their perspectives and experiences are severely marginalized by their limited participation in interfaith events and formal theologizing. The "Christianity" and "Judaism" and "Buddhism" that interact dialogically often bear little resemblance to the forms of these traditions lived by women and poor people. This is a feature of the structures of interfaith dialogue—which are typically modeled on highly centralized and bureaucratic world institutions like the United Nations—as well as of the entrenched patriarchalism of the religions themselves. Recognition of these limitations is increasingly pronounced in studies of interfaith relations, and it is likely that more and more attention will be paid in the future to less formal, smaller scale open forums, as well as the dialogue encounters organized by women themselves.[10]

Reckoning with Multiple Belonging

Two generations ago, Wilfred Cantwell Smith, a historian of Islam and one of the most important theorists of interfaith understanding, made a critical methodological move to de-legitimize the reified notion of "religions" as separate, static, and competing entities, and replace it with the concept of interpenetrating "cumulative traditions" with complex histories and soft boundaries (Smith 1991 [1962]). While "religions" have certainly not disappeared from scholarly rhetoric, Smith's insight into the fluid quality of religious traditions and religious experience is a profound one—not yet adequately appreciated by theorists—that may help us to see more clearly the phenomenon of multiple religious belonging that has gained scholarly attention in recent years, and that is clearly critical to understanding contemporary religious affiliation.[11] Multiple belonging refers generally to those who explicitly identify with more than one tradition, maintaining a "hyphenated" religious identity. While many in Asia have long managed multiple belonging quite comfortably, it has only recently come to prominence in the west, the result of immigration bringing new populations into what were once Christian monopolies, along with the development of spiritual individualism and eclecticism fostered by the processes of secularization. For that reason, multiple belonging has generally been studied as a problem for Christian theology.[12]

But more radically, multiple belonging offers a model for understanding all religious experience at all times, and especially in this time of globalization. This came home to me as I was reviewing Paul Griffiths' (2001) incisive analysis of religious difference, in which he uses the terms "religious aliens" and "religious kin" to define the relationship between members of different traditions. It struck me as a Christian that I feel far more alienated from many of my fellow Christians, in my own neighborhood as well as in the Vatican, than I do from many Jews, Buddhists, Muslims, and others, who feel to me very much like kin. The usefulness of such terms is questionable in the face of our growing awareness of the complexity of our identities. Gender, ethnicity, geography, sexual orientation, class, clan, religion—identity is an intricate construct at the individual level; and much more so at the level of millennia-old religious traditions.

Jeffrey Carlson makes this point in his insistence that belonging to any tradition is a matter of "selective reconstruction from an array of possibilities" (2003, 78). As a Roman Catholic Christian, for instance, I am also acutely aware of being a woman, which makes me in many ways an alien in my own tradition. In order to inhabit this tradition, I must selectively interpret those aspects of its history, scripture, doctrine, and ritual that will allow me to remain whole. At the same time, I also inhabit, among other things, feminism and American political liberalism, which interact with my Catholicism in creative ways. In belonging to a religion, this is to say, we never belong entirely, and always belong in other places as well. Some of these places, of course, are religious; increasingly, we all inhabit multiple religious worlds, whether because of the character of our neighborhood, our own spiritual seeking, or our participation in interfaith events. Religious syncretism, or blending, has traditionally been the dangerous boundary that interfaith dialogue has taken pains to avoid, and for good reason. For many religious institutions, the fear that dialogue is aimed, explicitly or not, at developing a single world religion that would strip particular religious communities of their distinctiveness is the primary obstacle to interfaith participation. For that reason, insistence on maintaining the separateness and autonomy of each tradition typically figures prominently in interfaith literature and speeches. In reality, though, some form of syncretism is inevitable, and has gone on all along. As Carlson notes, "there is no whole Christian or whole Buddhist, untouched by and unmixed with the other—and indeed with so much more" (79).

This notion of multiple religious belonging has important implications for academic interfaith work, especially for those interested in affirming some version of pluralism. First, it keeps attention on the internal pluralism of all religious traditions, which deftly solves the pluralist's problem of deciding which religions qualify for admission to the dialogue table; the answer is, of course, all of them, in their own internal complexity. In this model there are no longer aliens or kin whose relationship must be established in order for comparison to begin. All of us, in our strange amalgamated particularity, are simultaneously alien and kin with one another in shifting patterns of belonging. This means, of course, that the comparative religions scholar must attend not only to those sectors of world religious experience that are obviously amenable to dialogical exchange, but also to less "dialogenic," if I may coin a word, forms of religion like fundamentalisms, new religious movements, and other marginal varieties. Peter Huff (2000) has suggested provocatively that if interfaith movements can move beyond the modernist assumptions on which they were founded, they might find fundamentalisms, for instance, to be valuable dialogue partners, "with a distinctive wisdom to contribute to the human community" (100), especially in the global context sketched earlier. Huff calls interfaith theorists, therefore, to a "measured appreciation for fundamentalism's critique of the profound limitations of modernity in all modernisms" (101). Such a focus on the internal pluralism of religions also puts scholarly interfaith work into the service of intrafaith dialogue, which, in these red-state/blue state times, may be a far more urgent project.

FROM THESE INTRICATE MAPS we now turn to the territory itself, the landscape of religious difference and interfaith encounter in the United States. As I have tried to show in this chapter, getting a sense of the big picture of the issues involved in American interfaith relations involves assembling a set of schemas that, like overlays on a map, may complicate as much as they clarify. Intricate questions of how and by whom interfaith encounters are structured, the official positions taken by religious institutions on questions of interfaith relations, complex theoretical analyses of the theological issues involved in those positions—all of these must be understood in the context of the often asymmetrical systems of power and privilege that are prominent features of global societies. Religious diversity, of course, is an age-old fact. Religious pluralism is a conscious reckoning with that diversity increasingly characteristic of American social experience. As new technologies and new demographics bring them into contact with more and more alternatives for religious orientation and practice, and as religious identity becomes more and more diffused into secular life, Americans are faced with profound questions about what was once mostly assumed: What do I believe? And what am I to make of others who believe differently? Whether or not responses to these questions will align with the theories and typologies of scholars is a wide-open question. When Evangelicals and Jews come together on a common conservative political agenda, what becomes of the Evangelical's exclusivism? When Catholics and Buddhists exchange ideas in an online forum, will their positions reflect the official teachings of their institutions? When a Muslim woman marries a Jew, what happens to her sequentialist inclusivism? Are pluralists really the best dialogue partners? The new data being produced by the interfaith religious experiences of ordinary Americans may well make the old maps obsolete; instead of exclusivists, inclusivists, and pluralists, we may find that we have become "shoppers," as sociologist Robert Wuthnow suggests (2005), or eclecticists, or bracketers, or synthesizers, or something else yet unnamed and unmapped. The following chapters explore some of the most interesting places in American society where new ways of thinking about religious others are being generated.

2

Strange Bedfellows

Multifaith Activism in American Politics

In the presidential election of 2004, Americans suddenly discovered color as a defining mark of their political identities—not black and white this time, but red and blue. From its use in network news graphics to represent Republican and Democratic voting patterns, "red state" and "blue state" quickly came to serve as shorthand for broad cultural divisions on everything from gay marriage and prayer in schools to fashion and music tastes.[1] The instant ubiquity of red state/blue state parlance lends credence to the theory, popular since the early 1990s, that the United States is engaged in a culture war (Wuthnow 1988; Hunter 1991) in which the opposing factions are defined not by traditional religious denominational identities, but by a new alignment of liberal Americans (as detailed by Wuthnow) or progressive Americans (discussed by Hunter) on one side and conservative (Wuthnow) or orthodox (Hunter) Americans on the other. Culture war analysis suggests that on either side of this great divide those of diverse faith traditions might be finding common cause and developing interesting alliances, and in the process developing a distinct mode of interreligious interaction. This chapter explores this possibility by examining the efforts of interfaith activist organizations to shape public policy from religiously informed positions, whether it is Jewish and Evangelical Christian joint advocacy for Israel, multifaith efforts for environmental preservation, or interfaith organizations promoting Bible courses in public high schools.

The unique structure of the American political system and the character of American religious pluralism have always conspired to throw religion and politics together in distinctive ways. Today that intersection involves not only Protestants, Catholics, and Jews, but also Hindus, Muslims, Buddhists, and Native Americans who find themselves encountering each other as they try to establish coherence between their religious and civic lives. Interfaith engagements occur in many contexts in the United States today, but it is in political activity that the tension between Americans' adherence to the religious virtue of committed faith and the civic virtue of tolerance emerges most starkly. What are the implications of collaborations between religious groups that have sharply divergent theologies and often a history of mistrust? Are such collaborations purely strategic—calculated compromises necessary for success in the leviathan of American politics—or do they represent authentic interfaith engagements? How are religious conflicts negotiated in the work of political activism? As they collaborate on these political projects, interfaith activists stand to make a distinctive contribution to the changing role of religion in American public life.

Religion and Politics in a "Secularized" Society

Faith-based political activism, both by individual religious groups and interfaith organizations, has increased in volume and prominence over the past two decades, taking many observers by surprise. For the first three quarters of the twentieth century, some version of secularization theory held sway in most intellectual assessments of the role of religion in American society. In its simplest form, secularization refers to the diminishing significance of religious institutions and explanations in human existence, and a corresponding increase in the prominence of scientific and social-scientific accounts of experience. As secularization proceeds, the theory goes, religion becomes a separate sphere of activity, defined by personal beliefs and private practices, and less and less relevant to activities in the public arena—education, law, politics, etc. To a casual observer of American life, secularization might be readily evident: Popular communication forms (television, newspapers, music, film) give minimal attention to religion;[2] Americans tend to trade in psychological rather than theological explanations of inner experiences; our behaviors are more reliably predicted by the logic of a consumer-driven marketplace than by the ethical codes of any religious system; and we remain profoundly suspicious of anything that appears to institutionalize religious belief. The secularization thesis's primary component—the increasing *differentiation* of the religious sphere from other aspects of life—is hard to contest.

It may even, ironically, go a long way toward explaining the renewed vigor of religion in American public life. José Casanova, for instance, compares the relatively flaccid quality of religious life in societies with a history of established religion with the cultural flourishing of religion in places, like the United States, where religion is disestablished, differentiated, and relegated to the sphere of private, socially inconsequential meaning. The autonomy of religion in these circumstances can actually be empowering to religious entities, spurring a process of *deprivatization,* in which "religious institutions and organizations refuse to restrict themselves to the pastoral care of individual souls and continue to raise questions about the interconnections of private and public morality to challenge the claims of the subsystems, particularly states and markets, to be exempt from extraneous normative considerations" (Casanova 1994, 5).

America in the past thirty years offers compelling evidence for Casanova's case. By the early 1980s, it was clear that religion had no intention of staying out of the American public square. The Moral Majority, a coalition dedicated to advancing a conservative Christian agenda in America politics, was formed in 1980 under the leadership of Jerry Falwell. U.S. policy in Central America under Ronald Reagan drew progressive Catholic and Protestant activists, especially those informed by Latin American liberation theology, into both direct actions and sophisticated lobbying efforts. By 2004, a presidential campaign could be won on a direct appeal to "morality," widely understood to refer to the specific position on selected social issues taken by conservative Evangelicals and Catholics. While we may not be in a process of "desecularization," as some scholars have suggested (e.g., Berger 1999), clearly we must understand secularization to mean something other than the disappearance of religion from public affairs, something able to account for this reemergence of religion in American politics.

In its most obvious meaning as "nonreligious," secularism is also hard to square with American reality. For in spite of many popular characterizations of Americans as "spiritual but not religious," the evidence suggests that Americans actually remain *religious*—in the sense of main-taining specific theological beliefs, identifying with specific religious in-stitutions, and participating in regular worship services—at a remarkably high rate, at least as compared with the rest of the developed world, where secularization seems to have carried the day. According to the 2001 American Religious Identity Survey (ARIS), 80 percent of Americans iden-tify with a particular religion and 79 percent believe in God. Robert Wuth-now's 2005 study of American religious diversity puts regular worship service attendance at 42 percent, as compared, for instance, with Great Britain, where a recent survey reported that only 49 percent are reli-giously affiliated and 46 percent have never attended worship services at all. Survey data on religious attendance is notoriously suspect, as people tend to report much higher rates of participation than are actually ob-served, but even if this 49 percent figure is wrong by half, Americans are still involved with religious institutions at a rate much higher than else-where in the industrialized world.[3] Kenneth Wald's study of American re-ligion and politics brings this home with the observation that more Americans identify with a religious denomination than with a political party (Wald 2003, 10).

Secularization in the United States, then, is a highly ambiguous pro-cess, better understood as a kind of *adjustment* of religion to modernity rather than an acquiescence to it (Wald 2003, 14). Casanova helpfully dis-tinguishes between the basic thesis of secularization as a process of dif-ferentiation and emancipation of religion from the secular spheres of the state, the economy, and science, and two sub-theses often assumed to be consequences of that differentiation: the decline-of-religion thesis and the privatization thesis (1994, 17–18). The United States may well be demonstrating the truth of the primary thesis but disproving the sub-theses, pointing to one of the most salient frictions in American social life. As recent, very public, and often strident, conversations about the place of religion in American democracy suggest, the removal of religion from public life is unlikely to occur, and individual involvement in reli-gion remains high. But most Americans are intensely resistant to any-thing that smacks of the establishment of religion, and popular discussions of religion tend toward the generic, inclusive, and inoffensive. There is thus a riddle at the heart of American public life: How does a profoundly religious, and religiously diverse, society reconcile that faithfulness with its nonreligious habits and its firm commitments to pluralism, freedom, and tolerance? This question is nothing new to American life; the tension between these two aspects of American identity has been a deep and productive force in American history.

Chosenness and Diversity in American Religious Consciousness

As Americans responded to the horrifying images of the aftermath of Hurricane Katrina in New Orleans in 2005, many commentators and ordinary observers expressed shock that such a scene could be unfolding "here in America." Subsequent analysis explored the ways in which the disaster removed blinders from many Americans about the depth of race and class divides in their society. Something even more basic can be heard in that initial response, though, than the shock of middle class reckoning with the faces of American poverty. At some very fundamental level, things were supposed to be different "here in America." A vital part of American self-understanding throughout its history has been a belief in its distinctiveness from other countries, a conviction that America would somehow be the exception to the pattern established by the rise and fall of other societies. At its best, this exceptionalism has generated extraordinary displays of egalitarianism and opportunity, self-sacrifice and global generosity; at its worst, imperialism and resistance to international law. Sustaining this belief in the unique role of the United States in the world has been a deeply embedded sense of the sacred nature of its destiny.

It is not uncommon for a human community to conceive of its destiny as uniquely linked with a higher, divine purpose—the Jewish notion of being a chosen people set apart for special responsibilities in history, the Mormon Church's understanding of its mission to establish in America "the moral, social, and political conditions necessary before Christ's reign could occur" (Arrington and Bitton 1992, 37); even some indigenous peoples' self-understanding as uniquely connected with certain sacred places in nature. In the United States, however, this sense of divine purpose was early on attached to the society not only as a religious but also as a political entity, giving rise to the concept of "civil religion," whereby secular symbols and institutions are invested with sacred meaning. Certainly the Puritans who believed they were establishing a model "City on a Hill" in fulfillment of a divine plan for the American wilderness identified themselves as a religious body, but as the nation formed itself into a secular state, the Puritans' sense of sacred mission persisted as a vital element of national consciousness, so that "that cluster of ideas and convictions, the special practices, and sense of peoplehood that belong to America" (Wentz 1998, 57) continue to wear the cloak of the sacred.

Until quite recently, public discourse has tacitly assumed that America's special status is linked to its special relationship with God as a Christian nation. Even today, fully half of the American public, according to a 2002–2003 study, believes that the United States was founded on Christian principles and that its faith has made it strong (Wuthnow 2005, 198). Disestablishment notwithstanding, at times of national crisis and political opportunity, the religious rhetoric of America's divine purpose is heard again and again. Even when the language is not explicitly religious, it is easy to hear Protestant themes in what have come to be accepted as "American" values. The Protestant conception of the human person as an autonomous individual in unmediated relationship with God (as opposed to the corporate understanding of personhood characteristic of Catholicism) informs American individualism. The Protestant critique of the power and ritualism of the Roman Catholic Church lives on in the deep American suspicion of institutions and the insistence that their power always be checked by other forces. The eighteenth- and nineteenth-century revivalists' confidence that God could suddenly initiate dramatically new and better lives finds echoes in contemporary Americans' fondness for psychotherapy, entrepreneurship, and makeover shows. And the persistent understanding of America as the "land of the free" is rooted not only in the Declaration of Independence, but also in the Protestant conviction that Christian freedom could not be bound by any earthly entity. The assumption that America embodies a special divine purpose, then, is coupled with some specific religiously informed ideas that, in secular form, have become major elements in defining that purpose, one also marked by the Enlightenment values of tolerance and equality enshrined in the Constitution.

For much of Protestant-dominated American history, this coupling went mostly unchallenged. But assumptions about the sacred quality of American values and purpose have become more problematic, in part because they now involve critical reckoning with who the "we" of American destiny is. Whenever a group of people regard themselves as special, their self-understanding becomes bound up with their understanding of those others who are not so marked. As Robert Wuthnow puts it, "Regarding themselves as special necessarily implies that some other group is not special and thus raises the question of why this should be so. The question is not simply a matter of idle curiosity but is integrally connected to a people's sense of identity and purpose" (Wuthnow 2005, 9). Throughout American history, the dominant religious group, Protestant Christians, developed multiple ways of answering this question, seeing those others in terms of "a mission to fulfill, foes to conquer, visions of evil to avoid or go to war with, intellectual puzzles to resolve, opportunities to exploit, and reassurance about our moral goodness and cultural progress" (10). Increasingly, these are terms unacceptable to those others, who have grown in number and voice in the past half century.

As immigrant communities of Muslims, Hindus, Buddhists, and others come to define themselves as Americans in their own ways, many resist identifying the United States as a sacred model. American Muslims, for instance, who are tied by religion—and sometimes by national origin and family—to parts of the world targeted by the United States in a "war on terror," are often highly ambivalent about exalted expressions of global American purpose. Statistics indicate that they have good reason to be anxious about their full inclusion in conceptions of American identity and purpose. A 2006 poll found that, four years into the Iraq war, 46 percent of Americans held negative views of Islam (Deane and Fears 2006). A 2003 survey showed that 43 percent of Americans see Muslims as "anti-American" and 44 percent believe Islam encourages violence, up from 25 percent just a year earlier (Pew Forum 2003). The Council on American-Islamic Relations reported in 2004 that incidents of anti-Muslim harassment, violence, and discriminatory treatment rose by 70 percent in the previous year. Questions about what it means to be American, then, are questions that necessarily involve religious referents, as much as we celebrate our official secularity. The negotiations that define a society—how it will educate its children; what counts as science, or as a family; how to regulate the economy—are in the United States negotiations that still bear the weight of these referents. Critical questions now deal with which religious voices are participating in those negotiations, and how their diversity might recast the conversations going on in the public squares of our legal and educational systems, political campaigns, and other national settings.

The Public Role of Religion in America

A study of interfaith political activism lands us squarely in the confusing morass of religion and politics in the United States. As described above, this is a society that is deeply religious, sees its national purpose in sacred—historically Christian—terms, yet celebrates religious diversity as part of its national mythos and is committed to religious freedom and the non-establishment of religion. How are we to make sense of this apparently schizophrenic disposition, and how can it possibly work in political practice? It helps to distinguish the several principles that allow these commitments to coexist. Derek Davis (2004) lays out three sets of rules that govern the complex relation between religion and state in the American society. First, the system specifies the *separation* of church and state, requiring that "the institutions of church and state in American society not be interconnected, dependent upon, or functionally related to each other" (Davis 2004, 34). Second, it encourages the *participation* of religious voices in the political process, inviting "the active involvement of religious persons, faith communities, and religious organizations that vigorously enter public discourse, seeking to persuade government officials of the merits of framing law and public policy to reflect their distinctly religious outlooks" (36). Finally, the American system *accommodates* civil religion, as "a kind of theological glue that binds a nation together by allying the political with the transcendent . . . without getting bogged down in theological differences" (40). The first of these rules is clearly established by the Constitution, the second instantiated by the unique structure of the American political system, and the third, the least explicit, is largely a matter of tradition and habit, and increasingly contentious as the complexity of American religious pluralism surfaces.

Interfaith political activism, though, can draw effectively on the tradition of civil religion to the extent that it has legitimized and accustomed us to generic expressions of religious faith in political settings. These three "rules" are often in tension, if not outright contradiction, with one another, Davis notes, yet the ability to move among them appears to serve the diversity of the nation's constituencies fairly well.

That religious entities have always been public players in the United States is often obscured by more consistent focus on the principle of institutional separation. In fact, the secular and the sacred have been thoroughly mixed in American culture, as historian R. Lawrence Moore argues, both before and since the Constitution prohibited the government from establishing a national religion and protected the free exercise of religion itself. Moore explains that the lack of an established religion in fact contributes to flourishing of multiple religions, or at least, in the early years of the nation, multiple denominations, which in turn fosters a very public role for religion:

> The only certain thing was that religion, without any government sponsorship, was very visible in American public life. The energies that had drawn more and more Americans into organized religions, at the same time driving them, were the forces of market competition. Americans who wanted to build churches had to drum up business. They had to find ways to sell their product and to engage in what would later be called product differentiation. Religious leaders called this activity proselytizing, and many of them became extremely good at it. Their efforts placed religion in the center of America's marketplace of culture and guaranteed that much about American religious life was enacted in public rather than within the church walls of individual denominations. (2003, 17–18)

When modernity pressed for the privatization of religion, then, it was already up against tough odds in the United States, where market forces had long been honing religion's public skills.

Both the motive and the opportunity for religious voices to make themselves heard in American politics are easy to recognize (Wald 2003, 27–31). The free exercise of religion means that religious groups may

lobby, engage in direct actions, and even work to put their own representatives in office at every level of government. They may be driven to participate in these various ways by perceived threats to their religious
freedom, as in Native Americans' efforts to protect the ritual use of pey-
ote in the face of restrictive drug laws, or by institutional self-interest, as
in Christian and Jewish activism on school voucher initiatives, or by deeply
held religious beliefs relevant to public policy, as in conservative Christian groups' advocacy of anti-abortion Supreme Court nominees.

There is thus no "wall of separation" between church and state (a
phrase found not in the Constitution but in a letter of Thomas Jefferson to
a group of Connecticut Baptists), but rather a prohibition against the
state's acting to grant establishment status to any particular religion. On
the face of it then, all religious players are equally free to engage in the
kind of participation in public affairs noted above. In practice, however,
that equality is elusive. "Establishment" of a particular religion is not per-
mitted by the Constitution, but as historian William Hutchison notes, in
much of American history, more subtle forms of establishment have functioned: "Terms like 'establishment' also denoted cultural, literary, educational, and journalistic entities that were Protestant in leadership and
outlook; and a personal network of Protestant elites that extended across
the churches, dominated most of the nation's political life, and managed
virtually all of the 'secular' institutions and social movements in American society" (1999, 39). Even the meaning of religion itself carries this
deeper sense of establishment, with serious consequences for particular
minority traditions. Rita Brock writes of the underlying assumptions
about religion embedded in American law: "When the term 'religion'
appears in the Constitution, it is used self-evidently as referring to something that does not need definition. The implicit definition is androcentric and based in Enlightenment Protestantism, the religious worldview
under which the secular-public/sacred private divide is most intelligible.
Religion is reduced to belief, or faith, and freedom of thought or belief. . . . Religions that resonate with this definition receive greater constitutional protection. Dissonant religions are not free to practice"
(2002, 856–857). Brock makes this point in particular reference to Native American groups, but it applies more widely as well. When "dissonant"
groups seek to make their voices heard in the public sphere, they face

greater suspicion and resistance than do "established" groups to whose presence, rhetoric, and values we are more accustomed. Interfaith alliances on political matters must be understood in the context of this asymmetry of influence. On the one hand, groups representing established religions can lend access and legitimacy to more marginalized groups, while those minority groups can help protect mainline groups against charges of elitism and insularity. Thus interfaith collaboration can have strategic value, as the cases considered below show, even when the broader social visions of the groups involved differ significantly.

An Overview of American Interfaith Activism

Approaching interfaith activism as a site of interreligious encounter involves exploring three interrelated sets of issues: First, which religious groups get involved in interfaith activism and what are the causes that draw them into the political fray? Second, what goes on in these encounters? How are religious differences negotiated? Does any interfaith dialogue actually occur, or are the alliances only strategic and superficial? Third, what is the effect of these alliances? How are they working to reshape the public role of religion and conceptions of religious identity in America? An overview of interfaith activism and a close-up look at three organizations dedicated to multifaith political work show just how complex the role of religion in the pluralistic American public square has become. While interfaith activism thrives at the local level in countless community-based prayer services, demonstrations, and other direct actions, the focus in this chapter is on national activist efforts, given the community focus of the following chapter and in an effort to make sense of the current prominence religious voices now seem to have in political conversations affecting the entire country.

Interfaith political activism today tends to focus not so much on issues pertaining to the legal status of religion and church-state boundary issues as on social issues on which religious perspectives are brought to bear (Wald 2003, 112). As in most dialogue settings in the United States, Christians are by far the most widely represented religious group. Indeed, the rosters of most groups involved in interfaith political initiatives bear witness to the persistence of the tripartite Protestant-Catholic-Jewish conception of American religion. It is typically the presence of Jewish groups that qualifies these initiatives as interfaith (as opposed to ecumenical Christian efforts); only occasionally are Muslim or, even less frequently, other religious communities listed as official participants.

We live in a binary political system, and interfaith organizations, like other activist groups, can generally be characterized as either liberal or conservative, progressive or orthodox. But it is important to note that interfaith activism occurs on all sides of the political spectrum, as well as across political divides. It is often noted, especially since the 2004 presidential election, that the political Left has tended to concede the public role of religion to the Right, focusing instead on vigilance against the state sponsorship of religion (Brock 2002, 858). In many progressive communities, religion is seen as part of the problem, not a potential ally in building solutions.[4] And yet a survey of activist organizations identified as interfaith suggests that there are far more interreligious alliances for progressive causes than for conservative ones.

Several factors may help explain this apparent anomaly. First of all, it is simply inaccurate to equate political liberalism with secularism. While they may be less visible than the Religious Right, there are many progressive Democrats who are deeply involved in religious institutions. And while Americans on both the Left and Right have been active lobbyists, protesters, and influence-seekers throughout United States history, the civil rights, antiwar, and women's movements of the 1960s and 1970s established both networks and strategies for popular political action that have empowered progressive causes ever since.[5] Thus while many on the Left reject a public role for religion, those who do want to enact their religious values in the public sphere find plenty of structures in place to help them. At the same time, certain strains of Evangelical Protestantism have since the late nineteenth century espoused a doctrine of dispensationalism that teaches that conditions on earth will progressively deteriorate until the second coming of Christ, sapping efforts at social reform of their religious significance. More recently, conservative Christians have made a dramatic reentry into political affairs at all levels of government, but theological concerns inhibit the likelihood of their engaging in interfaith efforts, even where common cause is readily evident. Exclusivist conceptions of religious truth and salvation, combined with a spiritual tradition of maintaining personal and institutional separation from what is "ungodly," make it challenging for some Christians to ally themselves with non-Christians, regardless of a common political agenda. "Be ye not unequally yoked together with unbelievers," Paul writes in the Second Letter to the Corinthians, "for what fellowship hath righteousness with unrighteousness?" Under this injunction, it is not surprising that relatively little conservative Christian activism is done in an interfaith context.

Since the 1980s, however, conservative Christian politicking has grown exponentially in volume and sophistication, and today there is considerable interfaith engagement among what had been rather insular groups. Conservative Christians have tended to form interfaith alliances—almost exclusively with Jews—around abortion, religion, and education issues (school prayer, state support for religious schools, etc.), and, most visibly, support for Israel. Conservative Christians share many social values with Orthodox Jews, including opposition to abortion and homosexuality and support for vouchers for religious schools. Liberal and secular Jewish groups tend to align much more consistently with liberal political causes, although support for Israel is a consistent priority among almost all Jewish organizations. Many conservative interfaith efforts are one-time, informal collaborations, as in interfaith pro-life rallies and conferences, or joint position statements on ballot measures. More sustained and structured conservative interfaith activism is supported by such groups as the International Fellowship of Christians and Jews, founded by Orthodox rabbi Yechiel Eckstein, which aims "to promote understanding and cooperation between Jews and Christians and to build broad support for Israel and other shared concerns" (IFCJ 2004).

Liberal interfaith action is more institutionalized, and most commonly focuses on issues of poverty and economic justice, racism, the environment, and war and peace. The Chicago-based National Interfaith Committee for Worker Justice (IWJ), for instance, traces its roots to the 1968 Memphis sanitation workers' strike and "calls upon our religious values in order to educate, organize, and mobilize the religious community in the United States on issues and campaigns that will improve wages, benefits, and working conditions for workers, especially low-wage workers" (IWJ 2004). In 2005, IWJ called on Congress to establish an independent Ethical Reconstruction Commission in the wake of Hurricane Katrina to "ensure that those who were left behind in the evacuation of the Gulf Coast Region will not be left behind again in the rebuilding effort" (U.S. Newswire 2005).

More broadly, there are a number of liberal interfaith initiatives that seek to mobilize liberal people of faith for a range of political causes. The *Tikkun* community, a project of Rabbi Michael Lerner, editor of the bimonthly progressive Jewish magazine *Tikkun*, sponsored a Spiritual Activism Conference in California in 2005 and 2006, aimed both at building a Network of Spiritual Progressives and at promoting greater awareness and appreciation of religious perspectives among the secular liberal and progressive communities. Speakers at the conference included Jim Wallis, John Shelby Spong, Arun Gandhi, and a host of Jewish, Christian, Muslim, Buddhist, Pagan, Sikh, and other religious and nonreligious leaders. Session topics at the Berkeley conference ranged from "Environmental Policy: Sacred Stewardship of the Earth" to "Healing Israel/Palestine" to "Writing on the Wall: The Art of Spiritual Culture Jamming," giving some sense of the ambitious scope of this effort.

Single political issues have sparked interfaith initiatives on both sides of the political divide. Environmental issues, not surprisingly, have drawn together progressives from a wide range of religious traditions that recognize care for the natural world as a religious responsibility. The National Religious Partnership for the Environment brings together Catholics, Mainline and Evangelical Protestants, and Jews "to offer resources of religious life and moral vision to a universal effort to protect humankind's common home and well-being on earth" (National Religious Partnership for the Environment 2005). While this is an alliance of institutions (The U.S. Conference of Catholic Bishops, the National Council of Churches U.S.A., the Coalition on the Environment and Jewish Life, and the Evangelical Environmental Network), others are coalitions of individuals from different traditions.

New Jersey–based GreenFaith, for example, believes that the core values of its approach to the environment—spirit, stewardship, and justice— are religious universals. "All our programming grows from these values, which can be found in all the world's great religious traditions" (Green-Faith 2005). GreenFaith defines as its mission "inspiring people of diverse spiritual backgrounds and religious traditions to deepen their relationship with nature and to take action for the earth." Its members or "partners" are not only those affiliated with religious institutions, but also those in the wider environmental movement who understand a spiritual dimension in their work. Based on this mission, the group works in three program areas. Under the heading of "Spirit," GreenFaith speakers work to educate and inspire religious communities about environmental issues as well as sponsoring Days of Interfaith Environmental Restoration, which bring participants together for hands-on labor and interfaith liturgy. "Stewardship" programs aim at changing the practices of individuals and congregations toward greater environmental responsibility, including increased use of renewable energy and eliminating the use of toxic maintenance materials. Finally, under the heading of "Justice," GreenFaith targets key pieces of legislation each year that it believes can make a significant difference in the lives of those most affected by environmental degradation. The organization lobbies for such legislation and encourages faith-based institutions to do so as well.

While GreenFaith is open to all, its Board of Directors reflects the reality of most interfaith organizations. Of its fourteen board members, five are identified as Jewish (Conservative and Reform), one as Roman Catholic, four as Mainline Protestant (two from historically black churches), and one as Quaker. Two have no religious affiliation identified. While this is an impressively diverse group, it is notable that there are no representatives of religious communities whose concern for the environment is at least as prominent as it is for Christians and Jews. Buddhists, for instance, have a long history of reverence for the earth and engaged activism on its behalf. Native American spirituality is defined by the human interconnection with the earth. Pagan belief and ritual are focused on the life-sustaining power of the earth and its cycles. Demographics can perhaps explain the absence of Buddhists and Native Americans on such a roster; groups that form only a tiny segment of the local or regional population tend to direct their energies inward and can ill afford to expend resources on such broader partnerships. The case of Paganism, however, raises a slightly different issue. GreenFaith's open and inclusive self-understanding and the centrality of nature in Pagan belief and practice would seem to make them natural allies. Lacking a central denominational structure, it is difficult to measure the size of a Pagan community in a given area, but as a very fast-growing religion, drawing significantly on urban, educated populations, New Jersey surely has a sizeable population.[6] The absence of Pagans on the Boards of Directors of progressive groups like GreenFaith speaks to the fact that we have not caught up institutionally with the kind of religious diversity that now characterizes the nation. Especially for groups seeking to make a political impact, issues of legitimacy and credibility are critical concerns. While it is possible that many Pagans are still hesitant to assume such public roles because of persistent prejudice and discrimination, it is also likely that Pagan membership on an interfaith roster would compromise that group's ability to win support in many quarters, and could even jeopardize the affiliation of other members. In the land of disestablishment, we are constantly reminded, some groups remain more established than others.

On the other side of the political divide, another interfaith environmental coalition raises a second set of issues. The Interfaith Council for Environmental Stewardship (ICES) could be the name of countless progressive religious initiatives to protect the environment. Instead, it is the initiative of twenty-five conservative theologians, economists, scientists, and policy experts to provide a "credible alternative" to what they see as a misguided religious approach to religion and the environment. Explicitly a Catholic-Protestant-Jewish alliance, the ICES uses the language of a common "Judeo-Christian heritage" to promote an approach to environmental issues that puts human agency, rather than human restraint, at the center. "The Cornwall Declaration on Environmental Stewardship," released by ICES in 1999, criticizes religious approaches to the environment that fail to acknowledge human dominion in creation and that exaggerate threats to environmental well-being. According to the Cornwall document, neither global warming, overpopulation, nor rampant species loss are scientifically validated concerns, and free market economies, leading to "growing affluence, technological innovation, and the application of human and material capital," are the key to responsible environmentalism (Interfaith Council for Environmental Stewardship 1999). Signatories to this document include very high-profile religious conservatives, including Father Robert A. Sirico, founder and president of the Acton Institute for the Study of Religion and Liberty; James Dobson, president of Focus on the Family; Charles Colson, chairman of Prison Fellowship

Ministries; Richard John Neuhaus, editor of *First Things* and president of the Institution on Religion and Public Life; and Rabbi Daniel Lapin, president of Toward Tradition. Positioning itself primarily as an intellectual initiative, ICES is not an activist organization in the sense of taking direct legislative action. And yet the powerful influence of these and other signatories and their allied groups makes its potential political impact very significant. More recently formed in response to a high-profile "Evangelical Climate Initiative" aimed at galvanizing Evangelical support for efforts to fight global warming, the Interfaith Stewardship Alliance takes a more activist approach by serving as a clearinghouse for speakers, videos, Sunday School curricula, and other materials, and offering spokesmen to news and religious media. As they issue competing calls for support or opposition from the huge and influential National Association of Evangelicals, initiatives like these on both sides of environmental issues, while they do demonstrate the possibility of conservative interfaith political work, are perhaps better understood as internal struggles over the identity and direction of the American Evangelical mainstream.

Close-Up: The Interfaith Alliance

Perhaps the best-known interfaith activist organization is The Interfaith Alliance, a broad coalition formed in 1994 with the explicit mission of offering an alternative religious voice to the "radical religious right" that had come to dominate political discussions of faith. The Interfaith Alliance (TIA) claims membership of 150,000 people drawn from seventy faith traditions, as well as atheists and agnostics. In addition to its national base in Washington, The Interfaith Alliance also has forty-seven affiliates across the country engaged in grassroots activism at the local level. Through congressional lobbying, petition drives, press releases, and educational programs, The Interfaith Alliance seeks to influence policy on such "core issues" as government-funded religion, hate crimes, criminal justice reform, and workplace discrimination. To support its advocacy work, The Interfaith Alliance has also established a partner organization, The Interfaith Alliance Foundation, which "provides training, education, research and other support to a growing grassroots network of clergy and people of faith who are working to promote social justice in their communities" (The Interfaith Alliance 2005). With such venerable celebrity endorsements as Walter Cronkite, whose image appears on its mailings, The Interfaith Alliance has positioned itself as a champion of the "traditional" American values of tolerance, diversity, and civic participation.

Critical to that role is The Interfaith Alliance's establishment of a mainstream profile, maximizing the number of Americans who might identify with the group and minimizing the number who might view it as marginal or even offensive. But this goal of political effectiveness can run counter to the stated goal of embracing broad religious diversity. As with many politically active interfaith organizations, the religious diversity of the Interfaith Alliance is probably much greater among its general membership than its Board of Directors, which includes representatives of Protestant, Muslim, Jewish, and Unitarian Universalist groups, but no Catholics, Buddhists, Hindus, Sikhs, or members of other minority traditions who might support much of The Interfaith Alliance's work.[7] This kind of trade-off appears to be a consistent challenge for progressive interfaith activists.

In its opposition to the Religious Right, The Interfaith Alliance has made style, not just substance, a significant piece of its agenda. According to its original Mission Statement, The Interfaith Alliance "believes that religion best contributes to public life when it works for reconciliation, inspires common effort, promotes concern for the less fortunate, and upholds the dignity of all human beings." This mission also encourages active political participation by all people of faith and insists that "truthfulness, civility, and compassion should always characterize their words and deeds." Its challenge to the Religious Right, then, has not only been on matters of policy, but on the very nature of religious participation in public life. To that end, The Interfaith Alliance has sponsored such events as the "Civility Summit" it organized in New York City in 1999 to foster open dialogue on difficult issues that divide religious groups. Unfortunately, the alliance has so far been unsuccessful in engaging any but like-minded liberal groups to engage in such dialogues.

Leaders of the Religious Right view The Interfaith Alliance's efforts as cynical tactics to retake control of national values. In response to the 1999 summit, for instance, conservative syndicated columnist Cal Thomas insisted that liberals only became concerned about civility after Republicans took over control of Congress. "When the Democrats were in control, it was 'shove it down your throat.' Now we have to be concerned about 'civility'" (Marks 1999, 3). The Interfaith Alliance, for its part, has been vigilant in opposing the confrontational rhetoric of religious conservatives as a primary example of the "misuse of religion" by politicians. In April 2005, The Interfaith Alliance released a statement denouncing radio commentator Rush Limbaugh for stating that "the religious left in this country hates and despises the God of Christianity and Catholicism." Such comments are ignorant and inflammatory, Rev. Dr. C. Welton Gaddy, president of The Interfaith Alliance, said in a press release. "We remain gravely concerned about the continuing manipulation of religion for partisan political purposes. The fusion of partisan politics and religion arrogantly blasphemes religion and aggressively threatens the vitality of democracy" (Common Dreams 2005). Only a month later, however, The Interfaith Alliance found itself on the defensive against similar charges when two of its representatives in Colorado referred to James Dobson and Focus on the Family as "the Gestapo" and "an American Taliban." The Interfaith Alliance issued a formal apology to Dobson and his organization, which was accepted.

The Interfaith Alliance thus demonstrates two interesting challenges at the heart of this kind of religious activism. For The Interfaith Alliance, religious pluralism is a good in and of itself; its multifaith constituency is not merely a strategic means to a political end, but is itself part of the vision the group seeks to promote—a religiously diverse but civically engaged public. And yet, as its Board of Directors roster and participants in its public events suggest, such diversity can be harder to realize in practice than in mission statements. Minority religions other than Judaism are not represented on the board, and The Interfaith Alliance events have thus far been largely unsuccessful at generating dialogue *with* the Religious Right, instead of just about it. Similarly, its commitment to civil discourse and nonpartisanship is often met with cynicism by those whose positions the alliance lobbies aggressively against. Such are the dilemmas of a progressive interfaith group aiming for political success in a society marked by aggressive partisanship and dominance by only a few religious groups.

It is also not clear whether The Interfaith Alliance functions as a dialogical forum for its multifaith membership. As a political entity, the alliance's mission is to influence public policy; its multifaith constituency may not be especially interested in engaging one another in conversation about their religions. The organization does not have an interactive website where members might engage one another, but it does offer passive opportunities for interfaith encounter via its quarterly newsletter, which presents profiles of religious leaders from different communities and reports on interfaith events and lectures. The newsletter also encourages members to become more involved in interfaith activity. In one article, for instance, the Field Department recommends "Seven Simple Ways to Get Active with TIA" that include attending a worship service outside one's own tradition, encouraging one's spiritual leader to organize an interfaith event, and getting connected with those of another faith by joining a local Interfaith Alliance chapter. Given the likely readership of this newsletter, though, it may be hard to find deep differences among the religious communities likely to participate in such events.

Close-up: Evangelical-Jewish Alliances for Israel

If The Interfaith Alliance is one of the most visible interfaith collaborations on the progressive side of the American political spectrum, surely there is no more visible—and controversial—alliance among conservative people of faith than Jewish and Evangelical Christian joint advocacy for Israel. Jewish-Christian relations are notoriously complex, and challenged by a painful history of church-sanctioned anti-Semitism. Most Christian denominations have formally repented of this past, and major initiatives in Jewish-Christian dialogue since the 1970s have made significant strides in repairing that damage. The persistent and systematic effort of many Evangelical Christian groups to convert Jews, though, has left that relationship strained. The Southern Baptist Convention (SBC), for example, passed a resolution in 1996 calling on its membership to "direct our energies and resources toward the proclamation of the gospel to the Jewish people," provoking strong critical reaction from American Jewish organizations. More recently, the Anti-Defamation League has condemned an SBC proposal to use Jewish converts to Christianity as "an evangelistic mission to the Jewish people" (Associated Press 2005). Perhaps the lowest point in Jewish-Evangelical relations in the United States occurred in

1980, when then president of the Southern Baptist Convention, Rev. Bailey Smith was quoted as saying "God almighty does not hear the prayer of a Jew." This conflict was reinvigorated in 2003 when Mel Gibson's film *The Passion of the Christ* was released to enthusiastic praise by many Christian groups, who used it as an evangelizing tool, and strong opposition by many Jewish groups, who identified it as anti-Semitic. How in the world, then, have Jews and Evangelical Christians come together to form a powerful political force with influence at the highest levels of government?

Part of the answer lies in the growing force of conservatism in the American Jewish community. While it not statistically demonstrable that American Jews are voting more conservatively in any sustained pattern, conservative Jewish views have increased in media prominence, and the most conservative branch of Judaism, Orthodoxy, is increasing in both adherents and intensity of observance (Kress 2005). Abortion, homosexuality, school vouchers, and opposition to the perceived secularization of society may be drawing increasing numbers of Jews into common cause with conservative Christians. Central among their shared concerns, though, is U.S. support for Israel. For both Jews and proponents of an increasingly popular movement known as Christian Zionism, a secure Jewish homeland in Israel is theologically, not just politically, critical, although the theological reasoning behind their commitments differs sharply.

According to the "Proclamation of the 3rd International Christian Zionist Congress," adopted in Jerusalem in 1996, "Jesus of Nazareth is the Messiah and has promised to return to Jerusalem, to Israel and to the world," and "[a]t the time appointed by God, the Messiah will return to sit on the everlasting Throne of David in Jerusalem and will reign over all the world in righteousness and peace." For these Christians, the "in-gathering" of Jews to Israel, where they have "the absolute right to possess and dwell in the Land, including Judea, Samaria, Gaza, and the Golan" is a necessary prerequisite for the return of Christ. And while they reject "replacement theology" and insist that the Jews remain the "elect of God," they also see as "vital" the fulfillment of the "Great Commission," that is, the injunction in Matthew 28:18 to "make disciples of all the nations" (Third International Christian Zionist Conference 1996). And while Christian Zionists may be a relatively marginal group in the American religious landscape, their investment in the Christian theological significance of Israel is shared by a wide swath of American Christians. A recent survey shows that more than one third of Americans believe that "the state of Israel is a fulfillment of the biblical prophecy about the second coming of Jesus" (Pew Forum 2003).

For Jews, of course, the state of Israel holds very different significance, as the homeland promised by God in the Hebrew Scriptures and as a vital manifestation of the permanence of the Jewish nation in a world that has consistently pursued its destruction. Theological differences about the ultimate significance of Israel are put aside by Christian Zionists and their Jewish allies, however, given the urgency from both perspectives of protecting Israel in this historical moment. Christian Zionists are now estimated to number 20 million in the United States, and have funneled millions of dollars of donations into Israel, where they have formed alliances with Israeli politicians seeking an expanded "Greater Israel" (Lampman 2004). Israel-focused interfaith groups of Christians and Jews in the United States include Unity Coalition for Israel, Christian Action for Israel, and, most visibly, the International Fellowship of Christians and Jews (IFCJ).

Founded in 1983 by Orthodox Rabbi Yechiel Eckstein in Chicago, IFCJ now has an annual budget of 27.5 million, and in 2003 was listed by the Israeli newspaper *Haaretz* as the second largest charity in Israel. The mission of IFCJ is "to promote understanding and cooperation between Jews and Christians and to build broad support for Israel and other shared concerns. Our vision is that Jews and Christians will reverse their 2,000-year history of discord and replace it with a relationship marked by dialogue, understanding, respect and cooperation" (IFCJ 2004). The IFCJ operates four major programs: "Isaiah 58," a charitable initiative that provides aid to elderly Jews and orphans in the former Soviet Union; "On the Wings of Eagles," which supports the immigration of Jews to Israel; "Guardians of Israel," which provides aid to "victims of terrorism and poverty" in Israel; and "Stand for Israel," co-chaired by Eckstein, Ralph Reed, and Gary Bauer, which "encourages Christian churches, leadership, and individuals to support Israel through prayer and advocacy" (IFCJ 2004). This advocacy work is very high-profile; IFCJ's 2005 "Washington Briefing," a yearly event that brings together U.S. politicians, Israeli leaders, and pro-Israel Christians, included speeches by Joseph Lieberman and Rudy Giuliani, both of whom received the "Friend of Israel" award, as well as former House Speaker Tom DeLay, Senator Rick Santorum, and Israeli Ambassador Daniel Ayalon. Individuals who join "Stand for Israel" are given regular e-mail briefings in which they are encouraged to express their views to local, state, and national legislators; to write letters to local newspapers; and to fund the other activities of the IFCJ.

Much of the success of IFCJ can be attributed to Eckstein's strategic negotiation of religious and political boundaries. A registered Democrat, he voted for Al Gore in 2000, and George Bush in 2004. "Christians and Jews can walk together on separate paths," he says enigmatically, "hand in hand, up Mt. Sinai and accept God's Word" (Eckstein n.d.). According to a 2005 *New York Times* report, "In the last eight years alone, an esti-mated 400,000 born-again donors have sent Eckstein about a quarter of a billion dollars for Jewish causes of his personal choosing. No Jew since Jesus has commanded this kind of Gentile following" (Chafets 2005). If Christian Zionists, who, like most Evangelicals, have little time for inter-faith dialogue generally, are willing to walk this path with Jews, Jewish support for such initiatives is harder to explain. For many, it is seen as a cynical attempt to attract Christian dollars to the pro-Israel lobby. While American Jews as a group tend to fall on the left side of the political spec-trum, support for Israel, as Esther Kaplan notes, "has simply eclipsed other priorities" (2005). For many Jews wary of these alliances, there are three primary stumbling blocks to accepting much-needed Evangelical support, as identified by Carl Schragg in a recent study:

1. Fear of efforts to target Jews for conversion, and the implied lack of acceptance of Jews as Jews;
2. Discomfort with Evangelical notions of "end-times" scenarios;
3. Disagreement with Evangelicals on a host of domestic policy issues ranging from abortion to church-state separation. (2005, 1)

An increasingly popular response to these concerns in the American Jew-ish community seems to be to adopt the traditional approach of coalition-building that agrees to put aside areas of disagreement in order to promote more effective collaboration on a single issue. In this case, it also involves consistent and forceful insistence that Evangelicals desist from conversionary activities in their dealings with Jews. This view is made prominent by the national director of the Anti-Defamation League, Abraham Foxman, who has been a frequent and vocal critic of Evangelical efforts to convert Jews, including speaking out in numerous instances against the Southern Baptist Convention, but who has also been a defender of Evangelical-Jewish alliances for Israel, as laid out in a much-quoted essay, "Why Evangelical Support for Israel is a Good Thing." In that piece, he insists that Evangelical support is "overwhelming, consistent, and unconditional," and that within these alliances, "we will continue to articulate in forceful ways our significant disagreements on social issues" (Foxman 2002). In an era of rising anti-Semitism, many American Jews apparently concur with Foxman that this is no time to be picky about allies.

The political alignment between pro-Israel Evangelical and Jewish groups seems to rely not only on shared support for an uncompromised Jewish state, but also on a shared vision of common enemies. A general concern about rising secularism in the United States can be heard in the writings of both groups, but even stronger is their critique of "radical Islam." Rabbi Benny Elon, member of the Israeli Knesset and chairman of the right-wing National Union Party, has been a strong supporter of Evangelical alliances and is currently a member of the Knesset Christian Allies Caucus. Elon minimizes the differences between Jews and Christians by heightening those between both groups and Muslims. "I try to strengthen the common denominator, which has a scathing dispute with Islam," he says of his recent book on Jewish-Evangelical relations. "I'm not proposing to burn down mosques or make provocations, but neither am I suggesting that the common enemy be disregarded" (quoted in Guttman 2005). At the 2003 "Interfaith Zionist Leadership Summit" in Washington, Jan Willem van de Hoeven, founder of the International Christian Embassy in Jerusalem, said of the Jewish-Christian partnership, "we may have disagreements about who [the messiah] is, but He is not coming back to a mosque but to a third temple," referring to the prophesied destruction of the Muslim Dome of the Rock in a remark that drew a standing ovation (Duin 2003).

Like The Interfaith Alliance, the Jewish-Christian alliance represented by IFCJ uses the language of patriotism to articulate its interfaith vision. Stand for Israel's webpage is red, white, and blue, and displays the American flag prominently. Its supporters frequently make connections between support for Israel and American national purpose, as in this 2003 endorsement by former Attorney General John Ashcroft: "When we experienced the horror of September 11th . . . Israel was among those countries most capable of understanding our national pain and our national thirst for justice not merely as a result of shared pain and agony and sheer tragedy, but as a result of shared values and a shared understanding of freedom. . . . Stand for Israel is playing such a critical role today. Your ability to generate grassroots solidarity for the war against terrorism, here and in Israel and elsewhere around the world, helps the cause of freedom" (http://www.ifcj.org/site/PageServer?pagename=Endorsements). Similarly, respondents to IFCJ's weblog frequently make clear the connection they perceive between U.S. support for Israel, American success, and God's blessing:

> May America stand for Israel anew, so that God's blessing may be upon her. (Ranghild Sodahl, 9/20/05)

> May God be with the connections between America and Israel. (Amanda Chudyk, 9/21/05)

> Isn't it interesting . . . we helped evacuate Israel from the Gaza Strip now God is evacuating us from our land . . . New Orleans, Texas, etc. We had better be careful when we touch God's people. (Billie Norris, 9/23/05)

> God has blessed America because we have stood with Israel. This is God's covenant with America. (Dick Merritt, 9/16/05)

The language of American chosenness, which has for centuries been a feature of national political rhetoric, is here invoked to shore up not only conceptions of America as God's promised land, but also the distinctive link between American destiny and a particular position of the state of Israel.

Clearly the IFCJ and the wider Evangelical-Jewish alliance for Israel is a powerful instance of interfaith *encounter* among Jews and Christians. It is unclear whether it is also an instance of interfaith *dialogue*. The IFCJ website hosts a "Stand for Israel" weblog (http://standforisrael.blogs.com/stand_for_israel/) where one might expect to find substantive exchanges between Christians and Jews responding to the various blog topics, which include weekly messages from Gary Bauer. Blog topics tend to focus on threats to Israel's security, detailing recent Palestinian violence in Israel, and responses to coverage of Israel in the U.S. press. Reader comments on the blog are minimal, with each posting usually drawing only one or two postings. Where readers are engaged, they tend to reiterate sentiments expressed in the blog or, occasionally, express strong and hostile opposition, as in this comment on the enthusiastic response to the 2005 Washington Briefing, at which the indicted former House Majority Leader Tom DeLay was a speaker: "When you have people such as Tom DeLay in your midst, you are just Republican Right wing NUTS. WHEN YOU LAY DOWN WITH A DOG THAT HAS FLEAS YOU ARE BITTEN. AS FRIENDS OF ISRAEL YOU STINK" (Ben Packer, 10/7/2005). Equally vehement is this post from an anti-Israel poster, presumably not a part of the Jewish-Christian alliance at all: "You are symbols of evil at its worst. Your support of this evil entity would also backfires. There is no such thing as israel and will eventually be vanished" (Anti Zionist 10/31/05). There is no evidence on this site of Jewish-Christian conversation on issues that might be of common religious interest or tension—scriptural interpretation, the meaning of covenant, social values, interpretations of Jesus, the ultimate significance of Jerusalem and Israel. Instead, this very conservative group stays focused on a fairly narrow range of almost exclusively political topics, drawing in only those who are equally zealous in their agreement or disagreement with the group's positions.

Close-up: The Bible in Public Schools

The mailing lists, websites, and media campaigns that link interfaith members of groups like the International Fellowship of Christians and Jews, or The Interfaith Alliance, are mechanisms of voluntary connection for like-minded people of different faiths. Those who are not moved to participate in such enterprises may opt out simply by doing nothing. There is one place in American society, however, where people of different faiths are drawn into the public square out of no particular interest in interfaith cooperation: the public schools. Compulsory education in a multifaith society means that, except for those 11 percent of Americans who choose private education, the local public school is inevitably a place of interfaith encounter. And because there is perhaps no topic about which parents are more passionate than their children, this is a site at which those encounters are often highly charged.

In the United States, public schools have also historically served as places where civic values are inculcated, as represented in the curriculum by courses in U.S. government and ceremonially in the daily Pledge of Allegiance. Students tour courthouses and state capitals, report on "current events," hold debates and mock elections, and are encouraged to develop the attitudes of respect and responsibility that foster civic engagement in a democratic society. It is in the public schools, traditionally, that children learn what it means to be a "good American." As American identity has grown more complex due to increased immigration of more diverse populations and movements for greater awareness of and participation by women and minority groups, however, education for citizenship has become a highly contested enterprise, and religion is often at the heart of those contests.

Hot-button issues in schools today—debates about multiculturalism, sex education, school prayer, "character education," evolution and creationism, the "under God" phrase in the Pledge of Allegiance—reflect the high level of tension, and widespread confusion, about how religion and secular education can properly intersect in the United States. Suspicion runs high in conversations about religion and the public schools on both sides of the culture war divide. Some liberal parents and organizations worry that any mention of religion in public schools constitutes a stealth attack by the Religious Right. Many conservative Christians, on the other hand, feel so marginalized by what they see as anti-Christian sentiment and policy in the public schools that they have opted out of the public system for private schools or home-schooling, which increased by nearly 30 percent between 1999 and 2003 (Department of Education).[8] Many others, unclear about exactly what separation of church and state means in the context of schools, and wary of offending or being offended, are quietly caught in the middle.

Underlying this polarization is widespread American confusion about just what the Constitution and the Supreme Court actually stipulate about religion in schools. "Many Americans, both religionists and secularists," writes Bruce Grelle, director of the Religion and Public Education Resource Center, "continue to hold the mistaken belief that the controversial

Supreme Court decisions dealing with prayer and the public schools in the 1960s mandated the removal of all references to religion from the school environment" (2005, 25). In fact, the court has consistently distinguished, as it did in *Abington School District vs. Schempp*, between school sponsorship of religious *practices*, which is not constitutional, and academic study *about* religion, which is. Today, Grelle continues, "there is increasing recognition of the importance of including the topic of religion in the curriculum of public schools, but there also remains considerable confusion on the part of many teachers, parents, and members of the general public about what to teach regarding religion and how to do it" (25). Which religions must be covered in order to achieve impartiality? Can students be required to read the Qur'an? Play-act a religious ritual? Most public school teachers today have no nonsectarian training in the study of religion, and given its dangerous political charge, most opt to have as little to do with the topic as they can.

In this context, interfaith efforts to develop a curriculum for a constitutionally sound high school Bible course seems ambitious, if not downright foolhardy. And yet the interfaith Bible Literacy Project spent five years and two million dollars doing just that, releasing in 2005 its 387-page textbook, *The Bible and Its Influence*. The distinctive approach of this project can best be illustrated by comparison with what at first appears to be a very similar project. Since 1995, the National Council on Bible Curriculum in Public Schools (NCBCPS) has promoted its own Bible curriculum, using the Bible itself as the textbook. On the face of it, this program and the Bible Literacy Project have a great deal in common. Both affirm that their curricula are aimed at education rather than indoctrination; both explore the historical and literary significance of the Bible, and both take as their point of departure the Supreme Court's declaration in the *Schempp* decision that "The Bible is worthy of study for its literary and historic qualities. Nothing we have said . . . indicates that such study of the Bible or of religion, when presented objectively as part of a secular program of education, may not be effected consistently with the First Amendment."

But the similarities end there. While it insists that it conforms to constitutional guidelines, and its curriculum guide exhorts that "No public school teacher should ever endorse, favor, promote, or disfavor or show

hostility to, any particular religion or non-religious faith" (http://www
.bibleinschools.net/pdf/CurrTOB805.pdf), the NCBCPS program has some
clear Christian allegiances. Its Bible curriculum, now reportedly used in
over 275 school districts in 35 states, is produced "in cooperation with"
two conservative Christian organizations, the American Family Association and the Center for Reclaiming America. The links on the NCBCPS website direct visitors to sites promoting creation science, opposing "liberal"
media, and reclaiming America's "Christian heritage" and "Judeo-Christian
values" (http://www.bibleinschools.net/sdm.asp?pg=links). The rhetoric
of the NCBCPS reflects a starkly polarized understanding of American society, and presents the establishment of its Bible curriculum as a critical
step in reclaiming a culture under siege. As one enters the NCBCPS website, triumphant music plays as the words "it's coming back" move toward
the viewer and fill the screen. "The world is watching," the Council's president, Elizabeth Ridenour, writes on the site's opening page, "to see if we
will be motivated to impact our culture, to deal with the moral crises in
our society, and reclaim our families and children" (http://www.biblein-
schools.net/sdm.asp). The goal of this curriculum is "returning the Bible
to its rightful place in American schools," emphasizing "that the Bible is
the foundational document of our society and is the single most influential book in shaping western culture, our laws, our history, and even our
speech. It is a lesson in America's heritage" (http://www.bibleinschools
.net/img/ncbcpsbrochure.pdf). It is important to observe here that "western culture" is identified with "our society," and that both are seen to
have a single, normative relationship with the Bible. For this group, a particular vision of America as a society whose distinctive greatness is linked
with a specifically Christian foundation is the primary motivation behind
the public school Bible curriculum, the inclusion of a rabbi on its Advi-
sory Board notwithstanding.

A very different, explicitly pluralist understanding of American religious identity is at work in the Bible Literacy Project's curriculum initiative.
Whereas the NCBCPS curriculum uses the Bible as its textbook (King James
Version recommended), the Bible Literacy Project curriculum is based on
its textbook, *The Bible and Its Influence,* and does not require students to use
the Bible itself. The textbook contains selections from the Hebrew Scriptures and New Testament, taken from three different sources—The King

James Version, popular among conservative Protestant groups; the New Revised Standard Version, the translation most widely used by scholars; and The Tanakh, published by the Jewish Publication Society. The textbook's treatment of the Bible is primarily cultural; while it addresses many of the theological issues raised by the text and disputed among religious groups, its focus is on the influence the Bible has had on literature, art, and other cultural expressions. Richly illustrated with art from many eras and cultures, the textbook invites students to make "cultural connections," for instance tracking the allegorical parallels (and dissimilarities) between the Bible and the popular *Matrix* movie trilogy. This literary-cultural approach is one strategy for negotiating the constitutional challenge to *teach about religion* and not *teach religion*; students explore the cultural impact of the Bible without any direct or personal reckoning with its religious significance.

The interfaith credibility of *The Bible and Its Influence* is attested by both the list of reviewers and consultants (forty-one scholars, teachers, and religious leaders representing Judaism, Catholicism, Protestantism, Evangelicalism, Unitarian Universalism, and secular academic institutions) and the roster of those who have endorsed it, which ranges from Ted Haggard, then president of the National Association of Evangelicals, to Harold Bloom, Yale University literary critic. The textbook follows the guidelines developed in the report the Bible Literacy Project co-sponsored with the First Amendment Center entitled "The Bible in Public Schools: A First Amendment Guide" (First Amendment Center 1999). The remarkable list of endorsements of this guide cuts across both religious and ideological lines, and includes the American Jewish Committee and the American Jewish Congress, the Council on Islamic Education, People for the American Way, the National Education Association, the Christian Legal Society, the Anti-Defamation League, the Baptist Joint Committee on Public Affairs, the National Association of Secondary School Principals, and the National Association of Evangelicals.

In another publication of the First Amendment Center, *Finding Common Ground: A Guide to Religious Liberty in Public Schools,* the authors lay out strategies for finding common ground in school districts addressing conflicts on religious issues. The first three strategies seem to have been applied in the development of *The Bible and Its Influence,* and may explain its apparent early success. "Agree on ground rules," "include all of the stake-holders," and "listen to all sides," the guide advises (Haynes and Thomas 2002, 63–64). In the press conference following the release of *The Bible and Its Influence*, its general editor, Cullen Schippe, reported that the key tool that made the interfaith collaboration possible was maintaining simultaneous respect for the law, for religious diversity, for diverse faith traditions, for scholarship, and for teachers and students (http://www.connectlive.com/events/bibleliteracy/). Respect is one thing, but aiming to satisfy all of these constituencies is a daunting task indeed. The Jewish community, in particular, has been resistant to public school Bible courses because of their perceived christocentrism, as Marc Stern, general counsel of the American Jewish Congress and a content contributor to *The Bible and Its Influence*, noted at the same press conference.

It remains to be seen whether all will be satisfied, but editor Chuck Stetson reported that the process succeeded by careful avoidance of devotionalism and denominationalism, and, when disagreements arose, agreement to set them aside for the higher common purpose of giving the academic study of the Bible a place in public education. In the textbook, this takes the form of simply reporting on different groups' interpretations of contentious passages. In presenting the creation story in Genesis, for instance, the text notes that "Scholars and faithful readers differ on the date and authorship of Genesis. Even within the first two chapters, some see two distinct creation narratives. . . . Some read Genesis as a literal account of the mechanics of creation. Still others read it as a poem about God's relationship with humans. Many read the book as both" (Schippe and Stetson 2005, 28). Similarly, different readings of the "suffering servant" image in the Book of Isaiah are simply reported, with no effort to adjudicate among them: "In general, Christians see the servant songs as a specific foreshadowing of Jesus and his sufferings. . . . Jews often read the suffering servant as a portrait of Israel as a whole. Others . . . view the servant as a portrayal of the 'remnant' who remain faithful to God despite exile. Some Jews do see the suffering servant as description of the messiah . . . but others do not" (115).

Such solutions were achieved through the editorial process. Reviewers representing Jewish, Catholic, mainline Protestant and Evangelical perspectives were given galley sets for comment; when views were not in accord, the editors incorporated reports of the variance into the text (Weber 2005). This process goes a long way toward the goal of hermeneutic neutrality, but it should also be noted that the presentation of multiple interpretations of scriptural passage is itself a kind of normative move. All readings are given formal parity in this approach, which, while clearly appropriate to a public school setting, will not satisfy the most conservative religious constituencies, who might prefer no Bible study over one of this type.

It is perhaps not surprising, then, that this curriculum, though widely praised in the mainstream media, is not receiving universal acclaim. The National Council on Bible Curriculum in Public Schools, for instance, has released a brochure warning about "comparative religions" approaches to Bible curricula. While not naming the Bible Literacy Project specifically, the brochure identifies "groups and individuals with controversial pasts and questionable motives" behind such programs, among the "most troubling" of which is The First Amendment Center, which co-sponsored the production of *The Bible and Public Schools* guide with the Bible Literacy Project (NCBCPS). In several state legislatures, the two competing curricula are now the subject of rival "Bible bills," with both Democrats and Republicans eager to show their respective constituencies their commitment to one or the other of these very different views of the place of the Bible in public education (Haynes 2006).

When *The Bible and Its Influence* was released, a conservative news and discussion website, Liberty News Forum, broached the question of whether the Bible Literacy Curriculum was "good news or bad news." The site's host offered that "greater general knowledge of Christianity would be a plus, even from a strictly academic viewpoint. But I'm wary of the book's application by the lefties who run our public school systems" (Liberty News Forum 2005). Responses from discussion participants reflected similar views—attraction to the idea of a fair and balanced presentation of the Bible in public schools coupled with deep suspicion that that could ever occur, given the perceived secular, liberal bias of the educational system. On the other side of the cultural divide, many are suspect that the Bible Literacy Project's textbook represents a stealth move by the Religious Right. A contributor to the "Meat-Eating Leftist" blog, for instance, frames the new curriculum this way: "Since religious zealots have been having a difficult time getting public schools to teach courses on christian scripture, they have come up with an idea that they are now pitching that will try to circumvent the law and the separation of church and state: A textbook called '*The Bible and Its Influence*'" (bobriven, meat-eatingleftist.com, http://www.meateatingleftist.com/mt/archives/2005/09/the_bible_ and_i.php>, September 22, 2005).

With suspicion running this high, the coalition that came together to produce *The Bible and Its Influence* has understandably gone to great lengths to emphasize its religious neutrality. For this textbook, what is important is that students come to recognize biblical allusions in literature, trace the influence of biblical rhetoric in American politics and popular media, and come to appreciate the Bible's cultural significance, not that they do religiously sound exegesis. In this way the Bible Literacy Project reflects a common feature of pragmatic interfaith work: dialogue is pursued not to arrive at religious truth but to arrive at a common goal. Indeed, in this case, the producers of the Bible curriculum do not even want the "interfaith" label attached to their project (Weber 2005). Given the importance of its secular constituency and the need to appear absolutely neutral religiously, the Bible Literacy Project opts to avoid any faith referent in their self-description, even though the majority of the textbook's reviewers and advisers are religiously affiliated.

It is difficult to evaluate, then, in what sense the Bible Literacy Project and its new curriculum represent an enterprise in interfaith dialogue. Like the activist organizations described earlier, its participants apparently have little face-to-face encounter. The editorial process leading to the publication of *The Bible and Its Influence* clearly involved a degree of interfaith negotiation for a common goal, and at least one of the reviewers, Leland Ryker, an Evangelical scholar, reports having "learned something new on virtually every page" (Bible Literacy Project 2005a), but significant reckoning with issues of religious difference is more likely to be an unintended outcome than an intentional part of this project. While the process of producing *The Bible and Its Influence* might not have been deeply dialogical, it is possible that this textbook may *create* a site of interfaith encounter in a very unlikely place: the American public high school. Simply providing the structure for conversation about religion in a public place—where multiple religious and nonreligious perspectives are present and where ground rules are in place—is a significant act in a society in which anxiety about religion in public places has contributed to both ignorance and bigotry. It is interesting to ponder the possibility of an elective high school Bible class functioning as a kind of demilitarized zone in the midst of a raging culture war.

Making Public Space for Religious Difference?

The effort to bring religious ideas and values into public affairs is far more complex, as these cases show, than a simple crusade of religious Americans against nonreligious Americans for control of public life. Interfaith coalitions formed around public policy issues cross both religious and ideological lines. While most alliances link conservatives from one religious tradition with those of another, or liberals with their counterparts in other religions, some issues, like promoting academic study of the Bible in public schools, bring together those who might oppose one another on most conceivable ballot measures. Such coalitions add complexity to culture war analysis, for they remind us that red and blue can come together on a range of issues, and that so-called progressive and orthodox Americans do not always act as united blocs.[9]

As a context for open and exploratory interfaith dialogue, these public initiatives are also ambiguous. The work of The Interfaith Alliance, The International Fellowship of Christians and Jews, and the Bible Literacy Project suggests that the effort to affect public policy, while a powerful motivator for interfaith coalition-forming, may not be a venue well suited to interfaith (or political) dialogue. These groups speak *to* their political bases *about* their political opponents with little red-blue engagement, and even within their organizations they do little to foster serious interfaith conversation. As seen in the postings on the IFCJ website, the single-issue focus of the alliance tends to promote the language of politics—polarized and impassioned—over the open and exploratory language of interfaith dialogue. In a similar way, the rhetoric of The Interfaith Alliance, for all its endorsements of diversity and the healing role of religion in national life, sets up a binary opposition between its perspective and the "political extremism" of the Religious Right. As noted in the case of the Bible Literacy Project, however, serious interfaith encounter can be an outcome of such initiatives, even if it is not an explicit part of their mission. This may also occur in the case of Jewish-Evangelical advocacy for Israel, where events organized by groups like the International Fellowship of Christians and Jews—a prayer service in an American city or a tour of Israel—may lead members of the two communities into dialogue with others whom they might not otherwise ever have encountered. Such encounters may also occur at an interfaith event sponsored by a local chapter of The Interfaith Alliance. Dialogue, of course, is premised on awareness of the differences among participants that make conversation interesting; for political coalitions like the IFCJ, The Interfaith Alliance, and the Bible Literacy Project, internal (religious) difference is bracketed so as to maximize contrast with the political opposition, against which the language of difference is invoked for strategic purposes.

Another consequence of the strategic nature of interfaith political alliances is their tendency to limit the range of religious identities represented. Whereas some interfaith venues (local interfaith councils, university forums, etc.) seek to maximize the diversity of faith communities represented, in the case of those organizations operating in politically polarized contexts, a roster of participants that actually "looks like America" can be a strategic liability. It is very rare to see a major interfaith coalition aiming to affect public policy in the United States today listing Pagans, Mormons, or Jehovah's Witnesses, for instance, on its board of directors or staff. When the goal is to influence policy on a large scale, many groups have apparently opted to include only those groups whose presence or endorsement is not likely to alienate more supporters than it might draw. This mechanism is illustrated in the way that National Council on Bible Curriculum in the Public Schools criticizes alternative approaches to Bible education by highlighting their suspect affiliations, notably Harvard University's Pluralism Project: "This group is dedicated to the rejection of absolute truths, the advancement of a 'new world order,' and the blending of all religions into one. Among its board members is a leading Wiccan witch who authored a popular book advocating contemporary Paganism along with a leader of the Freedom Forum/First Amendment Center" (NCBCPS 2005). While most organizations use this strategy of politicking by association more deftly, the different combinations of Protestant, Evangelical, Catholic, and Jewish affiliations that typically define "interfaith" coalitions attest to the challenge of building widely inclusive interreligious alliances. Establishing distance between religious institutions, it appears, can be just as effective a political strategy as forming coalitions.

One thing these alliances already demonstrate is that interfaith activity is no more likely among those we might classify as pluralists than among those with exclusivist religious views. Theologies of religious difference are not articulated by most interfaith coalitions, and yet their language hints at their different ways of linking American diversity with common purpose. Conservative groups' rhetoric of moral clarity, individualism, tradition, reclaiming an idealized past, and defense against perceived threats complements exclusivist theological constructs of a solitary path to salvation that must be guarded against weakening compromise. Whether it is in the International Fellowship of Christians and Jews or the Interfaith Council for Environmental Stewardship, the coherence between these political and religious discourses facilitates alignments across religious divides. Similar correlations are at work on the liberal side. GreenFaith, The Interfaith Alliance, and other progressive interfaith organizations ally the political rhetoric of tolerance, diversity, and democratic participation with the religious language of pluralism and spiritual openness to mobilize diverse religious groups for common action. Thus without laying out a theology of religious difference, these groups use cultural codes that appeal to their different constituencies and subtly reinforce exclusivist and pluralist patterns of interfaith relations within the context of interfaith work itself. The most difficult challenges, then, lie with conservative coalitions whose political and religious rhetoric tends toward restricted conceptions of truth and righteousness. Justifying alliances with groups who do not share the same conceptions is delicate work, however strategically valuable.

The political context of these efforts also creates potential challenges for the theological integrity of member groups. Throughout American religious history, as R. Laurence Moore has shown, compromise has been the price of a public role for religion. Making the case for religion's social benefits "requires inventing public expressions of religion that give as little offense as possible" (Moore 2003, 23). This can mean not only limiting the roster of those with whom one is willing to collaborate, but also minimizing some of the particularities of belief and practice that distinguish one group from another. In the case of the Jewish-Evangelical alliance, for instance, a certain reticence about the ultimate status of Judaism comes to characterize the public expressions of Evangelical participants. On the liberal side, The Interfaith Alliance champions religious freedom and celebrates the United States as being "the most religiously diverse nation in the world," but does not call upon that diversity with any specificity. If good interfaith dialogue is contingent on maintaining one's own distinctiveness and engaging others in theirs, as most theorists of interfaith relations insist, the strategic avoidance of those areas in which particularities might collide is another reason to conclude that politics is not the best arena for real engagement across religious lines.

And yet the potential of these public alliances for enhancing the depth and quality of interfaith relations is very real. While they may not have dialogue on the agenda, coalitions like those described build relationships—institutional and sometimes personal—that are the foundation on which dialogue can be built. While familiarity with religious others may not necessarily breed harmony, it is clear that the reverse is true: ignorance about and lack of experience with members of another religion are correlated with negative views. The 2003 Pew Forum report "Religion and Politics: Contention and Consensus" found, for instance, that white Evangelicals have the most negative view of Muslims of all major religious groups (Pew Forum 2003), and the Religion and Diversity Survey conducted in 2002–2003 found that "exclusivist Christians" have the lowest level of interaction with Muslims (Wuthnow 2005, 213). As will become clearer when we look at local, community-based interfaith work in the following chapter, relationships formed in interfaith coalitions for political purposes can temper a group's tendency toward extremist views and intolerant attitudes toward religious others. It becomes harder to take a hard line against a particular religious group when you have worked in common cause with members of that group. For this potential to be realized among activist groups, of course, those relationships must actually be developed; as of yet, that potential seems largely unrealized. The public nature of these activities, though, has had the effect, as seen clearly in the case of The Interfaith Alliance, of moderating polemical rhetoric about the political opposition, a development that may contribute to improving the climate for contentious public conversations about religion.

A more interesting, and subtle, way that these activist alliances might contribute to new patterns of American interfaith relations is the way in which they work to define a space for religious ideas and activities in the public sphere in interreligious terms. One important basis for public co-operation among religious groups is the increasing sense of the trivialization of all religion in a society characterized by secular media saturation and extremely high rates of religious illiteracy. According to a 2005 study, only 10 percent of American high school students could even name five major religions of the world; 15 percent could name none (Bible Literacy Project 2005b, 37). For different reasons but with shared urgency, then, many American religious communities have a stake in augmenting the public presence of religion. As Wuthnow puts it, "diverse religious groups may band together despite their differences in hopes that preserving any religion is better than living in a world devoid of religion" (Wuthnow 2005, 102). American Muslims, Hindus, and Buddhists, he finds, are anxious for other Americans to better understand and respect their religions based on real familiarity and knowledge (72). Many American Christians want their religious values reflected in school curricula, abortion laws, and U.S. foreign policy. Other religious groups want to bring their religious principles to bear on policies pertaining to workers, prisoners, and the environment. Individually, every religious group in the United States is a minority, and thus pursuing these goals in coalitions with those of other faith traditions is politically savvy. As American identity grows increasingly complex and pluralistic, these alliances will need to negotiate more and more intricate issues of identity and purpose.

Interfaith activism as illustrated by the groups and initiatives considered here continues to draw on a powerful language of American distinctiveness and high purpose, the language of civil religion. But yoking different religious constituencies together for common civic purpose is now far more complex than invoking the "triple melting pot" of Catholic-Protestant-Jew. New religions, the religions of new immigrant communities, and the views of the large segment of the population that wants nothing to do with religion must all be taken into account if religion is to have a part in the reweaving of an American sacred canopy. In this light,

some of the interfaith efforts considered here, in which very little difference is actually encountered, might be read as cynical attempts to use
pluralism as a vehicle of antipluralism. And yet even in these cases, an
important move is being made to stake out a space for conversations
about religion in which multiple religious voices might weigh in on matters of public concern. Even where no interfaith dialogue is on the
agenda, these initiatives function as placeholders where such dialogue
might occur in a society in which such places are very rare.

3

When the Other Is Neighbor

Community-Based Interfaith Work

A "community" is a slippery thing to define. On the one hand, it has come to refer to any group of people with a common interest or identity—we hear of the "Asian American community," the "pro-life community," the "transgender community," even, in a trade publication I spotted recently, the "event-planning community." On the other hand, geographically defined communities—the towns and neighborhoods where we live—are often anonymous places where we know only a few people, where the stores are just the same as in neighboring towns, and where few of us can name a single city councilperson. Given this context, many Americans find—and create—their social networks in alternative places: at work, at church, at sports bars, online. Certainly technology has facilitated our ability to define our communities for ourselves; countless web-based organizations have links to click where you can find a "community" to discuss everything from weight loss to politics to the best brands of baby clothes. At the heart of this explosion of meanings is a riddle of contemporary American life: Is our community something we can assemble ourselves through careful processes of affiliation, or is it the people we are stuck with based on accidents of geography? This chapter examines the work of Americans dedicated to resolving that riddle through intentional efforts at community-building in place-specific contexts, through the mechanism of the community interfaith council.

If the true work of interfaith relations is the face-to-face encounter with the religious other to negotiate issues of mutual concern, then local interfaith councils certainly look like the real deal. Around folding tables in church basements, synagogue libraries, or community centers in cities and towns across the country, Catholics, Protestants, Jews, Hindus, Muslims, Mormons, Baha'is, Buddhists, Unitarians, Sikhs, and others come together on a regular basis to learn about each other, coordinate soup kitchen staffing, lobby local leaders on social justice issues, organize multifaith prayer services, coordinate staffing of prison and hospital chaplaincies, or respond to a community crisis.

Interfaith organizations have exploded in number in the past quarter century. In 1980, a study done by the National Council of Churches Committee on Religion and Local Ecumenism reported that there were a total of twenty-four interfaith councils in the United States (National Council of Churches 1980). Today, the Pluralism Project at Harvard University has gathered information on over five hundred such organizations (Pluralism Project 2006). There are obvious reasons for this dramatic growth: the increased prominence of immigrant communities bringing nonwestern traditions into closer contact with Christians and Jews; the growth of spiritual "seeking" in the post–World War II population; the increased need for interfaith cooperation on social services in light of dwindling public resources; and growing concern about the role of religion in local and global conflict. A unique set of circumstances pertains in each community, but it would be hard to find a city of over 50,000 people today without an interfaith organization of some sort, and countless much smaller communities are part of the movement as well. In addition to local organizations, there are now meta-organizations like the North American Interfaith Network (NAIN), which facilitates communication and support for interfaith organizations throughout the United States, Mexico, and Canada; and People Improving Communities through Organizing (PICO), an Oakland, California–based network of diverse faith-based groups dedicated to urban, suburban, and rural community problem-solving. It is clear that interfaith work in the United States is no longer the informal effort of a few open-minded communities but a well-established, organizationally sophisticated, and increasingly mainstream phenomenon.

Local Interfaith Organizations: A Snapshot

A survey of 25 randomly selected community-based interfaith organizations from across the United States offers a snapshot of who's involved in local interfaith efforts and how they conceive of their work.[1] Based on their mission statements, the rationale for such organizations is quite consistent. Of these twenty-five groups, eleven defined their purpose primarily in terms of social service programs—alleviating poverty, housing the homeless, community organizing and education, and the like (two of these had a more narrow programming focus, one on housing and one on youth issues). Eight were focused on building bridges of dialogue and understanding among different faith communities. Four presented an equal emphasis on social programs and dialogue. And two had distinctive missions—one dedicated to clergy support and one to GLBT outreach. The basic split represented here—between a focus on interfaith relations and a focus on community service work—represents a perennial issue for interfaith groups: Do they come together to achieve a common goal, or is coming together itself the goal? Responses to this question have far-reaching effects on everything from membership policies, to whether or not the group worships together, to the kind of profile it assumes in the wider community. The dilemmas involved in these responses will be explored in depth below in the close-up account of two very different interfaith councils.

Other studies of interfaith groups suggest that many arise in response to particular events; certainly there are far more interfaith councils in the United States since September 11, 2001, than there were before. The controversial 2004 film *The Passion of the Christ*, hugely popular among many Christian groups but charged with anti-Semitism by Jewish and other groups, generated a surge in Jewish-Christian dialogues, panel discussions, workshops, and clergy meetings (Edelheit 2005). In Marin County, California, an interfaith group came together in response to disastrous floods in 1982. What began as a joint emergency relief effort developed into a thriving interfaith organization, one of the relatively few in the country that were founded as interfaith, that is, truly interreligious, not just interdenominational. Today Marin Interfaith is driven by a three-part mission to celebrate religious traditions, promote justice, and build community.

Part of the success of local interfaith organizations can be attributed to the established infrastructure of the Christian ecumenical movement, whose organizational model many interfaith groups have adopted. Indeed, many interfaith organizations developed out of their communities' intra-Christian groups; the 1990s saw the reinvention of many "councils of churches" as "interfaith councils" with the added involvement of Jewish, Muslim, and other religious groups. Of the seventeen surveyed groups whose history is published, seven were originally ecumenical Christian organizations (interdenominational groups dedicated to intra-Christian cooperation). These groups typically moved to a truly interfaith structure in the 1980s or 1990s, and today reflect no less religious diversity than their counterparts that were interfaith from their inception. If there is a reason some groups have more success than others in achieving diversity reflective of their communities, then, it does not appear to lie in the presence or absence of Christian origins.

The makeup of community interfaith councils can be difficult to track, given the variety of organizational structures, and the frequent gaps between official membership and actual participation. Some councils restrict membership to clergy, so that religious leaders form the membership; others are a specified mix of clergy and laity; others define membership in terms of whole congregations, who are free to appoint their own representatives; and still others, particularly those dedicated to dialogue and mutual understanding, appear open to all interested parties. Several organizations have multiple tiers of affiliation: boards of directors (who form the core membership), supporting congregations, and "affiliates" (groups who may not, for a number of reasons, desire or be invited to official membership). Groups primarily dedicated to social action often have affiliate relationships with local secular social service agencies as well as with advocacy groups from constituent denominations.

The collective religious diversity of these organizations is extraordinary. Protestants, Catholics, and Jews, not surprisingly, show up most frequently on lists of faith communities involved. Of the twenty-three groups in my survey who listed their religious constituency, fifteen also included Unitarians, fourteen included Baha'is, and another fourteen listed Muslims. Nine listed other Christian members, eight had Buddhists, seven had Hindus and/or Jains; another seven included Sikhs, three had Orthodox

Christians, and two had Sufis. Native Americans, Zoroastrians, and the International Society for Krishna Consciousness (Hare Krishnas) were represented on one membership roster each.

The Politics of Dialogue: Who's at the Table?

These numbers suggest interesting dynamics that both pull some very small groups into interfaith work at a high rate and suppress the participation of other, larger groups. Baha'is, for instance, make up only one twentieth of one percent of the U.S. population, yet are represented twice as often on interfaith councils as Hindus, of whom there are more than ten times that number in the United States. The central concern of the Baha'i religion to promote world peace and racial harmony surely contributes to its relatively high profile in interfaith work. At the same time, Hinduism, while it has deep American roots through such groups as the Vedanta Society, is still closely associated with recent immigrant communities that are both less geographically dispersed than Baha'is and more focused on establishing their own American presence through temple construction, community building, and ritual adaptation.[2] Of course, affiliation with an interfaith council is not always a matter of choice for a faith community. American Pagans, whose religious beliefs correlate well with the work of interfaith groups in that they emphasize a plurality of spiritual paths, and who typically have a high level of community activism, were represented on none of the councils in my survey. Again, pure numbers cannot account for this, since Pagans, though notoriously difficult to count, are at least as numerous as Baha'is in the United States (Pluralism Project 2005). A more likely explanation is the marginal status of Paganism, which remains erroneously associated in many minds with anti-Christian and Satanic belief and practice. Still, Pagans push for a greater role in interfaith work, and are achieving it at the national and international levels. A Wiccan priestess was on the organizing committee of the 2004 Parliament of the World's Religions in Barcelona, and Pagans are active in the North American Interfaith Network and the United Religions Initiative, an international group that works on projects of human betterment, operating on a small-group "cell" model (Wuthnow 2005, 296–299). Grove Harris cites three reasons for Pagans' lower level of participation at the local level: the resistance of local communities; the perception that Pagans are a political handicap to an organization's efforts; and the risk that Pagan presence might split fragile alliances already established in an interfaith organization (70).

The complete absence of Pagans in any of the groups I surveyed attests to this pervasive suspicion, but in specific locales such suspicion might also attach to other groups who might be welcomed elsewhere. In her study of American Hindu communities, for instance, Diana Eck cites a letter from a pastor in suburban Boston opposing the invitation of the growing Hindu community to join the local Clergy Association: "I believe that the inclusion of the Hindu community into the Clergy Association is making either an explicit or implicit statement to the community at large that other religions are valid and that Jesus is not unique but one of many! Is that what the association wants to purport to the community?" (Eck 2001, 81). If this pastor is representative of his community, then indeed there is much at stake in extending community interfaith organizations beyond the widely accepted Protestant-Catholic-Jewish configuration. The association referred to in Eck's discussion sponsored a Domestic Violence Task Force, an interfaith Martin Luther King Day observance, and an interfaith Thanksgiving service; one could hardly accuse them of lacking a community spirit. But when cooperation in such programs is premised on theological affinity, they can only tolerate so much diversity. Thus it is often those groups who aim to be most socially efficacious that have the narrowest range of faith traditions represented on their boards; the possibility of alienating supporting constituencies by including more marginal groups is one that must be weighed carefully.

Gender can also function as a regulating mechanism in interfaith council membership. Some religious groups are resistant to joining an organization in which women religious leaders are recognized as legitimate, so the presence of a female minister or rabbi on a council, for instance, may preclude the participation of other, more conservative groups. At the same time, many traditions do not permit women to be ordained leaders, and thus if an interfaith group specifies a certain number of seats be held by clergy, women stand very little chance of achieving anything like equal representation. Roman Catholic women, for instance, may often sit on such interfaith councils as lay representatives, but can never achieve parity with their male clerical counterparts. Perhaps in response to this problematic status, there are now several well established interfaith groups specifically for women, like Syracuse's Women Transcending Borders, which started with two women talking over coffee following 9/11 and now sponsors monthly gatherings of over forty women, led by a governing council that includes Catholics, Protestants, Jews, Muslims, Pagans, and Buddhists.

This brief survey may suggest that interfaith work is a vibrant part of most religious congregations, but most studies indicate otherwise. Larger studies of the behavior of religious congregations suggest that all these interfaith efforts are actually a low priority for most religious groups. A 2001 study by the Hartford Institute for Religion Research, for instance, found that only 7 percent of the 1,400 congregations surveyed had held an interfaith worship service, and only 8 percent had engaged in interfaith social outreach programs (Dudley and Roozen, cited in Wuthnow 2005, 234). Robert Wuthnow's 2005 Religion and Diversity Survey showed much higher rates of interfaith activity, but these varied widely among different kinds of religious communities. Southern Evangelicals had the lowest rate of sponsoring interfaith activities (32 percent reported having done so), while mainline Protestants in the Northeast and West and Catholics in the West all had rates of 53 percent, and Jews overall had the highest rate, at 88 percent (Wuthnow 2005, 234). Possible explanations for this disparity will be explored below in the context of specific community interfaith organizations, but there are clear denominational patterns of participation. Wuthnow explores the "avoidance strategies" by which some Christian congregations even in highly religiously diverse communities account for their lack of deep involvement with those of other religions: the limits of overburdened schedules, a focus on ethnic rather than religious diversity, feared resistance of congregants, and, of course, specific theological objections to participation in structures that appear to grant equal status to all religions (244–247).

Even if interfaith programs are not major elements of most congregational programming, though, the expectations of a culture steeped in the language of tolerance and diversity makes complete rejection of such initiatives problematic. Thus many communities engage in ceremonial affirmations of pluralism—joining with other clergy to inaugurate a civic endeavor, holding an interfaith service in a time of crisis. As Wuthnow notes, such celebrations are typically "abbreviated, well defined, ceremonial events that do not occur very often" (248), thus requiring very little of congregants in terms of serious interfaith engagement. The theological underpinnings of such interactions are often vague or entirely unstated, and potential conflicts carefully avoided, leaving in place what Wuthnow calls the reigning national approach on religious pluralism: "easy tolerance and limited interaction" (257).

For many, however, such soft pluralism is unsatisfying, and the desire for deeper experiences of engagement with religious others takes them beyond gestural congregation-sponsored events to participation in community-based interfaith organizations. A close-up look at two of these organizations, one in a small city in an agricultural area, one in a large urban area, allows us to see some of what motivates such people, how the dynamics sketched above work in actual practice, and how interfaith work shapes both what it means to live in a community and what it means to be religious in America.

Chico Area Interfaith Council

Chico, California, is a town of approximately 75,000 people at the northern end of California's Central Valley, about ninety miles north of Sacramento, and about a three-hour drive from San Francisco. The town is home to a public university hosting 15,000 students and has a historic downtown surrounded by almond and walnut orchards, with rice farms dominating the landscape as one moves farther outside of town. In the face of rapid population growth spurred in part by skyrocketing housing prices in the Bay Area, the city struggles to maintain its small town charm and special sense of place even as "big box" stores and chain restaurants fill in the once open landscape. Chico's median annual income remains below the national average, at about $29,000 per household, and the city has very limited ethnic diversity—the Latino population stands at about 12 percent, while the African American, Native American, and Hmong populations stand at 2 percent each. Religiously, though, there is considerable variety. In addition to at least one church representing Roman Catholicism, Eastern Orthodoxy, and each mainline Protestant denomination, there is

at least one of each of a wide variety of other Christian groups including
Quakers, Seventh-Day Adventists, Jehovah's Witnesses, Mormons, and Christian Scientists. There are several Assemblies of God churches, an AME
church, and numerous nondenominational Evangelical churches. There
is both a Jewish synagogue and a Havurah community, a Unitarian Universalist Fellowship, a Baha'i community, an Islamic Center, a Zen Buddhist Sangha, and a Church of Religious Science. Local Native Americans,
including Mechoopda and other Maidu groups, are religiously diverse
themselves; many are staunch Christians, while others continue to practice what aspects of their traditional religion have been passed down to
them, including sweat lodges and Sun Dances.

Interfaith activity in Chico is well established, with organized efforts
going back nearly fifty years. Like many interfaith organizations, the Chico
Area Interfaith Council (CAIC) began life as an ecumenical Christian
group, the Chico Council of Churches. In its original mission "to witness
more fully our essential oneness in Jesus Christ," the Council of Churches
set itself three purposes: to express through its work the "essential unity
of the Christian churches"; to provide "an interdenominational agency
for cooperation of the churches" in education, social action, worship, and
evangelism; and to "provide a forum for understanding and building relationships" with other organizations serving the needs of the community.
This mission statement makes clear that from the outset the council's
focus was outward rather than inward, aiming at serving the community
more than fostering dialogue among the faith communities. When the
council did opt to redefine itself as "interfaith," in 1995, it was making
official something that was already true in fact; minutes of meetings
from years prior to the change record regular participation of both Baha'is
and Jews.

Structure and Membership

The move from an ecumenical to an interfaith identity was remarkably
uncontentious, and the changes to the by-laws minimal. The focus on
"the essential unity of the Christian churches" shifted to "the essential
unity of God's people," the word "churches" was replaced with "faith
groups," and one additional item was added to the council's purpose: "to
promote interfaith worship, dialogue and cooperative events." As in its

former incarnation, membership in the CAIC is congregation-based; members are defined not as individuals but as Chico-area "faith groups," any of which is welcome to join so long as it affirms the council's mission, is voted in by a majority of Board of Directors, and participates in supporting the council financially. Members of the Board of Directors are elected or appointed by the member groups, and may include a clergy person or professional staff member and up to two laypeople per group. Today, some groups are represented by a clergy person and a layperson, others only by lay members. Finally, the Board of Directors elect four officers for an annual term: a President, Vice President, Secretary, and Treasurer.

This consistency with its earlier life as a Council of Churches affords the Council the benefit of continuity, but also raises challenges for inclusiveness. Defining membership by institutions makes involvement difficult both for those with a deep interest in interfaith relations but no institutional affiliation, and those, like Pagans, whose religious traditions are decentralized and typically not institutionally structured. Within the member groups representation can also be problematic. In Chico, for instance, the local Islamic Center formally affiliated in 2004, but representatives do not regularly attend meetings. Other Muslims in the community who are unaffiliated with the mosque, however, are actively involved in interfaith work. With no sponsoring institution, these individuals are ineligible for formal membership on the council, leaving Islam officially invisible. This is certainly not desirable to the council, whose commitment to openness and diversity is attested to not only by its mission statement, but also by the sentiments consistently expressed in conversations with council members.

The working solution has been for these unaffiliated members to attend council meetings and participate in its activities as "associate members" with voice but without vote. The primary Muslim representative at council events is Ali Sarsour, a Palestinian immigrant who has lived in Chico for thirty years but who is not closely associated with the local Islamic Center. Sarsour is a faithful participant, and often a leader, in whatever interfaith activities are going on around town, whether it's a multifaith potluck or an educational forum. He is satisfied with his informal role on the council, having for years taken the initiative to build relationships with different kinds of people. One wonders, though, about other institutionally unaffiliated religious people who might be equally vibrant contributors to interfaith life in Chico, but lack Sarsour's enterprising personality. What's more, if a recent finding that less than 15 percent of American Muslims attend weekly mosque services is accurate (Wuthnow 2005, 60), the institutional basis of membership on the council may significantly limit who gets to speak for Islam. This arrangement also raises questions of authority; the individual members of a religious tradition who do sit in on council activities may represent idiosyncratic interpretations of that tradition that would not be affirmed by others.

Official membership in the CAIC has been fairly consistent over the past decade. Member faith groups include a wide range of Protestant churches (Congregational, Methodist, Episcopal, Lutheran, Baptist, Disciples of Christ), Roman Catholic churches, the Society of Friends, the Church of Jesus Christ of Latter-Day Saints (Mormons), the Christian Science Church, the Unitarian Universalist Fellowship, the Church of Religious Science, the Baha'i community, the local Jewish synagogue, and, formally, the Chico Islamic Center. Several nonreligious community organizations, the Chico Peace and Justice Center, Parents and Friends of Lesbians and Gays (PFLAG), and groups serving the homeless population, have also regularly attended council meetings. This roster is notable both for who is on it and for who is not. While Jews, Baha'is, Unitarians, and members of the Church of Religious Science are consistent longtime participants, the group remains predominantly Christian. While this is perhaps not inappropriate given the majority Christian population of the community, it is nonetheless an ongoing frustration for council members who would like the "interfaith" descriptor to carry more weight.

Perhaps even more noteworthy are the *Christian* groups not present on the Council. Neighborhood Church of Chico, a Christian and Missionary Alliance church, is the largest church in Chico, with 1,200 regularly attending its set of Sunday services and 2,000 to 3,000 on its membership rolls. It has never been involved in the council, nor have the other major Evangelical churches in town. Also absent are the ethnic minority churches. Neither of the two historically black churches nor any Hispanic congregation has been a member, even though one of the African American churches is a "sister congregation" with the Baptist church that is very active in the council. These gaps in the effort to accurately represent the religious identities of the community are the result of a complex set of demographic, political, and theological issues. Give the perpetual shortage of time and resources for congregation leaders, many smaller religious communities may simply place interfaith work very low on a long list of priorities. Particularly when a congregation is predominantly poor and working class, its leaders may see much less value in interfaith programs than in those that meet direct needs in their communities.

The absence of larger and wealthier congregations like Neighborhood Church, though, cannot be explained in this way. In this case a combination of political and theological factors comes into play. I spoke at length with Larry Lane, senior pastor of Neighborhood Church, about his view of interfaith work in the community. While he has been actively involved with an ecumenical group of Christian leaders, the Pastors' Prayer Fellowship, for years, he has opted not to work with the Interfaith Council both because he does not believe it accomplishes a great deal given the investment of time required, and because he believes that joining the council might force him to compromise certain positions he holds dear. "I've had relationships with different folks on the council, so there's no hostility," he said. "It's just that the kinds of things that are really important to me and the things I want to invest my time in, I don't think we have an agreement to go do some of those things." For Lane, it is important that his efforts to improve community life in Chico have a Christian orientation, and he believes that the strategies he and other Christian leaders would use "would not be agreeable" to members of the Interfaith Council. Lane also perceives the council as politically activist in a way that he is not comfortable with. "I guess I'm not into trying to make a difference by protesting or making statements. We've done a little bit of that, but most of what we do is underground, behind the scenes, caring for people."

Perhaps because of the common perception that Evangelicals emphasize personal spirituality over social service, Lane took pains to underscore that his community is deeply involved in local service work. Just as Evangelical theology stresses personal relationships with God over formal ecclesial structures, Lane referred consistently to the work of relationship-building as the most effective means of serving the community. "Frankly, there's a lot that we do that people don't know about because we don't make a big deal out of it. I'm not saying that they [the Interfaith Council] are trying to get attention, but because ours is so relationship-based, I can make a few phone calls and talk about things and do things and off we go. We don't have to have meetings or press conferences or things like that, or issue statements. We just go and get it done." Lane cited with pride the fact that his church raised $20,000 for the local organization that feeds the homeless when its building was destroyed by arsonists in 1996.

As far as community service work goes, then, this pastor's resistance to working with the Interfaith Council is more practical than theological. But when it comes to the council's other mission of promoting dialogue among faith groups in Chico, Lane's opposition is more clear-cut. For Lane, interfaith dialogue is apparently equated with a particular theology of pluralism, one that assumes all religions are equal. When asked if simply better understanding one another's faith traditions is an aspect of council work that might engage him, he responded, "Here's the deal: It seems to me that there is a passion among some, a belief that 'all roads lead to Mt. Fuji,' and if we just listen and understand each other we'll all find that we're on the same road." This "many paths to the same summit" model of interfaith relations is indeed common among some participants in the interfaith movement, but it is by no means a majority position, and is certainly not the position of the Chico Area Interfaith Council. But for many nonparticipants, including Pastor Lane, the assumption that this reduction of all faiths to the same common denominator is the reigning theology of interfaith work is a powerful deterrent, and evidence of the interfaith movement's continuing problem with public perception. Larry Lane, for instance, believes that participation in the council would likely require him to compromise some of his deeply held values. Citing the issue of abortion, he stated, "I have real strong feelings about that. It ties to my understanding of life . . . but there would be those in other faiths that would totally disagree. And I want to respect their right to believe and to vote and to do whatever they can, but golly, I'm not going to compromise something that's such a deep conviction for me." When pressed, he acknowledged that council members themselves were probably deeply divided on this issue and that therefore it was unlikely to be a topic of discussion, but reiterated that "I wouldn't want to participate in a place where drive and passion is so concerned with finding common ground that we have to surrender things we hold dear, that somehow this common ground is going to be a better place."

The one area in which Lane was certain he would have a specific conflict with the council's agenda is interfaith worship. He would never resist coming to a council meeting because of resistance to associating with non-Christian groups, and in fact decried groups who would take such a position. But while "hanging out with folks and talking" has appeal, he drew a sharp line at shared worship. "Who are we worshipping?" he asked. "To have this sort of benign civil religion that's watered down and insipid to anyone, or when you ask me to pray, but tell me 'we don't want you to pray this way.' I don't want to have to do that. Why should I?"

At the heart of Pastor Lane's (and thus Neighborhood Church's) non-participation in the interfaith council, then, are both a theology and a pastoral style. The informal, unstructured, Evangelical approach to church affairs goes a long way in explaining this resistance; Lane seemed to equate the work of the Interfaith Council with a certain kind of formality and political posturing, as opposed to his own community's commitment to "relationship-building." More deeply, though, he believes his theology would not be well received at the council. Like most Evangelicals, Lane is solidly exclusivist; he believes that Jesus is the unique son of God and the source of all salvation, and that the teachings of Christianity are uniquely meaningful to life in the world. He "would be thrilled" if someone left another faith and became a Christian, but would never seek conversion in a way that was disrespectful or compromised another's free choice. For him, structured interfaith work is symptomatic of a culture that no longer believes in any absolutes, and would require a kind of compromise in which substantive faith positions are stripped away. Ironically, Lane thinks it would be "awesome" to sit and talk with a Muslim or other non-Christian, and could think of no reason why people of different faiths shouldn't work together on issues of hunger and homelessness in the community, but is not especially interested in the community structure that makes such dialogue and such collaborations possible. His absence is no doubt a loss for the council, which aims to represent the diversity of Chico's community and could certainly be enlivened by his thoughtful critiques of a culture of uncritical tolerance.

Lane's objections notwithstanding, the Chico Area Interfaith Council is neither a vehicle of leftist activism nor a univocally pluralist body. Despite the absence of Evangelicals and ethnic minorities, there is real diversity on the council. Mormons and Catholics, who represent religious bodies that take quite conservative positions on issues of sexuality and gender, for instance, sit at the table with women pastors and representatives of congregations that are "open and affirming" of gays and lesbians. Interestingly, a representative of the national organization Parents and Friends of Lesbians and Gays (PFLAG), a retired university professor with over fifty years invested in the community, was an early and active participant in the CAIC. Meeting minutes show that he attended nearly every meeting of the council until his death in 1997, and that there were no contentious discussions of issues relating to homosexuality. For Bruce Grelle, former president of the council and an ongoing representative of the local Congregational church, this is a good example of the way in which the Interfaith Council does not line up neatly along ideological lines. "The whole issue of gay and lesbian rights is a very divisive issue in the culture wars, and it's a very divisive issue within and between denominations. And you see all positions on that issue represented in this organization. So while it's not as representative of all the issues in the culture wars as it might be, it's not entirely unrepresentative."

Purpose and Activities

A range of motivations prompts the members to serve on the Chico Area Interfaith Council. Bruce Grelle, who is also a professor of Religious Studies at the local university, was driven by intellectual questions about religious pluralism and social ethics. For Father Richard Yale, pastor of St. John's Episcopal Church, joining the Interfaith Council when he arrived in Chico nine years ago "was just simply an expectation," something he would not have considered *not* doing, and looks for opportunities for deep theological exchanges. Rabbi Julie Hilton Danan reports that being the leader of the only synagogue in an overwhelmingly Christian community makes maintaining good relations with the larger community a vital priority. Father Michael Newman, pastor of the Roman Catholic Newman Center, comes to interfaith work from the theological perspective of Vatican II, which stressed the Church's responsibility for promoting social

justice, the presence of truth in other religions, and the importance of interfaith understanding. Ali Sarsour finds interfaith work to be a vital
counterweight to the forces of fundamentalism in all religions, and likens
interfaith encounters to enjoying a wide variety of foods. For others the
council is a place to advance certain social causes on which religious
groups might find common ground, for still others it might offer a chance
to quietly witness to a religious perspective believed to be uniquely true.
The variety of these motivations means that the relatively simple purpose
of the council declared in its by-laws is in reality open to change, negotiation, and, at times, confusion.

While the Interfaith Council's by-laws give equal emphasis to social
service and interfaith relationship-building, in reality that balance has
been difficult to maintain. The council has been very effective over the
years in mobilizing the support of the religious congregations in addressing community problems, especially hunger, homelessness, and violence.
The group is always a generous supporter of the Church World Service's
annual CROP walk, was a major participant in the planning stages of the
community homeless shelter, and helped coordinate the temporary shelter program that served in the interim. It has also coordinated staffing of
the hospital chaplaincy program and been a vigorous advocate for a per-
manent chaplaincy position. The council has also sponsored presentations and forums on such issues as community violence, the effects of the
new prescription drug plan on the poorest seniors, and racial tensions in
the community. While it certainly contributes to the well-being of the
community, though, it is sometimes difficult to identify a specifically interfaith, or even religious, component to this work. Each council meeting
begins with an opening "focus" presented by a board member—a piece of
scripture, poetry, or other inspirational material. But if one were to enter
a meeting after this opening moment, one may not get any other clues to
the religious character of the organization, and what differentiates it, for
instance, from a Rotary, Kiwanis, or other service organization. While the
prospect of increasing interfaith dialogue and understanding may draw
people to the council, once there, the steady stream of community need
seems to absorb most of the available time and energy.

In part, this is a product of the council's success. Monthly meetings
draw representatives of numerous community groups looking for support

from the religious community, and the council itself has generated more initiatives than its already overscheduled members can accommodate. Out of the council's conversations over the past ten years have emerged a local chapter of the Fellowship of Reconciliation, an independent anti-hate group called the Human Relations Network, and, most recently, a local incarnation of Celebration of Abraham, a Jewish-Christian-Muslim dialogue program that originated in the rural community of Lodi, California, and was initiated in Chico by Rabbi Danan. "Most of our monthly meetings are taken up with reports from all these organizations," Grelle explained, "all of which are doing good work. By the time we get though all the reports, there will be discussion items left on the agenda, but the time for the meeting will have run out." The impetus for deeper conversation across religious lines remains strong among many council members, but in recent years there has been an observable shift, to the disappointment of several council members, away from that kind of activity toward the more practical work of serving the community.

But the need for more explicitly interfaith initiatives is widely felt. The turnout for the 2005 Celebration of Abraham event, at which community members were invited to listen to presentations from Christian, Jewish, and Muslim leaders and share a potluck supper, was far greater than expected. Instead of 50, nearly 300 turned out, and the organizers had to scramble to bring chairs from the sanctuary into the meeting hall of the Lutheran Church that hosted the event. This suggests to Rabbi Danan, who chaired the event, that there is a deep hunger in the community for interfaith learning and exchange. "It showed that people want to learn about other faiths. They want to feel good about their own faith and share it. I think there's a great need for that." At this point, the CAIC seems to have delegated this explicitly dialogical work to its protégé groups like the Celebration of Abraham (whose membership overlaps significantly with that of the council), which holds monthly events including tours of houses of worship, book discussions, and educational presentations.

Neglect of explicitly dialogue-oriented initiatives by the council itself may be due, in addition to shortages of time and energy, to ongoing uncertainty about what being interfaith is or ought to mean, an ambiguity rooted in the council's Christian origins and ongoing Christian majority.

Its by-laws call for promoting "interfaith worship, dialogue and cooperative events," yet true interfaith events of this nature happen very rarely.
When shared worship does occur, it is most often in reality an intra-
Christian program, like the ecumenical Good Friday services that have become a tradition in the community, the "Religious Music Festival" at
which only Christian choirs perform, or the "pulpit exchange" program
shared only by Christian churches. Jewish members of the council have
expressed frustrations with the council promoting, and even sponsoring,
events on Friday evenings, and it is not uncommon to hear prayers at
council events end with "in Jesus' name."

In reality, it is very hard to design an interfaith religious activity that
has any substance but does not require unacceptable compromise from
constituent religious communities. Across the country, I have found that
while interfaith organizations are often eager to come together in sacred
space to share their traditions, this is actually one of the most difficult
projects to take on. Interfaith services are often uncomfortable affairs,
asking people to do something nearly impossible—act in a ritually appropriate manner in a setting in which no ritual tradition may be normative.
At one event in I attended in the small town of Yuba City, California, the
recitation of a Jewish prayer was followed by applause; not knowing the
proper religious ritual response, participants fell back on the rituals of
entertainment, exposing just how hard it is to be generically religious. Beyond civic-oriented events like an interfaith service for Thanksgiving or
Martin Luther King Day, very few interfaith groups regularly worship together, and for many interfaith participants, that's as it should be. Richard
Yale, the Episcopal priest who led the CAIC Council in 2004–2005, is skep-
tical about worship across religious lines. "I just don't know if such a thing
is possible." If that were to be the work of the council, Yale said, it would
be difficult for him to participate. "I would have trouble associating with
a group that invoked both Krishna and Jesus Christ in worship." He is
very supportive of the council as "a place where we are intellectually con-
necting," but to worship together would be to act out a certain kind of
pluralistic theology that Yale finds unacceptable. "That's not what I
signed on for."

Apart from its offshoots, then, the Chico Area Interfaith Council functions primarily as a clearinghouse, a two-way conduit of information and

resources among the participating religious communities. And while that work may look quite mundane, it has a deeply spiritual quality recognizable to all the participants. As Ali Sarsour noted, doing the work of community service *is* a religious act, especially from the perspective of a tradition like Islam, which measures faith by the quality of the life one leads rather than by the orthodoxy of one's belief. In this sense, working together on the various social initiatives of the council is itself a kind of interfaith dialogue, and prompts important discussions about which projects ought to rise to the top of the agenda, and which ought best be left alone. Whether and to what extent to take political positions is a recurring point of discussion—though rarely outright contention—on the council. Given the diversity of the faith communities represented, and the range of their positions on social issues, the general policy has been to avoid taking positions on controversial issues and stick to matters about which there is unanimity. Shortly after the council established its interfaith identity, for instance, a proposal was brought forth to affiliate with the newly formed Interfaith Alliance, a national progressive interfaith coalition explicitly dedicated to countering the Religious Right. While many council members supported the work of the Interfaith Alliance, it was decided in August of 1995 that affiliation would be too polarizing, and that the council could be most effective by maintaining an exclusively local identity. Since then, when debate arises over a controversial decision to sponsor a speaker, make an alliance, or release a statement on a particular issue, the council has generally opted for the safer option of not acting as a council but rather referring the matter to individual congregations. While this strategy means that issues of great importance to many members are not acted on by the council, it also means, they believe, that the council is able to maintain respect and credibility with a wider spectrum of the community, and therefore be more effective in the work they do take on. As Ted Sandberg, pastor of the First Baptist Church, said in his address to the council at the end of his term as president, "the more united we are, the more powerful our voice."

Still, as one reviews the activities of the council, there does seem to emerge an implicit consensus as to the type of work that is appropriate to the council. Whether it is through support of structured community programs like the CROP walk, the hospital chaplaincy, or the Community

Shelter Partnership, or responses to specific events, like the burning of the Jesus Center or the destruction of a Hmong family's strawberry stand, the CAIC consistently acts out of what Bruce Grelle calls "a presumption for the poor," and what Jim Anderson, a leader in the local Quaker community and longtime council member, calls "the work of compassion and love." For Grelle, what distinguishes the work of the Council from that of other civic organizations is that, usually without much discussion, there is a consistent effort to pay attention to those the rest of the community may be disregarding. In the case of a cemetery desecration, for instance, the Council addressed the issue from a perspective of restorative justice, asking how the perpetrators as well as the victims might be included in any response. So while the Council may not have been able to speak out against the Iraq war or in support of gay clergy, on the one hand, or against abortion on the other, one sees in the programs they sponsor and statements they issue a commitment to promoting a climate of respect, nonviolence, and tolerance, with a special eye on the community's most vulnerable.

The Interfaith Conference of Greater Milwaukee

Milwaukee, Wisconsin—noted for cheese, beer, and a passionate devotion to professional football—is also a city of extraordinary racial and religious diversity, and home to one of the most vibrant interfaith organizations in the country. The city itself has a population of nearly 600,000, which rises to 1.5 million when the surrounding metropolitan area is included. Like many older manufacturing centers, Milwaukee has seen a population decrease over the past several decades, while the surrounding metropolitan area grows apace. The service industry is now the largest job provider in Milwaukee, with manufacturing coming in second. During the 1990s Milwaukee became a minority majority city, meaning that nonwhites make up a greater portion of the population than whites. African Americans are the largest minority group at 37 percent, while Hispanics make up 12 percent, Asians about 3 percent, and Native Americans just under 1 percent, and all of these populations are growing, whether due to immigration, as is the case of Hispanics and Asians, or growth in the established communities, as with African Americans and Native Americans. The consequences of a contracting manufacturing economy have been painful for Milwaukee. Its overall poverty rate of 26 percent is roughly comparable to that of St. Louis, Memphis, and New Orleans, but smaller statistics are perhaps even more telling. Milwaukee ranks fourth in the nation for child poverty, with 41 percent of its children living below the poverty line (Held 2005). Milwaukee also has the poorest Asian population in the country, ranks ninth among the fifty largest cities in the United States in the concentration of ethnic minorities in extreme-poverty neighborhoods (Brookings report), and has the lowest high school graduation rate for black men and the highest teen pregnancy rate for black girls. While it is racially and economically diverse, then, Milwaukee is also notable for the degree to which it is racially and economically segregated. It is in this context that The Interfaith Conference of Greater Milwaukee (ICGM) finds its mission and challenge.

Like Chico's Interfaith Council, the Interfaith Conference has its roots, at least in part, in an ecumenical Christian organization, but in Milwaukee's case these roots are solidly activist. In 1963, with help from the National Conference of Christians and Jews, a group of local Jewish and Christian leaders formed the Greater Milwaukee Conference on Religion and Race to address the issues of civil unrest and racial and economic disparities that were troubling the city. The migration of African Americans from the south came rather late to Milwaukee, expanding rapidly in the 1950s and 1960s. Significant racial diversity was thus relatively new to this city in the volatile 1960s, and as in other urban areas, tensions often resulted in violence. In the same period, the Greater Milwaukee Council of Churches (founded in 1911) established an Ecumenical Urban Cadre, consisting of metropolitan ministers and a small group of laypeople, to address the same issues. Marcus White, the Interfaith Conference's fourth executive director, notes the importance of religious activism in this era. White believes the impetus for interreligious organizing was in large part the initiative of the leaders of some white congregations— Jewish, Catholic, and Protestant—challenging their members to be open to this new diversity. In 1970, the Conference on Religion and Race merged with the Council of Churches to form the Greater Milwaukee Conference on Religion and Urban Affairs, which was renamed the Interfaith Conference of Greater Milwaukee in 1987 to more explicitly reflect its interfaith identity.[3] Thus the Jewish-Christian collaboration to fight racial and economic injustice was the originating force of this organization, which drew vital institutional strength from the older and more established Council of Churches.

The Interfaith Conference continues to define its purpose in activist terms. Its mission statement defines the organization as "the interfaith agency established by the religious community to address the social issues affecting the quality of life in the greater Milwaukee area." Like the Chico Area Interfaith Council, the ICGM founds its interfaith work on the basis of a common humanity, drawing on the language of civil rights, rather than on any distinctly theological premise: "The mission of the Conference is based on the religious value of the dignity of every person and the solidarity of the human community. The Conference enables individuals, congregations and the religious leadership to participate as an interfaith presence in the dialogue and action that impact on this dignity and solidarity." While both dialogue and action appear in this statement, this interfaith group has clearly made a priority of its programs and lobby efforts on such issues as racism, violence, poverty, education, employment, and children's concerns.

Structure and Membership

While Chico's Interfaith Council defines membership in terms of congregations, the Milwaukee group consists of member "judicatories," or denominational organizations. Each denomination is allotted up to three seats, though typically only one representative from each "denomination" attends monthly meetings. There are currently fourteen member judicatories: the American Baptist Churches of Wisconsin, the Wisconsin General Baptist Convention, the Milwaukee Diocese of the Episcopal Church, the Greater Milwaukee Synod of the Evangelical Lutheran Church in America, the Islamic Society of Milwaukee, the Milwaukee Jewish Federation, the Milwaukee Jewish Council for Community Relations, The Wisconsin Council of Rabbis, The Presbyterian Church (USA) Presbytery of Milwaukee, The Milwaukee Meeting of the Religious Society of Friends, the Milwaukee Archdiocese of the Roman Catholic Church, the Southeast Wisconsin Association of the United Church of Christ, the Metro North and South Districts of the United Methodist Church, and the Southeast

Wisconsin Association of Unitarian Universalist Churches. Together, these judicatories represent approximately five hundred congregations in the Milwaukee area. The "interfaith" identity of the conference was established by the Jewish, Christian, and Unitarian participation that extends back to the group's earliest years. The recent inclusion of the Islamic Society, a process initiated by executive director Marcus White within a week of assuming leadership in 2001, is the conference's first experience with a primarily immigrant community, one that has thus far been very successful by all reports.

These judicatories provide approximately one third of the ICGM's $300,000 annual budget, while the rest is generated by grants and individual donations. This judicatory model is not common among interfaith organizations, and comes with benefits and costs. On the one hand, these organizations are large, well established, and typically well funded, and so tend to offer stability and a solid base of financial support, although White reports that the portion of the conference's budget that comes from the denominations is shrinking, both because they raise more in private grants than they used to and because the denominations themselves have financial problems. Another strength of the judicatory model lies in its accountability structure. When an interfaith organization is made up of representatives of a local congregation, each of those representatives must continually justify the interfaith project—and its various activities—to its constituent communities. With the judicatory structure, participation is established at a higher administrative level, and thus members are empowered to act independently of potentially divided local congregations.

The flipside of this accountability structure, of course, is that the conference can only act in ways that are consistent with the positions of these large judicatory bodies, regardless of the sentiments of local congregations or individuals. More fundamentally, this system has difficulty accommodating religious traditions that do not have a centralized structure that authorizes a representative to speak on behalf of the whole. Buddhists, Hindus, Quakers, Unitarians, Pagans—even Jews and Baptists—for reasons of polity and/or theology, are not groups that are structured in such a way that one member can speak for others. Because the Interfaith Conference acts primarily as an advocacy organization, taking positions on social issues is critical to its mission. If a Conference member cannot speak for his or her constituency in taking such positions, the value of their participation in the conference is questionable. While Quakers and Unitarians in Milwaukee have accommodated this system by locally delegating representatives with the authority to speak for their communities, the efforts of the conference to draw in a more diverse membership will certainly continue to be challenged by this arrangement.

Like the Chico Area Interfaith Council, the Milwaukee Interfaith Conference thus faces its own challenges to becoming as inclusive as it might like to be. In addition to these structural inhibitions, there are also demographic explanations for the fact that the conference is still overwhelmingly Christian. As noted in Chico's case, many smaller religious communities lack the resources of time and energy to devote to interfaith work. As Mary Ann Neevel, ICGM cabinet member and senior minister of Plymouth Church (United Church of Christ), put it, many pastors have a "do-everything role," and interfaith work may simply not rise to the top of the pile of tasks.

This can also be true of an entire religious community. Ahmed Quereshi, corporate secretary of the Islamic Society of Milwaukee and member of the ICGM cabinet, explained that the fast-growing Muslim community in Milwaukee is still very much an immigrant group; of the 1,000 or so who attend weekly services at the mosque on the south side of Milwaukee, he estimates that a plurality are immigrants from South Asian and Arab countries. Islam in Milwaukee is still in what Quereshi calls a "brick and mortar" phase. Having outgrown the $800,000 worship facility they built in 1995, the community launched a $1 million expansion in 2000 and hired its first full-time imam. "So we were looking inward and trying to build up our community and meet its needs," he told me. "We're still trying to acquire property and we're going from one full-time imam to three within the year, so we're looking inward, but we're looking outward at the same time." That outward gaze, of course, got a major impetus from September 11, when the phone at the mosque began ringing off the hook with requests from community groups for presentations on Islam. But without this crisis, the Muslim community in Milwaukee might not have moved interfaith work to the top of its agenda for another generation. In this case, the Interfaith Conference's goal of diversifying and the goal of the Islamic Society to increase is profile in the community and better educate the community about Islam coalesced fortuitously. The move to include the Islamic community as a judicatory of the conference occurred by unanimous vote in 2003. The Hindu and Sikh communities remain unrepresented.

But it is not just immigrant religious groups that have been absent from the conference's judicatory roster. "The gaping hole, from my perspective, is the African American religious community," said Arlo Reichter, executive director of the American Baptist Churches of Wisconsin and currently chair of the Interfaith Conference. "It always concerns me when we gather for a Cabinet meeting; we're all Caucasian—in the midst of Milwaukee." This is a concern shared by Marcus White. Given the centrality of race issues to the conference's mission, White made bringing African Americans into the conference another of his top priorities. At the time of my interviews, he reported that they were "very close" to announcing the affiliation of two historically African American denominations, the Church of God in Christ and the African Methodist Episcopal (AME) church. That this development is occurring only now can be explained by several factors. Given the challenges faced by the black population in Milwaukee, the leadership of the black churches has been focused on activism in its own communities, for which interfaith work may not appear immediately relevant. Judi Longdin, vice chair of the conference and director of the Office for Ecumenical and Interfaith Concerns for the Roman Catholic Archdiocese of Milwaukee, believes that, while the conference and the African American religious communities are working on many of the same issues, they come at them in different ways. Speaking of the Church of God in Christ, she explains:

> They are doing an enormous amount of work with building homes and home-ownership and local community development, and then you look at the Interfaith Conference and we are trying to advocate for this Housing Trust Fund as part of a larger picture. We're trying to ask how can we look at the legislation, the funding, so we can begin to create a secure foundation for being able to provide housing for low-income people. Whereas, what we're seeing in the African American community is, right here, in my neighborhood, right now, there is this specific need. And so we have these incredible

ministries right now. They are absolutely amazing. But given the amount of energy it takes to do that, in that local community, there's not a whole of time or energy—or even, in some places, enthusiasm—for that bigger picture.

In this case the conference's work has been to engage these churches in conversations about the benefits of collaboration on issues like housing, poverty, and racism, and by all accounts those conversations have been very fruitful.

The other obvious empty seat at the Interfaith Conference is the Evangelical Christian community. As in Chico, interfaith work in Milwaukee has largely been the province of liberal religious groups, and here, too, some of the largest Christian communities are nonplayers. Milwaukee has its own set of Evangelical "megachurches," led by Elmbrook Church in suburban Brookfield, which draws over 7,000 to its weekly services. Elmbrook now has nine offshoots in the area, including its brand new downtown "Metrobrook" church, but has no involvement with the Interfaith Conference. The leadership of the conference speculates that this has to do with both politics and theology. In addition to the fact that the megachurches are nondenominational and thus lack the centralized structure that facilitates membership as a judicatory, there is also a perception that they do not share the values of the Interfaith Conference and its commitment to systemic analysis of and response to issues of poverty and racism. But there is also a deeper theological issue at stake. Arlo Reichter, whose own Baptist denomination is deeply divided on the issue of interfaith work, believes it comes down to a question of who can be saved. "Quite frankly, when it comes to Evangelical churches, one of the real core issues is salvation. You don't sit at the table and work with people that you don't believe are saved. On some level there is cooperation, but to be able to sit around the same table with a group of people who you honestly believe require conversion, that's a stretch." The conference's explicit prohibition on proselytizing clearly bars participation with a conversionary intent, but it also clearly excludes by definition those for whom this is the only conceivable mode of interfaith interaction.

The recent outreach to and inclusion of Muslim and African American denominational judicatories may prove an interesting challenge to the established liberal identity of the group. As Marcus White observes, the Islamic Center tends to be fairly conservative on social issues, and the local bishop of the Churches of God in Christ was a delegate to the Republican National Convention. "We tend to be more liberal. For instance, we vigorously oppose the death penalty. Will we now lose our unanimity on that issue? I don't know." This is precisely the riddle of inclusiveness. Does the organization lay out its vision and only invite like-minded groups to join? Or does it aim for diversity that represents the community and then negotiate policy positions from there? Historically, the Interfaith Conference has used the former model; increasingly it is shifting toward the latter, with unpredictable consequences for its activist agenda.

Purpose and Activities

The Interfaith Conference's primary mission to address "social issues affecting the quality of life in the greater Milwaukee area" takes a variety of forms. While its web site and brochures highlight such activities as sponsoring the annual Greater Milwaukee CROP Walk, helping to run a shelter for women and families, and representing the faith community on various community boards and coalitions, the daily activities in the conference's downtown office often look more like the work of a legislative lobbying operation. The day's agenda is often driven by stories in the morning paper. On the morning I arrived to interview members of the conference, for instance, Marcus White had already exchanged several telephone messages with the chief of staff of a state senator in response to the senator's comments that morning regarding a proposed concealed gun law. It was striking to see the head of a religious organization initiating so direct an exchange with a politician, but even more striking that his call was returned so promptly. It is clear that the conference's roots in community activism, especially on issues of racism and poverty, continue to inform its present identity. In addition to lobbying efforts such as the conference's work on gun control, the group also maintains a public presence in its responses to local events. When the Ku Klux Klan held a Milwaukee rally a few years ago, the Interfaith Conference followed with a counterprotest at the same location, and conducted an interfaith "cleansing" of the site. In collaboration with the Congregational Action Network, the conference also produces and disseminates frequent "Action Alerts" calling on community members to write letters and make phone calls opposing and supporting various initiatives and attend forums on local issues.

Its successful grant-writing efforts have also allowed the Interfaith Conference to take on longer-term projects focused on racial and economic justice. The two largest current initiatives are its work with a coalition urging the city to establish a Housing Trust Fund that would dedicate an ongoing source of revenue to support local affordable housing efforts, and a new project undertaken by the conference's Institute for Justice called the Racial Disparity Project, a three-phase initiative that includes (1) research on Milwaukee's racial disparities in poverty, crime, incarceration, etc.; (2) community education and partnership-building; and (3) legislative advocacy to advance the strategies that emerge from those partnerships. In this kind of work the Interfaith Conference makes clear that it aims to be more than a clearinghouse for charitable initiatives of the various religious groups, though it does that work as well through its support, for instance, of the Cathedral Center emergency shelter. More centrally, the group tries to understand and educate about the underlying structural causes of social problems and collaborate in developing long-term, systemic solutions to them.

Though on a much larger scale, the Milwaukee interfaith organization uses a similar strategy to Chico's in deciding which issues to take on and which to leave to individual members. "We've stayed away from the stickier issues," I was told by Paula Simon, executive director of the Milwaukee Jewish Council for Community Relations and cabinet member of the Interfaith Conference, "because we know that what unites us is stronger than what divides us." In response to a major pro-life demonstration about twelve years ago, then, the conference did not make a statement about abortion, but rather spoke with unanimity about the legitimacy of certain forms of protest. Simon recalled, "Although we knew that there was no agreement on the substance of the issue of abortion, we were able to say that violence, the use of children in protests, not allowing people to act with their conscience—these were a problem. So we were able to issue a statement during the protest." Given its explicit political work, the Interfaith Conference is more clearly identifiable as a liberal organization than the Chico Area Interfaith Council, but the presence of groups like Baptists, Roman Catholics, and Muslims complicates that identity in important ways. In addition to abortion rights, the conference has also never taken up issues pertaining to gays and lesbians, and has avoided any treatment of the Israeli-Palestinian conflict. As in Chico, it has paid to stay local.

What emerge as the consensus social issues for these religious groups are predictably similar to those in Chico: poverty, racism, and a commitment to fostering dialogue across (at least some) social divides. In Milwaukee, this has taken shape in the Interfaith Conference's work in community mediation, especially on labor issues, and its Restorative Justice Task Force, which works with crime victims and offenders to restore accountability and trust and to promote healing and forgiveness. While this focus may mean that the group is not able to act on issues of great concern to some of its members, it definitely enhances the authority of the conference when they do speak. Maintaining the diversity of its religious coalition means that the Interfaith Conference offers a credibly broad source to which community groups, politicians, journalists, and others can turn when they want to hear from the "religious community" on a given topic but avoid sectarian perspectives. "This is where the judicatory leaders are very important," Judi Longdin told me about the Milwaukee groups' efforts. "The Conference will organize the judicatory leaders to do press conferences. When you have that kind of visibility, when you've got bishops and directors and heads of different religious organizations from the community, you have a lot of clout there." If it is true that more Americans belong to religious organizations than to any other voluntary associations (Wald 122), it makes sense that community leaders and politicians are disposed to listen to such voices, particularly when they can claim this broad, inclusive base.

It is important to note, though, that for all their unanimity, the member judicatories of the Interfaith Conference are not all similarly motivated in their interfaith work. For several denominations, the conference functions as their social action wing; without the conference, they might not be otherwise engaged in work for structural social reform. But for groups like the Catholic Archdiocese and several mainline Protestant denominations with well-established offices for social concerns, the conference is an opportunity for networking with other religious organizations so as to maximize impact. In both of these cases, the primary value of membership in the conference is found in looking outward from the denominations, at what the conference can help them do to improve the life of the city. For smaller groups like the Islamic Society of Milwaukee, affiliation with the Interfaith Conference has an important internal function as well, helping to secure a more solid position in the community through education about Islam. "The level of knowledge about Islam in this country is abysmal," Ahmed Quereshi noted, referring to a series of recent studies. In that context, and especially following September 11, he seizes upon every opportunity to raise awareness about Islam and its teachings. "We believe that with greater knowledge of Islam, there will be greater understanding among non-Muslims. What we can do here, because we don't have a national network, is try to reach out to non-Muslims on a grassroots level." For Quereshi and many other Muslims, the stakes in this drive to educate others about their religion are extremely high. "We know that if we can reach the American public on a grassroots level and educate them, we won't have another internment like the Japanese in World War II." Thus while the public service work of the Interfaith Conference is of great value to the Muslim community with its social orientation, at this point in their American history, this Muslim community sees collaboration with other religious groups an important tool for survival. Speaking perhaps to one of the American anxieties about Islam, Quereshi made clear that proselytizing had absolutely no place in Muslims' work with other traditions. "We try to present information. We do not participate in Interfaith to proselytize."

What, then, of interfaith dialogue? While it is not as prominent a part of ICGM's mission statement as it is in Chico, creating "opportunities for people from different backgrounds to dialogue, build relationships, [and] increase understanding" is also on the Interfaith Conference's agenda. Yet its monthly meetings are at least as packed with practical matters as those of the Chico Area Interfaith Council, and beyond a similar opening reflection offered by one of the members, it might be hard to identify a religious basis to its agenda. Also as in Chico, the strong interest in interfaith dialogue and faith sharing that cannot be met at the monthly meeting is being met by an affiliated group, in this case the Milwaukee Association for Interfaith Relations (MAIR). Unlike in Chico, where the dialogue group emerged out of the council, the Milwaukee dialogue group had a prior existence independent of the conference. MAIR was formed in the early 1980s as an interreligious dialogue group, with a diverse membership from the beginning. It holds monthly gatherings, "visitations" to houses of worship, a luncheon series on interfaith issues, and interfaith worship services. For years the group existed alongside the Interfaith Conference, with no formal relationship. Mary Ann Neevel, one of the founders of MAIR, recalled, "For a while we lived parallel lives, but there came a time when it was apparent that we didn't have the staff, we didn't have the energy to keep things going on volunteer time. So it became clear that we needed a larger partner." The Interfaith Conference offered MAIR affiliation as a committee, and that arrangement has proved a clever solution to a number of challenges. It offers the dialogue group staff support, a place to meet, and a wider public presence, and it also allows the conference to expand the range of religious perspectives it engages. "MAIR is far more diverse than the Interfaith Conference cabinet," observed Paula Simon, another early leader of MAIR. For while conference membership is limited to denominational judicatories, MAIR is open to individuals of any religious tradition and does not require any formal affiliation.

Tonen O'Connor, resident priest at the Milwaukee Zen Center and an active member of MAIR, distinguished the role of MAIR from that of the Interfaith Conference. "Our job is not like that of the Conference which takes positions on social issues. What we do, in a sense, is promote an interfaith presence in town. Rather than proselytizing, we bear witness to a pluralist view." For O'Connor, this does not mean the view that all religions are basically the same, but rather the simple acknowledgement that there are multiple forms of faith. For her, the goal is to "encourage people both to follow their own faith *and* to understand that it is *a* faith. If we're promoting anything, it's interfaith understanding, respect for other faiths." Participants in MAIR also noted the value of a group like this in which, in a society in which religion is constantly referenced but rarely talked about in any depth, they can simply come together and explore questions about salvation, suffering, life after death, human community, and the divine, with similarly engaged people. For the Interfaith Conference, then, the "adoption" of MAIR has been a relatively effective way to handle the tension between the Conference's two distinct missions. Bringing the activities of MAIR under its auspices creates a space in the

Conference for more individual, exploratory, spiritual, and relationship-oriented interfaith work, while the Conference itself can continue to bring the clout of its member judicatories to bear on its social action work.

Community-Based Interfaith Groups:
Issues and Observations

The Chico Area Interfaith Council and the Interfaith Conference of Greater Milwaukee are two among hundreds of local interfaith organizations around the country today. While they are dramatically different in size and scope of activities, they share internal tensions over their identity and purpose, and face the common challenge of maximizing both diversity and effective social action. The theologies operative in these organizations reflect the range of theological positions in the wider interfaith movement, but the particular ways in which these theologies are actualized in face-to-face communities tell us something important about the nature of interfaith encounter.

Identity Crises

Mission statements are hard to draft and even harder to live by. Chico's and Milwaukee's interfaith organizations have both developed ambitious statements of purpose that require them in practice to establish a balance between the work of dialogue for interfaith understanding and the work of social justice (through activism or service) to which the affiliated religious traditions are committed. Both groups have discovered, though it is less explicitly acknowledged in Chico, that their regular meetings are not the ideal place for enriching understanding of different religious paths. The practical work that each group has taken on—staffing a hospital chaplaincy, developing programs to address racial inequities, coordinating support for various social service agencies, responding to social and political crises in the community—is more than enough to fill the agenda of monthly meetings and taxes the already overburdened schedules of participants whose contribution to the interfaith organization is, with only a few exceptions, strictly voluntary. It is no wonder that interfaith council meetings are not places of profound spiritual exchange.

But the simple fact of the groups' diverse make-up means that some kind of interfaith dialogue inevitably occurs. Marcus White observed that at the Interfaith Conference office, where the staff is Buddhist, Christian, and Muslim, theological exchanges occur all the time, more often at the copy machine than at the conference table. It is also clear that, in spite of their intense schedules, most members of these organizations maintain a strong interest in deeper interreligious encounters. Both groups have achieved partial solutions to the problem of their mission statements' double vision by delegating the interfaith dialogue activity to a subgroup, primarily Celebration of Abraham in Chico, and the Milwaukee Association for Interfaith Relations in Milwaukee. Members of the Chico Area Interfaith Council seemed less clear about this arrangement; visions of the proper function of the council differed more widely among those I spoke with in Chico than in Milwaukee, where the purpose of MAIR was recognized as important and relevant to but distinct from the primary work of the conference. In Chico, some council members were comfortable with the council functioning as a clearinghouse for noncontroversial good works, while others would prefer that the group take a more active role on matters of peace and justice, and still others pushed for a third kind of activity in which the council would sponsor more opportunities for interfaith dialogue and reflection on community issues. Given the relatively small size of the Chico community, the Interfaith Council still struggles, as a small group with no paid staff, to be all things to all members.

My observations suggest that both groups have acted wisely to the extent that they have separated the social service and activism efforts of their organizations from the explicitly dialogical, interfaith relationship-building work. Groups like Celebration of Abraham and the Milwaukee Association for Interfaith Relations are far better suited structurally to the work of dialogue than the Council or the Conference. The fact that membership in these smaller groups is individual rather than institutional, and wide open to anyone (admittedly limited, in the case of Celebration of Abraham, to a focus on Jews, Christians, and Muslims), regardless of affiliation or status within a religious institution, means that they are much more likely to attract the kind of diversity that makes real dialogue possible and interesting. There is no mission statement or set of by-laws to affirm, no long-term membership commitment. These groups are sustained simply by an interest in religious difference that might draw an individual to a forum, book discussion, lecture, or other interfaith event. Religious experience is ultimately personal, and so, it would follow, authentic interfaith experience must be as well. Studies of interreligious dialogue consistently show that for the encounter to be meaningful, it must somehow engage participants at a personal, existential level. Clearly this is more likely to occur in these kinds of informal settings than at a conference table at which representatives of institutions form policies.

Diversity versus Justice: Negotiating Difference

When people who have different perspectives on some of the most important issues in human experience—that is, people from different religious traditions—come together, a certain level of tension, if not outright conflict, is to be expected. Interestingly, very few of the people involved in interfaith work at the level of community organizations report experiencing such problems. The relative harmony these groups enjoy can be explained by both internal and external factors. On the one hand, interfaith organizations are self-selecting; no one joins who isn't open both to the premise of interfaith work and to the perceived character—liberal, conservative, activist, or apolitical—of the particular organization. Thus, to the frustration of many council and conference members, these groups tend to be, if not homogeneous, certainly less diverse religiously—and especially ideologically—than the communities they represent. As Chico Interfaith Council's perception among Evangelical leaders and the Milwaukee Interfaith Conference's careful wooing of historically black denominations show, the kinds of diversity that might generate productive friction are hard to achieve.

Both of these groups are also acutely aware of the potential costs to the efficacy of their missions of achieving the kind of inclusiveness they aspire to. Diversity is an integral value to interfaith organizations, yet the more truly diverse a group becomes, the less it can speak univocally on vital issues. As Chicago interfaith activist Eboo Patel puts it, "the relationship between inclusiveness and justice fares better in books than it does in the real-life world of interfaith organizing" (2005, 17). This problem is felt more acutely in Milwaukee, where an activist agenda has shaped the organization's history; but in Chico, too, the desultory efforts to draw in

Evangelical groups may be in part attributed to legitimate concern for how that presence might reshape the council's social agenda. As Patel argues, there are profound religious issues at stake in these decisions: "When we take sides on justice issues, justify our position by our theology, and assail alternative positions, we have to recognize that we are implicitly criticizing the theologies of others, and thus in some way, violating an important standard in interfaith work. But if we don't take sides on justice issues, then we are not being true to our own understanding of God, and thus violating an equally important ethic in interfaith work" (20). In their struggle with this central identity issue, community interfaith groups are reckoning in practice with what theologies of religious difference have long grappled with in theory: how to integrate authentic religious (and consequent social and political) commitment with genuine openness to and engagement with those of very different commitments.

The most exciting thing to observe in these interfaith groups, then, is when they do manage to include those with genuinely and significantly divergent worldviews, and those perspectives engage one another. In Milwaukee, the Israeli/Palestinian conflict seems to be one of the few issues that the largely like-minded Interfaith Conference has experienced tension while confronting, and how they have dealt with this is reflective of the larger strategy of this interfaith group. For years, the conference, in cooperation with the Milwaukee Jewish Council, sponsored popular interfaith trips to Israel. Several years ago, Palestinian members of MAIR argued that the trip rightfully ought to include visits to Palestinian as well as Jewish sites, and when no agreement could be reached, the trips were no longer offered. More recently, the Presbyterian Church USA, which, via the Presbytery of Milwaukee, is a member judicatory of the Interfaith Conference, has been wrestling at the national level with the issue of divestment from Israel in protest over its occupation of Palestinian territories. Support for Israel has had the interesting effect nationally of nudging Jewish and Evangelical Christian groups closer together, as discussed in chapter two, even while it has caused rifts between Jews and longtime allies in the liberal mainline Protestant community (Walsh 2005). In Milwaukee, Paula Simon, one of the Jewish members of the conference cabinet, acknowledged that this issue is troubling, but that it is not causing the kind of painful divisions that it has elsewhere. "I sometimes like to say it's the elephant in the room," she noted, but arguments about Israel are "certainly not happening at the Interfaith Conference," perhaps because "we just have an awful lot in common around that table." She believes that the kind of theological wrestling that the Presbyterian church and the American Jewish organizations are undertaking in their own communities are first and foremost internal struggles for each group, and that at the Interfaith Conference "the issues aren't being grappled with in the same way."

On the surface, then, it appears the Interfaith Conference's way of dealing with conflicts between member groups is to avoid them: cancel the trips, don't discuss divestment. More subtly, though, these issues are dealt with through the relationships that are built around the Conference table. For instance, Simon explained, the much-publicized protest by Episcopal bishops outside the Israeli consulate in Boston in 2001 would never have occurred in Milwaukee, in part because of cultural differences, but also in part because of the power of face-to-face relationships established in interfaith work. "I don't think we would ever see anything like that because it would be pretty hard for someone you have gotten to know and who has looked you in the eye [to do that]." She referred to personal conversations with Presbyterian leaders, and with leadership of the United Church of Christ before their national meetings. "We don't do it around the table of the Interfaith Conference, but we have the relationship that I can go to them if I need to." Marcus White explained that these relationships and the conversations that go on outside the formal conference setting mean that the stickiest issues rarely make it to the table, having been negotiated informally so as to avoid public expressions of division and potential embarrassment.

Nearly every community interfaith participant I spoke with, in California, Wisconsin, and elsewhere, referred to the relationships nurtured by these informal conversations as by far the greatest payoff in interfaith work. Judi Longdin reported that the most powerful interfaith encounters she has had have come in bilateral exchanges, when two religious groups have an opportunity to ask deep questions about each other's approaches to social justice. Paula Simon and Arlo Reichter both spoke fondly of the monthly religious leaders' breakfast meetings, an informal gathering that meets under the auspices of the Interfaith Conference but with no set agenda. The networking, support, and relationship-building that go on in these meetings has been invaluable to both of their efforts on behalf of the Jewish and American Baptist communities, respectively. "To me, that is the perk of my job," Simon said. For Reichter, "it was and continues to be a tremendous support group, where we really share issues that we're facing in our congregations or synagogues. To have that need met in an interfaith way has been very exciting." In Chico, Richard Yale, the Episcopal priest, credits a similar informal group for drawing him into the Interfaith Council in the first place. Mike Newman values this group for the freedom its informality affords. "Because it's informal, you see how people think and react. You know that you can ask each other questions."

In both communities, then, participants reported that their interfaith relationships were sustained by encounters outside the formal parameters of the interfaith organization, whether through these less formal breakfast and coffee gatherings, or simply the one-on-one friendships fostered by pre- and post-meeting conversations and peripheral events. In some way, it seems, the formal interfaith organization sparks an impulse for deeper connection that the organization itself cannot meet. Informal and spin-off arrangements in both cities have developed to satisfy that need. While these formal and informal encounters have the potential to compete with each other for the time and loyalty of participants, they appear instead to serve complementary and mutually sustaining purposes.

Theologies of Community Interfaith Councils

It remains then to ask whether or not a distinctive or consistent theology informs interfaith encounters that occur at the community level. Beyond their shared commitments to community betterment, do these religious people share a common view of each other, or the nature of religious truth? I was struck in the course of interviewing these people by just how hard it was to actually get to theology, how strangely far afield questions of religious truth or the possibilities of universal salvation sounded in the context of what they really wanted to talk about, which was their communities, local issues, shared values, and personal relationships. No theological

premise, beyond the very general affirmation of the oneness of the sacred or humanity, is offered in the founding documents of these two organizations as a premise for interfaith collaboration. The looseness of
this theological foundation, of course, is strategically useful in that it allows for a wide range of groups to participate. When probed, however, the
comments of participants and the materials and events sponsored by the
organizations do reflect, if not a shared theology, a shared approach to
doing interfaith work that tends to neutralize the potential conflicts of divergent theologies.

Contrary to much popular perception, most members of community
interfaith groups do not espouse the kind of pluralism that deems all religions equal or essentially the same. In fact, every interfaith event I attended, and every person I spoke with, took pains to emphasize that
religions are not reducible to a common core, and that the interfaith
movement is emphatically not aimed at the creation of a single world religion. Perhaps because these organizations are congregationally and denominationally defined, individual participants' theologies of religion
tend to square quite neatly with the official positions of their religious
institutions. Catholic representatives Mike Newman in Chico and Judi
Longdin in Milwaukee, for instance, expressed near textbook versions of
Vatican II inclusivism, with its emphasis on the pervasiveness of God in
all religions. "I think that engaging people at this level," Judi reflected,
"really encountering and understanding them, seeing them in their holy
spaces and dealing with them in those spaces, engaging with them at important life moments, all of that can't help but reaffirm what the Catholic
Church has pretty clearly articulated: that there is truth in other faith traditions, that there is something of God in all of those traditions." When
pressed on the Church's recent emphasis, in spite of the truth in other
traditions, for Catholics to evangelize, Mike Newman offered this response, "I think it's good to evangelize. But evangelism means putting it
out there, and if people want to take it, they take it. And if they don't want
to take it, that's a matter of faith." But Newman leans heavily on the
Catholic teaching that non-Christians can be saved by the power of God's
grace without knowing Christ, so it is difficult to imagine him actively
evangelizing in any interfaith setting.

By the same token, Ali Sarsour and Ahmed Quereshi consistently referred to the Muslim teaching of avoiding any compulsion in religion, and leaving questions of salvation to God. "We are not concerned with proselytization," Quereshi insisted. "Guidance is from God, not from me or anybody else." For Sarsour, the question of who can be saved is simply not interesting when there is so much else to talk about. In good Muslim form, his refrain on the question turned the focus away from the human back to the divine: "Let God decide!"

Mary Ann Neevel, the UCC minister in Milwaukee, takes her cue for a theology of religions from the gospels and the prophets. "I connect Jesus and the prophets because I see both of those speaking to a society that wasn't getting it. This has drawn me into wanting to see who the people are in society who are ignored or undervalued or are just strangers." For her, this orientation leads inevitably to interfaith work. "If we see our mandate to love God and love our neighbor, we have to know who our neighbor is. And in order to share the love of God, we have to move out from where we are." Arlo Reichter, whose Baptist tradition has historically been among the more conservative in approaches to other religions, found that entering an interfaith context while in seminary in Berkeley, California, opened up a new appreciation of the mystery of God and the value of openness that subsequent interfaith work has confirmed. "I think it was just confirmation of the fact that it's not my job to judge. I'm thoroughly comfortable with the fact that, while I know how I have found my way to God, that there may be other ways. It's not my job to decide who's in or who's out. I always get worried about people who have it so well defined."

Rabbi Julie Danan offered a more explicitly pluralist position, drawing on the work of her own teacher, Rabbi Zalman Schacter-Shalomi, who has developed an organismic model of interfaith relations. In this conception, each religion is like a different organ in the body, each with its own integrity to maintain and its own contribution to make to the organism as a whole. "In other words," she explained, "we're all related but we're all distinct. We're not trying to give up our boundaries." As with all the interfaith participants I spoke with, this matter of boundaries, or difference, or particularity, was a vital emphasis. For all their commitment to openness, tolerance, and cooperation, none was interested in making the leap to a universal conception of the divine or human religion.

But while not all of the participants in community interfaith work are pluralists, it is hard to find those with exclusivist theologies engaged in this work. It may be true, as defenders of more traditional theological positions on religious difference have argued, that exclusivist theological commitments are not incompatible with interest in interfaith dialogue, but I found no exclusivists actually participating in these groups or their activities. It must be acknowledged that the practice of interfaith work, while it involves no pluralist litmus test, does require of participants a certain level of openness to the authenticity of alien religious paths. This in itself is a normative position that will continue to inhibit the participation of many religious groups, however open and inclusive the interfaith organization aims to be. As Tonen O'Connor put it, "Those that are fanatically certain about their path will never join us. You have to have some sort of openness—that you don't have the only answer in the universe—if you're going to participate." Most of those involved in interfaith work seem content with this situation, hopeful that one day more conservative groups might choose to participate, but unwilling to sacrifice this foundational openness in order to make that happen.

What often distinguishes community interfaith encounters from those explored in other parts of this book, however, is the depth of the participants' commitments to their own paths, however open they also are to others.' By and large, those involved in local interfaith organizations are not spiritual seekers, but individuals deeply grounded in and quite knowledgeable about their particular religious traditions. This commitment can be attributed to the organizational structure of these groups; defining membership by congregation or denomination makes it very hard for unaffiliated seekers to participate in significant ways. But it may also be a feature of participants' faithfulness to a structure itself. The discipline of monthly meetings, administrative responsibilities, and required commitment to the long-term flourishing of an organization make community interfaith work well suited to those with an already established investment in community structures. It may, perhaps, simply reflect the accumulated wisdom of the interfaith movement. To quote

Tonen O'Connor again, "You can only really do this kind of thing, genuinely, if you're very secure in your own faith."

"Just Being Together Is Enough"

No one doing community-based interfaith work that I spoke with was completely satisfied with what his or her group had achieved. Lack of racial and religious diversity, limited time and resources, unmet programming needs, misperception among some sectors of the community, not enough time for dialogue—all of these are frequent frustrations of the community interfaith council. But modest successes are enough to sustain them. At community interfaith events—a synagogue open house, a forum on Islam, an interreligious Thanksgiving service—interaction is limited and questions tend to be more polite than deep, but people leave these events less alien to the space they have visited and the people they have met. Administrative agendas may drive meetings, but before and after those meetings, and at the spin-off groups they have enabled, relationships have been formed that participants refer to consistently as the biggest payoff in interfaith work. I was struck by the fact that in both Chico and Milwaukee, members of the interfaith organization also regularly came together in a parallel, unstructured gathering—a breakfast meeting in both cases—with no agenda and no record-keeping, and that so many participants referred to this gathering as one of the most rewarding aspects of their jobs. So while the interfaith organization itself may not be the site of sustained interpersonal and interreligious exchanges, it creates opportunities for such exchanges that are of great value to many.

It may be, in fact, that the greatest value of these organizations does not lie in interreligious dialogue, or even in the community programs and activism that absorb so much of their energy. Rather, it may lie simply in people of different religious identities being present to one another. If the goal of local interfaith groups is to create communities of trust across potentially divisive religious lines, it would appear that structured dialogue may not be a critical element. Like the theologians of religious pluralism who insist that working together on a common problem is the most authentic mode of dialogue, those doing local interfaith work seem to find their greatest connections and insights as they do the mundane work of community life—planning a potluck, writing a press release for the newspaper, hosting a forum. "Just being together is enough," Ali Sarsour told me. "It is like fresh air to meet people who are different. Just being together is enough to break down ignorance."

But being together doesn't just happen. It is the vital contribution of the community interfaith organization that it creates a civic space for encounter, and invites people to remain faithful to a structure that can allow interreligious relationships to develop. For Bruce Grelle, it is this place-holding value that makes the Interfaith Council unique, and why he does not regret that his own council has not developed a more overtly political voice. "For all my own sympathies with taking certain stands on certain kinds of issues, I think there are other ways of doing that. There's enough partisanship out there already. What's lacking is the idea of a meeting place, a common ground where people can come together who are otherwise engaged in this culture war." In a time of intensely polarized public life, these councils, while still dominated by the personnel—and many of the assumptions—of a less diverse time, offer to be a place for realizing what is at the heart of American pluralist aspirations—real diversity within real community.

4

Intimate Others

Interfaith Families Making a Space
for Religious Difference

Most interfaith work is a purposeful, intentional thing. Driven by intellectual passion, politics, or a commitment to community harmony, people of different religious identities find or create the structures that will allow them to explore their difference and find common purpose. But for interfaith couples, the work of dialogue is un-asked for and unmapped. It comes up in the messy daily life of families—what day to call off-limits for soccer practice, what to make for children's lunches during Passover, how to decorate the house at holiday time, whether or not to serve wine at dinner. Most Americans who make up the 22 percent who marry outside their own religious tradition (American Religious Identification Survey [ARIS] 2001)[1] come to this dialogue experience with no particular interest in interfaith dialogue (or perhaps even in religion itself), only in loving a particular person. For some, living with that difference involves nothing more than the ordinary negotiations of coupled existence; for others, interfaith dialogue becomes a matter of survival, raising profound questions about personal identity, family, and what to do with the gaps between the lives they expected to lead and the ones in which they find themselves. In the process, these families are creating a unique mode of interreligious encounter and experimentation that both reflects and advances important recent developments in American spirituality.

Access to this site of interfaith encounter is not easy to come by. Domestic life is by definition private, unavailable for outsiders' analysis except through the blurry snapshots taken by survey data, and through the limited insight that can be gleaned from the stories of family life others are willing to share—stories that are always filtered, of course, through the interpreter's own experience of the complex dynamics of partnering, parenting, and negotiating religious identity. Demographic data on interfaith marriage—which religious groups are most likely to marry outside their faiths, sociological factors correlating with intermarriage, and the like—are available but of limited use. While they can tell us, for instance, that interfaith marriage is more common among Jews than Mormons, or among college graduates than those with high school educations, they cannot tell us what it is like to *be* a Jew married to a non-Jew, or how higher learning might reshape traditional religious views in such a way that marriage to a religious "other" becomes intelligible.

Since the goal of this project is to understand interfaith encounters as they actually occur in real people's lives, rather than how academics or religious institutions theorize about them, it is vital to hear from people actually living in interfaith partnerships. To that end, I draw here on two sets of primary data: a series of interviews I conducted with nine interfaith families, and an analysis of exchanges among interfaith families in online discussions. These conversations tell small stories that both enliven and challenge the big stories told by demographers and sociologists of religion, as well as the normative narratives put forth by religious institutions. They also offer a provocative counterpoint to established ideas about who gets involved in interfaith dialogue, why, and what happens when they do.

Institutional Anxiety about Interfaith Marriage

"For that would turn away your children from following me."

An assessment of attitudes toward interfaith marriage in America through the lens of television and popular films would lead to the conclusion that mixed marriages are everywhere, normal, and beautiful expressions of American ideals of inclusiveness and painless multiculturalism.[2] If interfaith couples were to enter their relationships on this assumption, however, they would fast come up against a very different reality. Nearly every organized religious community endorses interfaith dialogue as a matter of good global citizenship. While different groups set different limits on the specific topics and goals of dialogical work, all are generally agreed that mutual understanding and communal harmony are enhanced by intentional encounters with religious others. When it comes to interfaith marriages, however, the rhetoric of openness and tolerance often changes sharply. Interfaith partnering presses religious institutions to the limits of their interest in dialogue, because it takes place at the heart of religious identity formation and propagation: the family.

Jewish and Christian Perspectives

Jewish-Christian pairings are by far the most common interfaith combination in the United States today, and both traditions have developed considerable reflection on the issue of mixed marriages. Anxiety about marrying outside the faith is embedded in the Hebrew Scriptures themselves, where a spouse of a different religion represents a temptation to idolatry. God's instruction against intermarriage in Deuteronomy, which occurs in the context of the conquest of the peoples of Canaan, is fraught with concern for the Israelites' faithfulness to their one God, and is backed by a powerful threat: "Do not intermarry with them, giving your daughters to their sons or taking their daughters for your sons, for that would turn away your children from following me, to serve other gods. Then the anger of the Lord would be kindled against you, and he would destroy you quickly" (Deut 7:3–4).

Among Jews today, a sense of threat still often attaches to intermarriage. For while divine retribution may not have fallen on the heads of those who have violated this injunction over the centuries, history has certainly made real the threat of Jewish annihilation. And many Jews today reasonably worry that what attempted genocide has not accomplished, assimilation in a Christian-dominated culture will. Jews who intermarry thus often face sharp criticism from a Jewish establishment concerned about the threat of extinction. As one defender of Jewish intermarriage colorfully puts it, marrying non-Jews is targeted as "the latest virus eating away at the last shreds of flesh on the corpse of diaspora Judaism, making Jews who marry non-Jews the demographic equivalent of Typhoid Mary" (McClain 1995, 124–125). On the other hand, sociologist Silvia Fishman argues in her recent book on Jews and mixed marriage that "many studies indicate that for both inmarried and mixed-married families, the most effective strategy for cultural transmission is for the Jewish community to enrich Judaic experiences and knowledge across age, denominational, and geographic lines" (Fishman 2004, 160). If this is the case, then interfaith families who make a commitment to such experiences and knowledge may well be better contributors to Jewish flourishing than their secularized inmarried counterparts.

But at the official denominational level, resistance remains the norm for Judaism. The rabbinical associations of Orthodox and Conservative Judaism prohibit rabbis from officiating at interfaith weddings, although a recent study found that almost a third of Conservative rabbis regularly referred interfaith couples to rabbis who would (Jewish Outreach Institute). There are no official barriers to interfaith marriage for the more liberal Reform and Reconstructionist branches of Judaism, where such policy is determined by individual rabbis, many of whom officiate at interfaith weddings under certain conditions.

It is important to note that in spite of strong ongoing institutional Jewish resistance to interfaith marriage, increased interest in greater outreach to interfaith couples is evident in all branches of Judaism. Indeed, Jewish ambivalence about interfaith marriage runs high. While potent rhetoric about intermarriage abounds—whether it is referred to as a "silent holocaust" or, conversely, opposition to it as racism (Weiss, cited in Shulevitz 2000)—one of the most interesting findings of a recent survey of the American rabbinate was the high level of internal conflict many rabbis expressed about their own position on intermarriage (Jewish Outreach Institute). Meanwhile, the rate of Jewish intermarriage increases apace. According to the National Jewish Population Survey of 2000–2001, intermarriage rates for Jews who married before 1970 stands at 13 percent, while for those married since 1996, the rate is 47 percent. The 2001 American Religious Identity Survey places the overall rate of intermarriage for American Jews at 27 percent.[3]

Clearly, in spite of institutional resistance or ambivalence, Jews are engaged in this most intimate form of interfaith dialogue in such numbers that it will inevitably continue to reshape American Jewish identity. And as in so many areas of religious life, Jews who are living in interfaith marriages take their cues for how to understand and practice their faith in this context not only from the statements of their religious leaders and institutions, but increasingly from each other, in a growing grassroots interfaith movement that offers support, educational resources, help in designing interfaith ceremonies, and even, in some cities, fully developed interfaith religious schools for children.

For Christians, institutional opposition to marrying outside the religion is felt far less intensely than it is for Jews, which is not surprising given the dominant status of Christianity in the United States. Intermarriage might be seen as a risk to personal, individual faith, but it hardly represents a threat to the survival of the religion. Even where official doctrinal statements oppose interfaith marriage, as does the Westminster Confession of Reformed-Presbyterian Christians, for instance, in practice most clergy in these denominations willingly officiate at and fully support interfaith marriages. Many mainstream denominations, including the Lutheran Church, take no official position on interfaith marriage, leaving individual clergy to guide parishioners according to his or her own judgment. Among major Christian groups in the United States, only the Southern Baptist denomination actively opposes interfaith unions. This opposition draws from the strict dualism expressed by St. Paul in the New Testament: "Do not be yoked together with unbelievers. For what do righteousness and wickedness have in common? Or what fellowship can light have with darkness? What harmony is there between Christ and Belial [Satan]? What does a believer have in common with an unbeliever?" (II Cor. 6:14–15). This opposition is consistent with the exclusivist position Southern Baptists hold on the value of non-Christian religions; since specific affirmation of faith in Christ is required for salvation, marriage to a non-Christian, or even a different kind of Christian, would generate enormous theological tension.

Yet it is important to note that theological perspectives on religious difference—whether a given denomination takes a pluralist, inclusivist, or exclusivist view—will not necessarily jibe with that denomination's statements on interfaith marriage. Roman Catholicism, for instance, has taken an inclusivist approach to religious difference since Vatican II, asserting that saving knowledge of God is available through non-Christian traditions, though the fullness of that knowledge is found only in the Catholic Church. While statements by Pope John Paul II and the Sacred Congregation for the Doctrine of the Faith have since put more emphasis on the

ongoing need to evangelize non-Christians than on the truth their traditions contain,[4] still the Catholic Church places very few obstacles in the
path of interfaith marriage for Catholics. Roman Catholics may marry
baptized non-Catholic Christians, or even non-Christians with a simple
dispensation, provided that they agree to accept children and raise them
according to the teachings of the Church.

Conversely, Judaism, which tends to affirm religious pluralism in a
theological context, expresses much more opposition to interfaith unions.
Here, factors such as perceptions of vulnerability become critical. Within
Christianity, groups like the Amish, the Mennonites, or, to a lesser degree, the Church of Jesus Christ of Latter-Day Saints (Mormons), which
make up only a small percentage of American Christians and which maintain a culturally distinctive practice, place more emphasis on in-group
marriage than do mainline Protestant or Roman Catholic churches. For
these smaller groups, marriage to outsiders is often seen as dangerous di-
lution of a distinctive identity already under tremendous pressure from
external forces. Where large Christian groups, like Southern Baptists, oppose interfaith marriages, they also tend to do so out of a sense of threat,
not to their numbers but to their doctrinal clarity and purity. We can distinguish, then, between the resistance of theologically conservative Christian groups to intermarriage, which is based on a rejection of the validity
of non-Christian paths, and that of Jewish institutions, which recognize
the legitimacy of non-Jewish faith traditions while resisting intermarriage
as a matter of Jewish survival.

As in the Jewish community, institutional perspectives on interfaith
relations are only of limited significance in guiding the actual practices of
Christians. Christians continue to marry outside their own faith traditions at increasing rates, although intermarriage rates generally reflect
the institutional positions noted above. The 2001 ARIS survey reports, for
instance, that Protestants intermarry at a rate of 33 percent, Catholics at
23 percent, Baptists at 18 percent, and Mormons at 12 percent. But because interfaith marriage is so much less a focus of pastoral concern than
it is for Jews, Christians, perhaps ironically, find themselves with fewer
denominational resources for dealing with the issue. Outreach to interfaith families, for instance, is far less likely to be on the agenda of the average Christian church community than it is for the average synagogue.

Christians thus tend to find their own way through interfaith issues, although those in partnerships with Jews in particular have a rich and growing network of support on which to draw.

Buddhist and Hindu Perspectives

The increasing complexity and diversity of America's religious landscape suggest that interfaith configurations other than between Christians and Jews are likely to increase in frequency. The large influx of Asian immigrants makes it important to consider the views of nonwestern religions on intermarriage as well. Both the Hindu and Buddhist traditions are generally very open to the claims of other religions. Hinduism can be understood to offer a kind of Eastern inclusivism that honors all spiritual paths but sees Hinduism as the straightest route to spiritual fulfillment. Buddhism is also known for its openness to other religions, as well as for reticence on the kinds of doctrinal disputes that typically generate interreligious conflict (McCarthy 1998, 90). Neither Hinduism nor Buddhism makes any formal pronouncement of religious opposition to interfaith marriage.

But this is perhaps to look in the wrong place. It is often observed that both Buddhism and Hinduism are better understood as cultural systems rather than strictly as religions in the western sense. For this reason, marriage between a Hindu or Buddhist and a partner of another religion, especially in immigrant communities, is better understood as an intercultural rather than an interfaith issue. Many first-generation Indian and Nepali Americans, for instance, try to maintain traditions of arranged marriages with those of the same ethnic (and sometimes caste) origins. But such efforts face enormous counterpressure. While Asian immigrant communities once lived in protective enclaves where in-marriage was the norm, young Asian Americans today are thoroughly integrated into the dominant culture, in which early dating across all lines is increasingly common. High rates of college education further increase the likelihood of American Hindus and Buddhists choosing partners of another religion. One interesting emerging pattern in this process is the large number of Hindu-Jewish marriages, traced to the influx of Indian men coming to the United States for higher education beginning in the late 1960s. Journalist Jeremy Caplan reports that common cultural traditions—dietary codes, home-based religious practices, family values—make Hinduism and Judaism congenial partners, and while most of these households end up identifying religiously as Jews, Hindu cultural values and traditions are preserved and passed on (Caplan 2004, 1).

While its growth seems inevitable, intermarriage remains problematic for many American Buddhists and Hindus. While the philosophical openness of these traditions and their lack of a centralized institutional authority make it hard to find any formal prohibitions of interfaith marriage, the commitment to preserve cultural identity of a tiny minority in a dominant culture may exercise even greater pressure. At the level of family and community, especially among more recent immigrants, members of these typically pluralism-affirming religions often experience considerable resistance to marrying someone outside their tradition, a resistance reinforced, of course, by the wariness or outright hostility of surrounding groups.

Muslim Perspectives

Unlike Buddhism and Hinduism, Islam does offer clear statements about the legitimacy of interfaith marriage, views that are commonly known among ordinary Muslims in the widely divergent cultural settings in which Islam has taken root. According to the Qur'an and Muslim legal tradition, a Muslim man may marry a Christian or a Jew, but marriage to someone of a non-Abrahamic religion is invalid. Muslim women may not marry any non-Muslim, unless her partner first converts. As part of a minority community in the United States, American Muslim women thus face a greater challenge than men in finding acceptable partners. What's more, the fact that marriage plays a central role in Islam, in which married life, rather than celibacy, is seen as the highest religious calling, and that marriage is traditionally understood as the union of two families rather than two individuals (Smith 1999, 114), means that the stakes in such decisions are very high. A Muslim woman who marries a non-Muslim often does so against enormous familial and cultural pressure, and effectively puts herself outside the religious community.

The traditional restrictions on intermarriage for women apparently derive from the assumption that a Muslim woman will fall under the authority of her husband, and therefore that she and their children will be subsumed by his religion. In the United States today, this assumption is highly questionable, and American Muslim women in interfaith relationships thus find themselves negotiating one of the most interesting intersections of religious tradition and cultural pluralism. There is a tension in Muslim societies between the gender equality articulated in the Qur'an and the patriarchal Islamic legal tradition of assumed male headship and strict regulation of female sexuality, expressed in dress codes, restrictions on interactions with non-family males, emphasis on sexual chastity, and relegation of the female to the private, domestic sphere. In immigrant communities in the United States, where such regulations run counter to the norms of the dominant culture, Muslim women are negotiating new identities—taking on more public roles, establishing greater equality in private roles—and doing so by drawing on the deep and wide tradition of gender egalitarianism in Islam that is often obscured by attention to the highly repressive gender systems of some Muslim societies. American Muslim women who marry non-Muslims while maintaining the own identity as Muslims can be seen as part of this larger movement of Muslim women who are redefining the meaning of gender in Islam.

As with Jews and Christians, then, there are significant gaps for Muslims between scriptural and institutional proclamations (and familial expectations) and lived practice, among men as well as women. The rate of intermarriage among immigrant Muslims has increased with every generation (Smith 1999, 56), and today, according to the 2001 ARIS report, American Muslims intermarry at a rate of 21 percent, roughly the same as American Catholics.

Demographic Snapshots of Interfaith Marriage

It may be that far simpler factors than denominational positions and levels of perceived threats to religious identity are at work in determining who intermarries. Quantitative research on interfaith marriages in the United States suggests strongly that, doctrinal positions notwithstanding, the key determinant of likelihood to marry outside one's own religious community is the relative size of that community in the larger social context. In a study of Catholic intermarriage, for instance, Davidson (1998) found that when Catholics are 50 percent or more of the total population in a geographic diocese, their interfaith marriage rate is 18 percent, while it jumps to 40 percent where Catholics make up only 10–19 percent of the diocese's overall population. This pattern appears to be consistent across religious groups in the United States (Lehrer 1998; Davidson and Widman 2002). Buddhists, for instance, who make up less than 1 percent of the U.S. population, intermarry at a rate of 39 percent, the highest reported for any group in the 2001 American Religious Identity Survey. The lesson is clear: as the pool of those who share our religious identity shrinks, we are more likely to find partners religiously different from ourselves. At the same time, as recent economic theories of religion have sought to demonstrate, having a small share of the religious market may prompt religious groups to generate higher levels of commitment among their adherents (Stark and Finke 2000, 219). If both of these observations are correct, those drawn to interfaith relationships are in a difficult bind: those in groups with a smaller number of adherents are motivated to maintain strong commitments to those traditions at the same time that they are drawn by demographic pressures to partners outside that tradition.

Education levels also appear to correlate with intermarriage rates. According to Sherkat (2004), higher levels of education increase the likelihood of intermarriage, and marriages in which the woman is more highly educated than the man are more likely to be interfaith. Lehrer (1998) found that education levels do not correlate strongly with intermarriage rates for liberal Protestants and Catholics, but do for exclusivist Protestants, for whom intermarriage occurs at a much higher rate among those with the highest levels of schooling. Lehrer explains this pattern as a trade-off made by conservative Christians: "Among the most highly educated exclusivist Protestants, the more elevated levels of intellectual development and socioeconomic attainment associated with greater schooling—which may be found more easily in a partner outside the religion—appear to represent an important aspect of compatibility which is traded off against religious homogamy" (257).

What all these studies agree on is that intermarriage is a growing phenomenon in American society, more for some groups than others, in somewhat predictable demographic patterns. For most scholars, the increasing rate of religious intermarriage is understood in the context of secularization theory outlined in chapter two—the observation that in contemporary society religious explanations and institutions have a decreasing hold on personal and social life, replaced by those of science and commerce. In fact, while it is certainly on the rise today, interfaith marriages are as old as the country, and may reflect deeply embedded patterns of American religious self-determination in a society committed to pluralism in principle but uneasy about it in practice.

As American as Intermarriage: The Deep Roots of Domestic Interfaith Encounters

American experiences of marrying across religious lines cannot be understood simply as the encounter of two individuals negotiating different opinions about sacred matters. These encounters exist in a complex social context, and grappling with religious pluralism has a particularly prominent place in the history of the nation's effort to understand and define itself. While there is little information available about interfaith marriage before the mid-twentieth century, American views of religious pluralism—whether they reflect toleration, inclusion, or participation, to use Hutchison's terms again—have always framed the experience of couples who intermarry, adding complex layers to the meanings of such pairings ascribed by families and congregations. Specific time periods stand out as critical in the development of the uniquely American take on interfaith marriage. In terms of institutional positions, the middle part of the nineteenth century is perhaps the most important era to consider, for as historian Anne C. Rose documents in *Beloved Strangers: Interfaith Families in Nineteenth Century America*, the postures of major American religious communities and institutions toward mixed marriages were formed in these decades. As immigrant populations swelled dramatically, non-Protestant groups established the critical mass that necessitated reckoning with issues of community identity and boundaries and generated the institutional structures needed to communicate positions on these ideas (Rose 2001, 49). Before this time, Americans of different religions certainly had opinions about each other, but the overwhelming majority held by Protestant Christians meant that interfaith associations were limited, informal, and typically uncontentious. Between 1840 and 1880, however, Catholics and Jews, the major religious outsiders in nineteenth-century America, engaged in sustained internal conversations, through denominational publications, sermons, advice books, and pastoral letters, about the threat of interreligious mixing and how to respond to it (50). In the process, they established formal positions and interpretive frameworks that persist to the present.

The documents Rose assembles reveal a Catholic Church concerned with maintaining the sacred order against the threat posed by outsiders. Marriage to non-Catholics was sharply censured; yet records indicate that priests performed them quite regularly (53), perhaps out of fear of the greater threats to the Catholic soul of cohabitation or marriage outside the Church (31). According to the popular Catholic rhetoric of the day, intermarried Catholics could be redeemed by public penance and prayerful efforts at spousal conversion (55). While the Church officially forbade intermarriage, in practice it offered dispensations, nurtured close ties with the Catholic spouse, and interpreted interfaith relationships in the context of a clear salvation narrative. "The Catholic Church seemed able to offer interfaith households a structure in which to function as religiously mixed homes. . . . Tolerance, evangelicalism, and, critically, an institution squarely facing mixed marriages had appeal in an era when couples seemed eager for public religious ties" (93).

Nineteenth-century Jewish leadership responded to the growing issue of intermarriage in a similarly defensive mode, yet with a different focus. While Catholic conversation about intermarriage focused on the drama of individual salvation and purity of doctrine, Jewish leaders' opinions were more varied and centered more around questions of Jewish identity, descent, and ritual observance. Questions Jewish partners in interfaith marriages struggle with today—finding a rabbi who will marry them, the Jewish identity of children, and levels of ritual observance—were all vital questions subject to animated debate in the American rabbinate by the 1840s (56–62). And while the more liberal leanings of Jewish thinking (as contrasted with Catholic concerns for orthodoxy and control) opened up important dialogue and granted considerable local flexibility for interfaith couples, it also meant that their status was hard to clarify. "It could not have been easy," Rose concludes, "for interfaith families to find their way" (62).

Remarkable in Rose's thorough analysis of nineteenth-century discussions of interfaith marriage is the silence of the Protestant majority.
According to the records of sermons, publications, and news reports,
Protestant leadership simply did not speak about interfaith marriages,
though they occurred in significant numbers. This silence can be understood as the logical response of the socially dominant group that had the
power to absorb, and thus erase, difference: "The Protestant majority
gained much and lost little by quietly absorbing interfaith families. In
crude terms of numbers, Protestantism added households. Declining to
mention strangers in their midst protected an impression of seamless
hegemony and exerted pressure on mixed families to honor Protestant
norms. . . . Far worse to lament intermarriage loudly, admitting threat, than
to manage it discreetly" (62–63). Rose's analysis places Protestant treatments of intermarriage squarely within Hutchison's understanding of the
era's prevailing view of pluralism as toleration: Jews and Catholics were
cordially but quietly welcomed into Protestant families and churches, without even being required to convert, so long as their difference made no difference in social fact, that is, so long as they suppressed the marks of their
otherness and submitted to a set of Anglo-Protestant norms that were presented as "American." "Protestant writing implied that if interfaith families
behaved like Protestants, religious issues would fall into place" (64). Interfaith marriages were thus not (only) about individual couples freely negotiating individual religious difference, but (also) about the intersections of
groups sharply differentiated in their social power. When a person of one
faith chose to marry an outsider (or if he or she was the outsider), he or she
moved not only across religious boundaries, "but up or down ladders of legitimacy and reward" (Rose 2001, 9).

To the picture of Protestant hegemony and its effect on interfaith
relations, Rose's study helpfully adds analysis of the role of gender ideology in shaping attitudes toward and within interfaith marriages. In
nineteenth-century America, religion came to be understood as part of
the female domestic sphere, while its role in the male public world was
more limited and often only a nominal formality. Rose describes three intermarried senators at the center of public life in Washington, D.C., all of
whom seem to have dealt very tolerantly, even lightheartedly, with their
wives' religious difference; it apparently made very little difference to the

public lives by which the men defined themselves (100–109). Conflict in the interfaith home seems to have been minimized by the practice of leaving family religious leadership to women. In this sense patriarchal systems functioned in tandem with Protestant hegemony to minimize the contentiousness of interfaith marriage. Women's religious otherness, while profoundly influential at home, was largely invisible and impotent in the male world of public social power, and therefore to be tolerated, even celebrated as an emblem of American liberal ideals.

While American women no longer subscribe in significant numbers to anything like the nineteenth-century doctrine of womanhood, there is nonetheless much in the conception and practice of interfaith marriages established in the nineteenth century that continues to inform contemporary practice. First, institutional resistance to interfaith marriage remains stronger among groups, like Catholics and Jews in the nineteenth century, who are smaller in number, the objects of prejudice, and therefore concerned with protecting community boundaries. Today this resistance is still evident among Jewish communities, as well as in more recently arrived religious minorities like Hindus and Muslims. The Catholic Church continues its pragmatic approach of formally discouraging interfaith marriage while granting dispensations liberally, focusing instead on doctrinal clarity and maintaining the integration of intermarried Catholics and their children within the Church. These institutional solutions that were forged 150 years ago echo in the reports of interfaith couples today as they speak of pressures from family and clergy to avoid intermarriage, or, once in it, to manage it in particular ways.

A second legacy of this formative era is the need to continue to examine the perhaps more subtle but persistent ways in which power differentials—those of ethnicity, class, and gender—shape interfaith relationships. When the American children of Muslim immigrants from Asia or the Middle East, for instance, seek to marry white Christian partners, they enter a complicated web of familial and cultural expectations and anxieties about roles of husbands and wives, the meaning of family and culture, and movement up or down systems of status and privilege. Theological conflicts are easily lost in the fray.

Finally, the socially conventional and highly decorous nineteenth-century couples that are the subject of Rose's study established a profound precedent for contemporary interfaith families in their assertiveness in putting distance between the official positions of their religious institutions (to which they remained loyal) and their own religious lives. A century before secularization theory would be intelligible, these couples took advantage of the opportunities an open society afforded for religious self-determination and extra-institutional experimentation. In such interfaith homes, Rose shows, religion changed—as it would do again and again in American culture—"from a set of precepts to a series of possibilities" (13). These developments would be intensified by twentieth-century changes in American religion, notably the movements toward more individual religious meaning-making, decreasing adherence to traditional religious institutions, and new understandings of pluralism that do not demand assimilation but support the integrity of competing beliefs (Hutchison 2003, 235). Americans living in interfaith partnerships today are, as they were 150 years ago, unintentionally pressing the culture toward new ways of understanding its religious differences, with traits shared by their forbears—"religious curiosity, family loyalty, and a taste for the unexpected" (Rose 2001, 190).

Listening to Interfaith Families

The interfaith families whose lives I want to share glimpses of—couples I interviewed, and the people who are involved in or products of interfaith marriages who have written or posted online messages on the subject—are a small and distinct subset of those involved in interfaith marriages. In engaging in these activities, they reveal a level of reflectiveness about their interfaith experience that may not characterize all or even most religiously plural families. For many, certainly, the challenge of interfaith relationship ends with the successful negotiation of a wedding ceremony, after which religion ceases to be a topic of interest. What's more, this is a collection of partnerships whose goal is somehow to *live with* religious difference, not resolve it through conversion or dissolution of religious identities entirely. Couples in which one partner converts, or in which all religious ties are cut would make for another interesting analysis, but they are not the focus here, where I am aiming to see how the family can be a place of real interfaith encounter. It is my hope that, while perhaps not fully representative, the deeply thoughtful comments shared by these families will bring dimension and life to the limited information available about interfaith marriages, and prompt further reflection on the family as a significant site of interfaith dialogue.[5]

I spoke in depth with fourteen people involved in interfaith partnerships, ten as couples, four individually. Denise and Jeff are a young couple from New Jersey who have been together for four years. She is Catholic; he's Jewish. Janet and Susan, from Northern California, have been together over twenty years. They were both raised Catholic, but Janet is now a practicing Zen Buddhist, and Susan has returned to the Church after many years away. David and Amina are recently married and living in Northern California. He is Jewish, she's Muslim (originally from Pakistan). Laura, who is Jewish, has been married to her Presbyterian husband for over twenty-five years. They live in New York. Joan, from Connecticut, is Protestant and has been married for over twenty years to Peter, who is Jewish. Deborah, who is Jewish, lives in the San Francisco Bay area with her husband, who is a Catholic originally from Latin America. Ben is a Reform Jew who grew up in Detroit and now lives in northern California with his wife Saba, a Coptic Christian from Eritrea whose spiritual pursuits could also classify her as something of a "seeker." Bill and Sarah are raising their two young children in Chicago; he is Catholic; she's Jewish. Aaron and Petra, who live in northern Washington State, have the most complex religious identities of all the couples I spoke with. She's an immigrant from the Czech Republic who was raised by "adamant atheists" but now pursues an eclectic spirituality informed by Chinese medicine, meditation, and insights about energy processes gleaned from the Berkeley Psychic Institute. Aaron was raised as a secular Jew and still identifies as Jewish though he acknowledges that his practice, which also includes meditation, is highly eclectic.

These pairings are by no means representative of the incredible range of religious combinations now found in American households, though the prominence here of Catholics and Jews remains consistent with the focus of most American conversations about interfaith families throughout the nation's history. To supplement the stories told by these couples, I include references to five years of online exchanges between interfaith families on topics ranging from theology to ritual design to in-law relationships.[6]

The Everyday Work of Religious Difference

If one theme could be said to be universal among interfaith couples, it might be the value they place, in the present moment or in retrospect, on facing their religious difference head-on, as early as possible in the relationship. Many couples credit early, honest, and ongoing conversations about religion for the success of their marriages. Others, in hindsight, express regret that they had not reckoned, before marriage, or before having children, with the depth of their individual faith commitments and the conflicts they would generate.[7] One parent in an interfaith marriage writes in an online discussion group about the growing difficulty she feels in accommodating her husband's faith, and offers a warning to unmarried interfaith couples: "I was so 'in love' in my twenties when I married my hubby that I went along with his promise to raise HIS children Catholic. I can honestly say that as our child has grown and I've spent more time learning about his church, I am less inclined to want my child being raised with some of the beliefs of that church. I just keep telling him 'Jesus told us to "love one another." There were no stipulations.' I hope that will hold him until adulthood. I feel very accountable to God for his soul. It is very difficult. Singles, take note!" (niceguy, January 26, 2000).[8] By contrast, this Muslim woman reports that she and her Christian partner are moving forward successfully based on a shared perspective on their religious difference achieved through extensive conversations: "My sig other and I talk about religion all the time and the meanings of religion and have established that religions (islam, christianity, judaism) all produce the same love, belief, hate, poverty and despair in the world. Yet they all lead towards the same one god. . . . Islam and Christianity are mere words that come between interrelated faith. I love my family very much but if they can't accept a marriage based upon faith in god, morals, and values, then they cannot accept me" (ds103n, March 22. 2005). In this case, dialogue before the marriage has led the couple to a shared pluralist view of religious truth that allows them, at least at this point, to proceed with confidence in their relationship even in the face of her family's forceful opposition.

Aaron and Petra are perhaps unusual in the extent to which spiritual themes fill their conversations. She's an acupuncturist and herbal healer by profession; he's a former history teacher now pursuing an advanced degree in the history of religion. For them, it has not been money or sex but metaphysics that has fueled the most intense arguments in their four-year relationship. Long car rides have been filled with intense exchanges over issues like past lives and the subjectivity of ultimate reality. While they have not come to agree on these matters, they have found a vocabulary, a way of speaking that allows them to both account for their many shared spiritual experiences and beliefs, and also step aside when they encounter ideas that they apparently do not share. For them, staying focused on the function of their religious ideas and practices has been key; "Whatever it actually *is*," Aaron says of the energy that is at the heart of both their spiritual paths, "it works."

Another member of an interfaith partnership, further along in the relationship, makes a comment frequently heard among successful interfaith couples—that the marriage was preceded by a great deal of discussion of religion issues, particularly concerning children: "I'm in an interfaith marriage (I'm Wiccan, he's Christian—13 years this past May), and though it is hard work, it *can* work. When dh and I got married, we had talked and talked about how we would raise our children. So when we had our daughter, we already knew the plan of action" (harmonyfb, August 29, 2001). Not surprisingly, the value of open and early conversation about religious difference is one of the most universal themes in guidebooks for interfaith couples (e.g., Hawxhurst 1998, 2–4). But if interfaith couples aren't hearing that advice, they are not alone. A survey conducted by *Child* magazine, for instance, recently reported that only 41 percent of parents with children under age thirteen discussed the religious upbringing of their kids before the children were born (Brown 2002). Here as in so many areas, the idiosyncratic and unpredictable quality of interfaith family discussions contrasts sharply with other dialogue formats in which structures are in place, goals and guidelines established, and end results foreseeable.

When it occurs, one of the most frequently reported outcomes of communication among interfaith partners is a commitment to preserving each other's individual religious identity. This may be one of the most compelling features of this mode of interfaith dialogue: Whereas in formal interfaith settings, members of different religions are advised and encouraged to develop respect for one another, in a marriage setting, most partners come to the dialogue pre-equipped with the mutual respect that grows from love. For many, it is the commitment to the other that makes the spouse's conversion an unacceptable option. "Wiping out someone's identity, like a spouse's identity, with their faith," said Bill, a Catholic from Chicago about his marriage to a Jewish woman, "that just wasn't an option." Similar views are voiced online. "My husband is now a Muslim," one dialogue participant reports. "He will never convert to Christianity and I will NEVER convert to Islam. My beliefs, however misguided they potentially are, are dear to me, and so are his" (Tejana13, September 17, 2003). "When my husband and I got married," another woman explains, "I didn't believe in anything. But now, as I learn more things about different religions he stands by me in whatever I want to do. He is always telling me that no one has a monopoly on the truth, and that I should do what is best for me" (Akhiris, November 12, 2003).

Establishing that both traditions will be respected as part of each partner's identity is the foundation on which many interfaith families are built. Just how that respect materializes, though, is as varied as the families themselves. Until children are born, most interfaith couples simply pursue their individual religious practices on their own, attending separate services and observing different holidays, while others adopt many of each other's observances. Couples like Ben and Saba and Petra and Aaron, for whom the conscious creation of a meaningful spiritual practice is a prominent part of individual and partnered life, often make interfaith or hybrid religious activities—a community interfaith dinner and lecture, a workshop on healing techniques, shared meditation practices—the focus of their spiritual lives. But for most of the couples I spoke with, blended activities require more careful negotiation.

Jeff and Denise, a Jewish-Christian couple from New Jersey, had been married three years when I met them, and were still working out what shape their married religious life would take. They often attend each other's services out of respect and affection for each other, even if it raises eyebrows among friends and family. "If a christening comes up, I go to church with her family, and she comes with my family," Jeff reports. "But still, I know that there are friends and family that still think it's probably strange that I go to church; deep down . . . there is just something

visceral about that that they think is odd. For me it's not odd anymore."
Denise, who is Catholic, explains that when they were dating they established the pattern of taking both sets of religious holidays off from work,
and attending services with their respective families. "We don't really
look at it as my holiday or your holiday," she says. "It's just kind of what
we do." But as their relationship develops, they are now struggling to
identify what their own practice, apart from their families, will look like.
As Jeff says, "I guess we're at the point now in our marriage where we're
really trying—and it's a struggle—we're trying to figure out how we want to
celebrate religion for the two of us rather than just with our families." Almost all couples find that the first years of a committed relationship en-
tail careful renegotiation of relationships with their families of origin; for
interfaith couples like Jeff and Denise, religion is often the major catalyst
in that process.

As family life gets more complicated, many couples who are committed to maintaining both religious identities find the double set of observances burdensome from a purely practical perspective. Laura, who
helped form an interfaith family organization in New York nearly twenty
years ago to meet the needs of her own and other Jewish-Christian families, notes that for many busy Manhattan families, "doing both," while desirable, was simply impractical, and for many families the interfaith
community became the only venue for religious activity. Equity is also a
challenge, she explains. Learning Hebrew takes a greater time investment
than do most Christian catechism programs, and so it can be difficult to
achieve parity even when equal time is given to both activities. Deborah,
a Jewish woman from the San Francisco Bay Area married to a Roman
Catholic originally from South America, observes similar challenges in
her suburban community. While she and her family participate in activities in both the synagogue and the Catholic Church, they worried that
requiring their children to attend both Jewish Sunday School and
Catholic catechism would risk alienating them from both. "We never felt
that the kids would be confused. It was more of [a concern about] rebel-
lion. If you have too much of something, it would turn you off to the
whole thing."

Rather than rely on the traditional structures of weekly worship and institutionally based religious education, then, these families and countless

others have developed their own ways of accommodating their separate religious traditions. For some this means attending each service less frequently but together; for others it means worshipping separately. "We go our own ways," says David, a young Jewish man recently married to Amina, a Muslim. Another Jewish man says in an online post: "I light my menorah on Chanukah and my wife goes to Mass at her church on Christmas Eve (and every Sunday). I put a tree up, decorate it and put presents under it for her. She gives me eight presents for eight nights. No problem. I don't ask her to go to shul with me and she's not offended when I decline going to Mass" (windbender, December 24, 2004). For still others, the entanglements are more complex, as for the partnership described by a secular Jewish man in this online advice to a younger interfaith couple: "No question it has taken some growth on both our parts and we are still working at it. There are lots of ways to support someone without agreeing with them on all points. I watch my son sometimes so my wife can go to church. I go to church with her on special occasions (which can be tough, sometimes). I help her with some church activities she participates in. We have various religious stuff in the home. (I don't reject a xmas tree or a cross in our house. It's her house too.) So, it takes some growth but you can do it" (lancef, January 11, 2001). Regardless of how they arrange their patterns of religious observance, all the couples I encountered have found themselves, to varying degrees, distanced from their own religious institutions and simultaneously drawn into a relationship with a tradition not their own.

This is not always a smooth process. Because the learning about another religion occurs in the context of an interpersonal relationship, the occasions for hurt feelings are abundant. For Deborah, it is very important that she and the children observe the dietary rules around Passover, including having no bread in the house, though she accepts that her husband Luis can eat what he chooses outside the home. One day near the end of Passover a number of years ago, she came home to find Luis serving their kids sandwiches for lunch. "And I said, 'How could you do that?' That was a big thing for me, because it showed to me 'You don't take it to heart. You don't really care.'" Luis was able to convince Deborah that he really had simply forgotten, and they were able to resolve the conflict. Now, she reports, he has become a bigger stickler for dietary observance than she is.

"There's No 'Half' about Them": Raising Interfaith Kids

As their comments have already indicated, interfaith couples tend to experience most deeply their religious difference when they face the question of how to raise their children. It is here, too, that the variety and
creativity of individual family arrangements emerges. Many couples
"agree" at the time of their marriage to raise children in one tradition or
the other, and this is clearly the preferred option for most religious institutions. In most cases, the partner whose religion is the more strictly observant "wins" in this arrangement. What looks like a simple resolution,
though, is often complicated by the unexpected turns of real life. It is not
uncommon for the partner whose religion "loses" in this arrangement to
experience painful conflict when the child becomes a reality rather than
an abstraction. "What I didn't anticipate," one online participant writes,
"was the way my feelings would change after childbirth, which is an intensely spiritual experience. (And a very physical one too.) So things we
had agreed on rationally before having children began to seem rather different after they were actually born" (rabirtwistle, May 4, 2005). Another
factor complicating this choice is that, having agreed to raise the children
according to a partner's religion, the "outsider" parent may not ultimately
be viewed as an appropriate source of religious instruction and guidance
by his or her partner's religious community.[9]

Revisiting religious identity following childbirth is a common pattern, and for many it involves a revitalization of religious traditions that
were given up at the time of the wedding. One Christian woman who converted to Judaism when she got married reflects: "I . . . had my own crisis
when we became parents because you cannot in all sincerity bring up
your children in a way that is not right for you to live . . . and one cannot
really know how one will feel about how to raise one's children until one
has children to raise. Once we had two little ones I found my religion and
it felt like coming home" (grin/cho, February 6, 2000). This couple
worked out an arrangement in which each supported the other in taking
the children to separate religious services; ultimately, the children decided for themselves to be Christians.

A second approach to raising children in an interfaith marriage is to
offer no explicit religious training, just simply expose the children to

different worldviews and let them form their own religious identities as they grow up. According to one survey, 35 percent of children in mixed households were being raised with no religion (Kosmin and Lachman 1993, 248). One interfaith father explains his approach this way: "My philosophy is to try to provide the tools and knowledge needed to help my child make his own decision when he is ready to" (Iancef, February 29, 2000). For some, this looser approach is a reaction against negative experiences of religious indoctrination in their own childhood. Among this cohort, the widely observed patterns of individual and conscious choice in American religious identity are clearly in evidence; this is also the outcome so feared by religious communities who face demographic or doctrinal erosion.

And in not a few cases, a sense of regret attends this choice as parents observe their adult children's lack of explicit religious identity: "My background is New England Protestant, my husband is a southern Jew, and our children (both grown) are so far not involved in religion at all, as far as we know. Our 'solution' was no religious training, only the briefest of explanations, and I pray that God will forgive me and help them if this was wrong on my part. I came to believe in Jesus years after we'd been married, while my husband has remained a total atheist. We try to be respectful of our differences, so hopefully our kids absorbed that" (Rivanna, August 10, 2000). For this woman at least, trading firm religious identity for respect for difference is a less than satisfactory bargain.

But a third, widely adopted option complicates things much further. The more deeply invested they are in their own faiths and in the interfaith quality of their partnership (as evidenced by participation in online discussion groups, attending interfaith conferences, and the like), the more likely couples seem to be to attempt to raise children with dual religious identities. In spite of the challenges of doubling the expenditure of time and energy for religious training, a growing number of American interfaith families are attempting to raise their children as both Christian *and* Jewish, both Hindu *and* Catholic, both Pagan *and* Buddhist, and they are developing rich networks of support for doing so. While many religious organizations offer support groups for interfaith families in their own communities, the Dovetail Institute for Interfaith Family Resources (www .dovetailinstitute.org) is an independent organization offering publications, conferences, and a wide network of local links to help interfaith families find their own religious solutions. This is distinct from the approach of another large Jewish-Christian interfaith effort, InterfaithFamily.com, which encourages mixed families to live and raise children as Jews. The growth of Dovetail, which is unaffiliated with any religious institution, is one measure of the growing appeal of maintaining two religions in one home.

All of the couples I interviewed expressed this kind of dual religious citizenship as their ideal, though they acknowledged that in reality it is very difficult and the outcome unpredictable. David and Amina, whose friends have called them "poster children for world peace," hope that any children they have will identify as both Jewish and Muslim. For them, being engaged in both religions, which they see as essentially very similar, is akin to being bilingual, a cultural advantage they would relish passing on to a child. A father who is raising his children as both Jewish and Christian offers the same analogy in an online offering of advice to another couple: "Why not let them be both? This is not a Zen Buddhist koan, but a serious proposal. . . . The dogmatists of both faiths say it's impossible, but on the contrary, it's very enriching—like being bicultural or bilingual. . . . The alternative—choosing one religion—often creates lasting resentment. Someone dominates; someone imposes his/her religion on the other. Why should your husband's children give up being Episcopalian? Why should your children give up being Buddhist?" (davidhoward, January 12, 2001). The language of fairness and individual spiritual prerogative used here is common in American interfaith discourse, but it is also often accompanied by deep commitment to religious traditions.

Joan and Peter, an interfaith couple from Connecticut who have been married twenty-three years, have made careful and conscious choices throughout the lives of their children to preserve both her Congregationalist and his Jewish identities. Joan insists that her children are and always will be all Jewish and all Christian. "There's no 'half' about them," she told me. Joan was raised in a very liberal Christian community, and found little trouble incorporating Judaism into her Christian faith. But she met strong resistance from her husband's family, both at the time of their wedding and the birth of their children. They had both a baptism and a bris for their son, and committed to a full Jewish education for him.

For Joan, it was more important that they meet the ritual and educational requirements of Judaism than those of Protestantism, because she felt the greatest potential for exclusion from the Jewish community. "They may not believe the full creed of either one, but by the standards of Judaism (which is the proving ground they will be most hurt by, I think, in the long run), they are Jewish. I chose to run things by their standards, to give them at least that option some day." At fifteen, her older son has now decided to be exclusively Jewish, and has had a bar mitzvah. They all worship together now, "under one roof" in a Reform synagogue that welcomes her as a member, though she remains a committed Christian involved in various church activities. While others may find this arrangement strange, and some are frustrated by the answers she and her husband provide about their religious identity, Joan insists that "we are perfectly not confused."

The Wiccan mother cited above, who talked extensively with her partner about how they would raise children before they were married, reports that there is no confusion for her Wiccan-Christian daughter, either: "I take her to circle with me, and she joins me in my at-home devotionals. She also prays with Daddy and attended a Christian-run preschool. . . . She isn't 'confused' and she doesn't have to worry about 'pleasing' one or the other of us. We parent together, and we both have the right and responsibility to share our religious beliefs while respecting one another" (harmonyfb, August 9, 2001). The assertiveness of these voices recalls the boldness of interfaith families of centuries ago, who resisted conventional wisdom and, wittingly or not, pressed the culture to think about religious difference in new ways. Anne Rose's observation that nineteenth-century interfaith families changed religion "from a set of precepts to a series of possibilities," while it referred only to the relatively modest differences of Jewish-Protestant and Catholic-Protestant pairings, could just as easily describe the approach of this Christian-Pagan family today.

While there is little structural recognition of Wiccan-Christian partnerships, in several metropolitan areas across the United States, Jewish-Christian interfaith family organizations have developed to support the work of couples like Joan and her husband. The Family School in Chicago, the Interfaith Families Project of the Greater Washington, D.C. Area, and the Interfaith Community of New York all offer structures for interfaith child-rearing that are attracting many families who see their dual identities as a resource to be developed, not a problem to be solved. These organizations offer educational programs for children and adults, community celebrations, workshops, lectures, and discussions to help Jews and Christians honor and pass on each other's traditions without preference. Some groups, like the Interfaith Families Project, offer regular spiritual gatherings and function for many families as an alternative religious community; many participants are affiliated with no synagogue or church. Others, like the Interfaith Community, place much stronger emphasis on education, while holiday services, though inclusive, maintain a distinctive single-tradition focus. Chicago's Family School, which has clergy support and strong ties to a local temple and a Catholic church, offers an extensive K-8 curriculum, group baby-naming ceremonies, wedding planning sessions, and adult education. While some groups encourage children to adopt one religion at the end of their curriculum, others are comfortable with children continuing to identify as "interfaith," even if there is no box for them to check on demographic forms.

But for all this support, raising interfaith children remains a difficult challenge. Many couples report that their first religious conflicts surfaced when it came time to plan ceremonies for the birth of their children. Janet, one of the many U.S-born converts to Buddhism who account for the majority of Zen Buddhist practitioners in the United States, has been with her Roman Catholic partner Susan for over twenty years. For Janet, coming to terms with Susan's return to the religion she herself rejected in her youth has been a struggle greatly intensified by Susan's desire to have their daughter Lucia baptized in the Church. Because there is no local opportunity for their daughter to receive comparable training in Buddhism, their commitment to a pluralist household is hard to put into practice. "I have a judgment about the Catholic Church," Janet admits, "and that's not very Buddhist of me. But that's how I feel a lot of the time. It was really, really hard when Susan wanted Lucia baptized. Because there's a lot of basic ideas of the Catholic Church that I just don't really agree with." In spite of profound respect for a partner's spiritual choices, then, when it comes to children, many people come up against the edges of their tolerance. "When she's doing her thing, she's doing her thing. But when it involves my child, I'm really afraid that I just don't want her to be burdened with so much of the guilt that Catholicism had for me." Susan, in turn, feels hurt by Janet's judgment, and fears discussing the next steps in Lucia's religious education. "I don't see how she can see me as this smart and good, and still reject a part of me." Both Janet and Susan accept the pluralist model of religious truth; both admire aspects of each other's religion deeply, and want their child to make her own religious decisions as she grows. But in the meantime, a relationship that had been characterized by mutually supportive spiritual seeking now involves conflict and negotiation. They are confident, however, that the foundation they have built of careful introspection and open dialogue will see them—and their daughter—through.

Those who are further along in the parenting process than Janet and Susan report great admiration for what they see as the extraordinary qualities in interfaith children. "Children are so much smarter than we give them credit for," one online mother writes, a view shared by Joan, who has worked with interfaith kids throughout most of her marriage: "My experience with interfaith kids across the last twenty years has been that they are extraordinary human beings, and I hope my kids turn out that way. . . . It seems like the fact that they're exposed to the two different religious beliefs, in some loving way or other, has made them extraordinary human beings." But we don't need to rely only on parents' appraisals. Interfaith families have a long enough history in the United States that it is now possible to do a kind of outcomes assessment by listening to the children of these partnerships themselves. At a recent Dovetail conference, a panel of three interfaith young adults spoke frankly about their experiences and their current religious identities. All were raised by Jewish and Christian parents who aimed to immerse them fully in both traditions. All three expressed gratitude for having been exposed to both religions and for not having to choose between Mom's and Dad's faith. But they also expressed real ambivalence about the effects of interfaith upbringing. While there was none of the confusion often predicted by opponents of interfaith marriage, they often felt rejected by both communities, and two of the three do not have a strong religious affiliation at present. Because she had no reason to prefer one religion over the other, one young woman reported, "I never found a home for myself." And while one of the three plans to raise any future children interfaith, the other two said they hoped to marry someone with a stronger religious identity so as to offer children something more definitive.

Adult interfaith children in online discussions are generally more positive about their experiences:

> I am a "product" of a mixed marriage, both in terms of race and religion, my father being an Indian Hindu, and my mother, a Chinese Catholic. . . . From an early age, we (my sisters and I) were exposed to both these religions. We (all as a family) observed all major Hindu festivals at home, and went to church on major Catholic festivals like Easter, Xmas, etc., dad went to church with us, just as mom followed us to temple. . . . My sisters and I decided to follow Hinduism, but at the same time we did not forsake Catholicism altogether. I still attend church, and observe Catholic holy days, as much as I observe the Hindu ones. . . . I thank my parents for having the vision to share their faith with us. (jmk, November 26, 000)

Another discussion group participant also expresses appreciation for her parents' choice, and challenges those who extol the virtues of single-faith homes:

> As someone who was brought up in an interfaith home and who is about to enter into an interfaith marriage, I must disagree with many of the points that you all have made. Yes, the interfaith marriage of my parents ended, but it gave my sisters and myself a tremendous advantage over people brought up in a single-faith home. We learned a great many things about tolerance, understanding, prejudices, and the one thing missing from a single-faith home . . . choice. I have 5 sisters . . . 2 are Baptists (like our mother), 2 are undecided/too young to decide, and one sister plus myself are something else altogether. (Monkey-Manders, May 24, 2005)

A similarly unexpected outcome is reported by this child of a Buddhist-Catholic marriage:

> The irony in this is that now I have found the faith that is right for me, and my father, the Catholic, is uncomfortable with it. I am converting to Judaism. . . . I think that interfaith marriages are

difficult, but all marriages are difficult, at times. . . . The beautiful
thing about being multicultural is that you get to celebrate life in
many different ways and from many different aspects. I love having
Japanese, German, French, Buddhist, Catholic, Jewish influences in
life. This makes my world rich and my future children are going to
be rich in the way of knowledge and culture because, it is difficult,
but a thing to be celebrated. (kikue26, May 19, 2005)

Operative here is a clear sense of religion as a cultural skill set, akin to
language or dress codes, valuable social assets that can be acquired with
minimal costs. But the fact that many of these products of interfaith marriage are now religiously affiliated suggests that interfaith upbringing,
while unpredictable, is not necessarily a net loss for institutional religion.

The unpredictability of that outcome, however, is a source of anxiety
for many interfaith parents, and several I spoke with expressed sadness
about either the prospects or the reality of their children's choosing religious identities different from their own. "I think it's going to be hard for
me," says Deborah, "when my son turns thirteen, if he doesn't have a bar
mitzvah. My friends and my niece are all starting to plan and talk about
that and part of me feels, I want to have that. But it doesn't feel right to
me for him to have just the Jewish bar mitzvah. That doesn't seem right."
In Jennifer Kaplan's film *Mixed Blessings*, which explores the way four interfaith families deal with the choices and conflicts involved in their religious lives, Mary Rosenbaum, a longtime proponent of interfaith parenting,
stands by the way she and her husband decided to raise their children,
but recalls feeling twinges of sadness at not getting to see her children
move through their life passages in the Catholic church. For all the richness of double religious lives, then, interfaith parents know that there is
often also personal loss.

Robin Margolis, the child of an Episcopalian father and Orthodox
Jewish mother, and longtime writer on interfaith issues, offers advice for
interfaith parents based on her own experience. Many of the concerns
raised by parents—that their children will be confused, that they will turn
out with no religion, that they will choose one faith over another—are
borne out in Margolis' comments in a recent online article. "Please don't
raise us as 'nothing' with the idea that we can choose when we grow up,"

she writes. "It guarantees that we won't fit into either the Jewish or Christian communities. If you're not religious, take us to secular Jewish or Christian groups, but don't leave us with no information at all." She is equally leery of what she sees as "compromise" options like Unitarianism, which, she believes, "usually means Christian," or various forms of Paganism or Eastern religions. These, she believes, "will create a Jewish-Christian child with a coating of Paganism or Hinduism. Is that what you want?" Margolis insists that if parents do want to raise children in both traditions, they should do it thoroughly, not with "superficial smatterings" of each, and should be prepared that this kind of education may well lead a child to pick one religion over the other (Margolis 2003). While one might quibble with her assumptions about Unitarianism and other religions, what Margolis distills seems to represent an emerging consensus about raising interfaith kids: it can be done, but must be done well, and that requires extraordinary effort by parents and the presence of a supportive—or at least not hostile—religious community.

One especially intriguing aspect of the spirituality of interfaith children is the way in which they embody a pluralistic worldview as part of their essential make-up. While many religious people come to affirm pluralism based on ethical or philosophical reflection or experiences of religious others, interfaith children are raised with pluralism in the water, so to speak. In this sense, they offer a kind of test case for the plausibility of pluralism as a lived reality, not just a philosophical position. One of the young Dovetail panelists, Kate Cohen, made a powerful case for this possibility: "When an interfaith kid hears Mom say, 'I believe Jesus is the Son of God, and Dad doesn't,' that kid concludes that Jesus both *is* and *is not* the Son of God." This is the kind of thinking that philosophical pluralists have promoted, while critics have challenged that it is untenable as a basis for faith. Yet what appears impossible for adults may be viable for children. When you give children both worldviews, Cohen argued, they naturally integrate them.

Making a New Space: The Fruits of
Interfaith Family Dialogue

Interfaith families are pushed, not drawn, to dialogue about religion. There is little reason to suppose that many of these couples would have become as deeply literate and reflective about religion had they not been forced to reckon with differences when planning a wedding or raising children. Having done so, however, young people like Kate Cohen and their interfaith families are contributing in a distinctive way to new paradigms in American religion. The most basic but perhaps most significant way in which being in an interfaith partnership affects individuals is that they become more conscious and reflective about their own religious identities, advancing the trend in American culture toward thinking of religion as a matter of personal, conscious choice, akin to political or aesthetic preferences. While many forms of interfaith dialogue invite and encourage the kinds of engagement in which participants are open to change, the focus in other venues tends to be on coming to understand and appreciate the other. For interfaith families, the effect of the encounter with the other is profoundly reflexive; nearly every interfaith partner I encountered reported significant shifts in their own thinking about religion as a consequence of their interfaith relationship. "Talking about my religion with someone who does not always agree with me expands my horizons and makes me understand myself and my religious beliefs better" (Monkey-Manders, May 25, 2005). "One thing I've learned in this relationship," says Bill, "is that there is not one way. Catholicism is not the only way. . . . I can't understand that anybody could sit through the High Holiday services and not learn about Judaism; you spend two days during services. I can't understand how there could be hatred toward the Jews because the whole system is based on being good to your fellow man and loving your neighbor." Amina puts it another way; for her, being involved in an interfaith relationship means coming to see another religion "in 3D." She says that she now "question[s] everything, which makes it harder." For Denise, having a Jewish partner has led her to question her understanding of Jesus. "I have to say for me, obviously I believe in Jesus, but now, going to the synagogue and spending more time there, I have to wonder, maybe Jesus really wasn't the savior. Because you can't have all these people thinking that he wasn't. So I think I've questioned things along those lines."

Questioning one's own religious identity in the context of an interfaith relationship in many cases leads not to a dissolution of faith, but to clarification of beliefs and intensification of religious observance. David,

Amina's husband, notes that her Muslim influence has reinvigorated his Jewish practice: "From the age of twenty until I was about thirty, I was fairly non-practicing. And non-believing, too. But then I've gotten more into it as we've been together, and one of the things is about dietary laws—I haven't eaten a bit of pork since we've been together. So in that way," he says, turning to Amina, "you've made me into a better Jew than I was. I've started, you know, studying the Bible a little bit and going to synagogue." Deborah and her family carefully considered what it might mean for their children to have a first communion or bar mitzvah, from both their own and the institutions' perspectives. Recalling their discussions, she remembers telling her son: "Then, as a family, we will discuss, do we agree with that and what it means to us? So we can all be comfortable with it. From the outside, somebody might say, 'Oh, you can't do that, you're Catholic.' But to us, that's not what it means. . . . I don't care what the priest is thinking in his mind when he says these prayers. We've always looked at it like, 'I don't care what the structure says, what does it really mean to us?' " This shift in thinking about religion from an inherited set of assumed ideas and practices to a consciously selected and personally tailored worldview is often observed among the American religious subset known as "seekers" (Roof 1993, 1999; Wuthnow 1998; Fuller 2001); interfaith marriage may be advancing this shift among a different population who, but for their choice of partners, might never had questioned their inherited faith traditions. This is an especially interesting development for the current teenagers and young adults who are the "first fruits" of the highly intermarried previous generation. Recent studies of the religious lives of American youth suggest that this is a generally complacent generation not particularly motivated to religious exploration (Smith 2005); young people growing up in interfaith households where spiritual matters are the stuff of weekly negotiation, experimentation, and often deep reflection may represent a powerful countercurrent in that trend.

When a family's relationship with a religion is experienced in this way—not as a pre-established set of beliefs and behaviors in which one is more or less comfortably enmeshed but as a set of cultural commodities available for selection, rejection, and recombination—extraordinary creativity and idiosyncrasy come to characterize religious life. Joan is a non-Jewish, unconverted full member of her local synagogue. Bill and Sarah are part of an otherwise all-Catholic Croatian tamburitza orchestra that now plays for seders as well as Masses. Many couples beamed as they described the unique interfaith wedding ceremonies they created. Jeff and Denise explain that unlike a wedding based on a single religion in which, as Denise says, "we just kind of sit there and go through the motions," theirs took much more planning and effort, but the outcome was a source of great pride. "We had to get out the workbooks; we had to argue about it," Jeff says. "It was definitely a process. At the end we had this finished product that we used, and it was *our* wedding, *our* ceremony." Denise notes that they made a special effort to educate guests about both traditions with an informative program. "And really, I have to tell you, at our wedding so many people came up to us and said, 'That was a beautiful ceremony. It was the most beautiful wedding I've ever been to.'" Weddings are always potent ritual negotiations of change and continuity; for these interfaith couples, they were early opportunities to sharpen skills of religious autonomy and creativity that they continue to use in their marriages.

Redefining ideas of sacred space is another interesting aspect of interfaith families' religious creativity. For many of these families, the physical space and material culture of religion become both objects of interfaith conflict and symbols of its resolution. For instance, nearly every couple I spoke with, even one in which neither partner was Christian, referred to the Christmas tree as a potent and often contentious symbol in their household. For American Jews, in particular, the Christmas tree is a powerful icon of Christian cultural dominance, and very few are comfortable with the "Hanukah bush" gloss. Redefining the meaning of this symbol is a solution for some, although its powerful associations with the commercialization of Christmas—the piles of gifts underneath—make that a daunting task. For Laura, early solutions to the problem of holiday equity in the home involved setting apart separate spaces for the two religions. "Christmas and Hanukkah were hard at first, on many levels. I used to clear this little shrine area with a white cloth and menorah over on the side somewhere, while the rest of the house was festooned with green and red." But as their understanding and appreciation of the shape their interfaith arrangement would take grew, segregation ceased to be necessary. "After a while," Laura says, "I got to like the tree, I got to like the smell, and there was never any issue about religious decorations on it; that was never anything that my husband cared about . . . so pretty soon I became accustomed to it as just seasonal decoration." Just as Deborah's family moved to redefine the meaning of religious rituals for themselves, Laura became comfortable with "Christian" holiday symbols when it became clear that their meaning for her husband was no threat to her Jewishness. While this is a redefinition that many Jews have made in interfaith relationships, it is by no means universal. Petra, who has never been Christian, has always had a Christmas tree, and wants one in the home she has now made with Aaron. While Aaron is happy to give Petra a Christmas gift, the tree remains a point of conflict. "When I think of a Christmas tree," Aaron says, "I think of pogroms." So far—for Aaron and Petra—no tree.

Many interfaith couples come to realize that, more than theologies, the physical space of religious institutions—churches, synagogues, mosques—are powerful triggers of anxiety and discomfort for outsiders. A young Catholic man in an online discussion sought advice in planning a wedding with his Buddhist fiancé, who he says is "open to Catholic wedding, as long as it is outdoors (not in the building of the church)" (billwood 323, August 2, 2003). When Sarah and Bill were planning the "blessing ceremony" for their daughter—a Hebrew baby-naming and a Catholic baptism—they knew that their families would be uncomfortable in one or the other of the religious structures. Instead, they held the ceremony in their home, performed by the same priest and rabbi who married them. "I think the key to making our families comfortable was that we haven't done things in a church or a temple. No one ever feels that they are in foreign space." In this way, whether it is setting up different displays in different parts of the house, redefining the meaning of religious objects, or designing at-home rituals, interfaith families are creatively making their homes into alternative sacred spaces able to accommodate their particular religious circumstances.

Of course, it must be said that these families' choices to conduct their religious life at home is often a matter of necessity. Many interfaith couples, especially when they are unwilling to commit to an exclusive affiliation for their children, find themselves unwelcome at their houses of worship. Amina defines her spirituality quite eclectically, in part because "the minute I married him, I was technically kicked out of the religion. . . . I'm an infidel." Joan acknowledges that she and her family could have found a Congregational church that would honor their interfaith choices, but "we had a much longer search and evolution in finding a place where our children could be Jewish. And, in fact, we never really found one until [their son] decided that he wanted to be identified as Jewish, and have his bar mitzvah as well." In their distancing from their own religious institutions as a consequence of their interfaith partnerships, these families stand in the tradition of their nineteenth-century predecessors, who similarly offered silent challenges to their institutions in the self-determination and creativity of their religious lives. For twenty-first-century families, there are now some support systems in place for these moves, from Internet discussion groups to formalized interfaith education programs and para-religious organizations, but for many a sense of wistfulness, sadness, regret, or anger still attends the alienation from their own religious institutions.

This, then, is one site at which the *constructed* character of American religious identity is highly visible. Generations ago, the religious identity of an American citizen was an assumed thing, a matter of inheritance closely connected with family, ethnicity, and community. Today, as noted in the introduction, Americans are much more likely to change religious identities, and to assemble customized spiritualities from the wide array of resources now available to them. The answer to the question, "What religion are you?" is no longer so much a matter of checking a box as of conscious self-analysis and -formation. Pushed by institutional limits and drawn by personal initiative, interfaith couples embody this trend as they come to inhabit systems of belief and practice of their own design.

Otherness within Otherness: Race and Gender in Interfaith Relationships

But it is important to note, as William Hutchison does in his study of American religious pluralism, that this approach to identify formation as a matter of choice does not extend equally to all groups. He makes this observation primarily in terms of race, which remains a powerful mechanism in American experiences of difference. Interfaith couples who are also interracial or intercultural know that prejudices that have nothing to do with religion are often the greatest challenges they face in their families and communities. When I asked Ben if his liberal Jewish family had any problem with his marrying a Coptic Christian, he replied, "No, they had a problem with the fact that her skin was a different color." For Ben, being part of an interfaith partnership has involved much more exploration of cultural differences and resources than religious. When they were dating, he remembered with a smile, "she would always tell me how much more cultured the Eritreans were than white Americans." In this sense, it can perhaps be said that race trumps religion as a marker of difference, both positively and negatively. It was the form of difference that problematized the relationship for his family, and it is the dimension of difference that has most enriched Ben's life with his partner. In fact, Ben's first serious interfaith encounters came as a result of his intentional crossing of racial lines as a teenager in Detroit in the early 1960s. Drawn to hear speakers like Martin Luther King and Malcolm X, he found himself increasingly exposed to the Christians whose churches hosted such events. The kind of easy racial mixing he found there did not, by and large, occur in his own Jewish community. Interfaith encounter, then, has in this case been an aspect of a much more highly fraught—and in Ben's mind more important—interracial encounter, both at the personal and the societal level.

In the context of this study, it appears that gender also remains a powerful limiting factor in the ability to choose freely one's religious identity. Anne Rose argues that throughout history, anxiety about sexual mixing has been expressed as doubts about women (Rose 2001, 9). Whether they are labeled as seductresses who might tempt men to idolatry or, more typically, as passive, malleable beings who would be easily drawn, and thus draw their offspring, into alien practices, women from biblical times on have entered into interfaith arrangements with disproportionately onerous assumptions. Today, the consequences of acting outside normative religious patterns remain much higher for women than for men. In the course of this study I encountered multiple reports from women of being threatened or disowned by family members and cut off from their religion; no comparable accounts came from men. Sociologists may document that religion is now part of the free market of American ideas and practices, but as in all markets, the real costs are still higher for some than for others. Explicitly in Islam, more subtly in other traditions, women who marry outside their religious community, or the cultural group for which the religion comes to stand, are seen as betraying that community in ways that do not apply to their male counterparts.

Interfaith Families and the Question of Truth Claims

Precisely because marital interfaith dialogue begins with relationship, not theological platforms, the philosophical grounding of the positions that emerge is often much less clear than in more formal interfaith settings. Most couples don't know, before they are deep in the relationship, if at all, just how they conceptualize the relationship between conflicting religious truth claims. Interpreting their comments, though, it becomes evident that mixed-faith families demonstrate, not surprisingly, a high rate of pluralist thinking in matters of religion. Of the couples I spoke with, all expressed the importance of tolerance and respect for all religions, and most, when asked, affirmed an explicitly pluralist view of the nature of religious truth, that is, that no one religion has access to absolute truth, and that multiple spiritual paths are legitimate. Janet and Susan both like the metaphor of many paths up the same mountain, one Laura finds also effective in her interfaith community. "I think most of the people in our organization really do not think there is only one kind of truth. And when they hear someone say that there are many ways to God, they may not have heard anybody say that before they came to something that we offer, but that really does click for them." Unlike other forms of dialogue, where many participants enter into conversation on the basis of an established pluralist view, here the relationship comes first. Laura recalls Christians coming to say as they become more involved with their partners' religion and her interfaith community, "No, I'm not really sure I believe that Jesus was God on earth, but if I do, I also understand that it's not exclusive."

For Deborah, "all religions (and now we have friends from many different religions) are all a different way of making sense of the world. Nobody knows the right answer. . . . To me, now, in our society, especially after being in this relationship, it doesn't really matter, when it all comes down to it." Bill and Sarah have come to see their particular faith commitments as accidents of birth rather than matters of ultimate truth. "I'm Jewish because that's what I was raised as; Bill is Catholic because that's what he was raised as," Sarah says. For them, different religions are different ways of "keeping grounded" and gaining strength. Bill's openness to other paths is clear when he speaks about his children's religious future: "I think that I want them to appreciate both Catholicism and Judaism and take from that that they can appreciate other religions as well. Maybe they'll decide to be Buddhist, and if that's what gives them strength, wonderful."

This kind of affirmation of the equivalence of all religions might be disparaged as a kind of soft pluralism in which religious affiliation becomes one more lifestyle choice for American consumers. But many interfaith couples are deeply sensitive to this problem and, like those who have been involved in interfaith work in other settings, these pluralists are insistent that what they are creating in their families and in their communities is not any kind of syncretism or watered-down, least common denominator version of the religions involved. In her guide for interfaith families, Joan Hawxhurst offers this advice against syncretism: "Religious scholars and clergypeople agree that religious syncretism detracts from the meaning and autonomy of both faiths. While their histories are doubtless intertwined, Christianity and Judaism each exist as independent and vital traditions, and their separateness should not be ignored. An interfaith couple runs the danger of syncretizing, or combining, Christianity and Judaism when it places Hanukkah decorations on a Christmas tree and dubs it a 'holiday tree,' or when it teaches children that the two faiths are interchangeable save for differing opinions on Jesus" (Hawxhurst 1998, 12). This kind of blending or diluting may in fact occur in interfaith households, but it is rarely expressed as the family's intention. It may also occur in interfaith Sunday schools, whose stated mission is to offer education but that in practice often serve as interfaith children's only religious activity.

Maintaining the particularity of their faith commitments while affirming pluralism is an existential rather than philosophical challenge for these families, played out in curriculum planning, holiday liturgies, and family celebrations. Different families will solve the problem in different ways. Some are comfortable with ceremonies that simultaneously baptize and give the child a Jewish name; others are not. For some the interfaith organization becomes the primary religious community; for others, it does not. The Interfaith Community of New York, for instance, encourages members to maintain relations with traditional religious institutions, reflecting a concern I heard often in conversations with interfaith families to avoid "going Unitarian."

But pluralism's particularity problem remains. This became most clear to me in listening to interfaith couples in their recurring references to a phenomenon that I came to call the amazing disappearing Jesus. While all religions make distinctive truth claims, the unique claims Christians make about Jesus make integration with other religious views challenging. While it is relatively easy for Christians or Muslims to integrate Jewish rituals and traditions into their practice, and while Islam's central teachings about the oneness of God and the prophethood of Mohammed can at least make harmony with Jewish and Christian belief, the odd specificity of Christian beliefs about Jesus of Nazareth as a unique instantiation of the divine is more problematic, and frequently a stumbling block in acceptance of interfaith partnerships.

Deborah recalls her frustration with Jewish friends who could not see the common ethics binding the Jewish and Christian religions, but who instead only asked her, "What do you do about Jesus?" Sarah remembers growing up Jewish and believing that "the whole Jesus concept made absolutely no sense." Indeed, as I tried to show in chapter one, the theological moves required to harmonize the traditional Christian claims about Jesus (the "Jesus concept") with explicit affirmation of the truth claims of other traditions have been the work of academic theologians, not, by and large, ordinary religious people. So while interfaith marriages in which one partner is Christian may aim to avoid a "least common denominator" religion, it does seem that frequently the easiest solution to religious conflict is to let Jesus, at least in his divine aspect, quietly recede from the picture. A recent article about interfaith holiday strategies describes the approach of Clare Hirsch, a Catholic raising a Jewish-Christian child: "During the holidays, Kirsch says she emphasizes family gatherings. She focuses more on cultural aspects such as the food or decorations around the house, and she'll shy away from talking about Jesus Christ" (Associated Press 2003). In planning their wedding, Jeff and Denise knew that it would be a challenge to make Jeff's family comfortable, so "we both agreed that there was going to be no mention of Jesus," Denise recalls. In their own relationship, though, the significance of Jesus rarely surfaces as a problem. Jeff says, "On the issue of things like, is Jesus really the savior, and the things a Christian says, I mean, it is a really important issue . . . but in terms of the marriage, I don't think it means anything." Denise agrees. "Sometimes I'll joke with Jeff and I'll say, 'Well, Jeff, what if Jesus really is the savior? Then what are you going to do?' But it's true, maybe I'm not right, maybe we're both wrong. . . . I just don't think you really know these things until the final hour." Joint religious activities for these families tend to include those elements in which overlap is easiest to see; for Christians this means that Jesus often appears as a teacher of wisdom, rarely as the Son of God.

The disappearance of the particular significance of Jesus is a high price to pay for interfaith harmony; in this sense interfaith families may validate the concerns of critics of pluralist approaches to interfaith dialogue. But to read their reticence about Jesus only in this way may be to make a category mistake. Interfaith dialogue is an encompassing phrase for many different activities with multiple purposes. According to Kusumita Pedersen, the three main motives of interfaith work are (1) to live more harmoniously with religious others; (2) to engage in a common task; and (3) to resolve questions of religious truth in the context of pluralism. The last of these drives most academic interfaith activities; the first two motivate most local and regional collaborations between individuals and organizations of different faiths (Pedersen 2005). Bearing this distinction in mind may help clarify that when Christians in interfaith relationships make minimal references to Jesus, they may not be making any statement at all about his salvific significance, because they are not at all engaged in motive #3. It may be that this kind of solution reflects patterns in interfaith work at the community and institutional level, that of bracketing the search for ultimate truth (motive #3), and proceeding instead on the basis of common values to work for more harmonious relations (motive #1) and foster commitment to shared tasks (motive #2). At the community level this might mean forming partnerships to deal with problems of homelessness or racism; at the family level it looks more like raising children with open minds and generous spirits, and creating holiday celebrations that allow diverse families to celebrate together. In witness to this, the successful interfaith families I encountered all had to be prodded to express their views on religious truth questions, but readily volunteered the importance of their shared values. "We're politically identical," David says of himself and Amina. Janet and Susan credit their shared Catholic background with providing a solid moral foundation that continues to connect them in spite of their different spiritual paths. "On the things that really matter," Jeff says, "Denise and I are in the same camp."

Because these are not philosophers or theologians but ordinary people for whom religious difference is interwoven in the fabric of intimate relationships, then, they have not (in most cases) developed fully formed and perfectly consistent positions on questions of religious pluralism. But in doing the real day-to-day work of interfaith dialogue, they are roughing out a model of pluralism that slips through the categories mapped out by scholars, one based on the deepest of familial bonds. This became clear to me as I listened to Joan's take on the metaphor of many paths up the same mountain in her reflections on Judaism and Christianity: "The peak of the mountain is higher than either of those truths. I've walked the path of Christianity all my life and it's a wonderful path, and there's no way I wouldn't want to walk my child on it as well. If my child said, 'I want to walk more paths,' why wouldn't I take their hand and walk those paths also? Judaism, to me, this is a tremendous path. This is a spirit-filled, amazing place that I could never ask them not to go. So, my choice is to say, 'Yes, go ahead all by yourself,' or 'take me along!' " Out of the profundity of her love for her "all Jewish" children, Joan has found a way to be Christian that some would call syncretic or simply not Christian. "I wish there was a better vocabulary for it," she says. This is a pluralism that insists neither that all religions are essentially the same, nor that they are irreducibly different and therefore incommensurable. Instead, it insists—by demonstrating—that unity in religious difference can be *lived* in a single, coherent life, even when it cannot be explained. And if this mode of religious experience is syncretistic, it challenges assumptions about the superficiality of the American tendency toward religious blending.[10]

Sociological studies based on survey data correlate interfaith marriage with lowered levels of religious participation (e.g., Iannaccone 1990). The interfaith families whose lives I have been able to glimpse might suggest that new ways of thinking about religious participation are in order. For in reality, while parish and synagogue rosters may shrink as a result of interfaith marriages, these families are one of the places in the culture where religious thought and practice are most alive. A 2005 study of young adult children of interfaith couples in which one parent is Jewish found that a large majority affirmed both that "being Jewish" was very important to them, and that they had a strong desire to "transmit a Jewish ethnic identity" to their children (Siegel 2005). It is significant that it is not an explicitly religious identity as measured by synagogue membership that these young people are maintaining in such large numbers, but it is clearly not true that interfaith families are a black hole for religious identity. In fact, deeply American patterns of creativity and self-determination are evident in interfaith families' theological reassessments, ritual inventions, and willingness to live with ambiguity and tension in relation with their religious institutions. A child of Jewish and Christian parents who was raised interfaith calls attention to the American character of his experience, relating his own experience to the American struggle with diversity and identity: "A double-faith upbringing is an essentially American experience because of the way America was founded as a country of immigrants. . . . I am an experiment in religious cohesion and the American experience. The way I learn to deal with the blessed both-ness that God has given me can, God-willing, be helpful to a world racked with religious strife. It already has allowed me to confront and penetrate the American experiment, to engage more deeply in the promise of America" (Goldstein 2005, 1, 4, 6). In exploring the question of whether Americans can find a mode of pluralism that moves beyond the binary options of assimilationist, melting pot models and individualistic, "raw" diversity, interfaith families may be a good place to look.

In the end, the significance of these couples' religious difference may be less than imagined. In truth, all marriages are mixed. Democrats marry Republicans, blacks marry whites, rural people marry urbanites. Most of the interfaith couples I studied are in fact profoundly united in many ways. They share values, political views, and a commitment to deal with a challenging issue against often intense and painful pressures. They are also united in *being religious*—that is, critically engaged with the particularities and disciplines of a specific religion—in conscious and committed ways, which makes them a distinctive presence in American culture, where "spiritual but *not* religious" has become such a popular self-identification.

5

Meeting the Other in Cyberspace

Interfaith Dialogue Online

The statistics are becoming familiar: 137 million American adults—more than two-thirds—are now online (Pew Internet 2005). Nine out of ten American school children have access to computers. More than four out of five households with computers also have Internet access. And clearly, one of the things people are doing with all that connectivity is learning and talking about religion. According to a 2004 report from the Pew Internet and American Life Project, 64 percent of wired Americans have used the Internet for spiritual or religious purposes, up from 25 percent just three years earlier, from sending e-mail with spiritual content to seeking information about other religions (Pew Internet 2004, 4). Religion-related websites abound, from denominationally sponsored pages to academic resources to chat groups to idiosyncratic personal spirituality portals. Shopping for Muslim headscarves, finding lyrics to Evangelical hymns, posting diatribes against other religions, joining a prayer circle or virtual coven, even participating in a Catholic Mass in an interactive simulation game—the potential modes of "doing religion" online appear limitless. Indeed, the Internet brings to our fingertips the dizzying reality of the American religious marketplace in a way that no survey or academic analysis ever could. If we really want to move beyond official pronouncements to get an accurate picture of everyday American interfaith engagement, the virtual world of the Internet may be one of the realest places to look.

Religion and the Internet

Since the Internet became a significant presence in American society in the mid-1990s, the possibilities of online religion have fascinated scholars, journalists, and religious people alike. But just what online religion actually *is* can be tricky to define. An entry on Buddhism in an online encyclopedia? A forwarded e-mail about guardian angels? Religion appears to be just as messy a category online as it is offline. Interpretations of religion on the Internet range from seeing it simply as a new medium for extending the presence of traditional, offline religions, to the "internet-as-religion" view that there is something inherently spiritual about Internet practices themselves, because of the parallel incorporeality of virtual space and sacred space (Maxwell 2002, 344).[1]

Assessments of the impact of online religious activity are similarly complex and wide-ranging. Some have imagined the Internet as a replacement for traditional religious institutions. Christian market researcher George Barna, for instance, predicted in 2001 that millions of Americans would "drop out of the physical church in favor of the cyberchurch" (The Barna Group 2001). Others, like sociologist Brenda Brasher, have celebrated the potential of the Internet to reduce fear and misunderstanding of religious others and promote interreligious understanding and cooperation (Brasher 2001, 6–7, 29).[2]

Useful classifications of online religion are now emerging that help make sense of the very different religious activities that occur online, and that facilitate an assessment of their impact on religious identities and relations. Christopher Helland's theoretical framework, for instance, distinguishes "religion-online" from "online-religion" (Helland 2000; 2002). The former is defined as a top-down, hierarchical mode of Internet communication, "an organized attempt to utilize traditional forms of communication to present religion based upon a vertical conception of control, status and authority" (Helland 2000, 207). The classic example of religion-online is the official website of the Vatican, where one can—in multiple languages—peruse Catholic doctrine, explore the riches of Vatican art, and check out the latest pontifical statements, among other things. But the site contains no links to other sites, and offers no opportunities for visitor interaction. This is very different from "online-religion," which Helland sees as a novel phenomenon defined by many-to-many communication and reflecting the Internet ideal of "unstructured, open, and non-hierarchical interaction" (2000, 207). Online-religion might be found in chat rooms, on bulletin boards, and even on the official sites of religious organizations, so long as visitors to those sites "are afforded the ability to interact with the belief system, contributing their own experiences and views to the religious group while receiving feedback from other participants" (217). To the extent that this kind of interaction is possible, online-religion becomes a truly new spiritual option, what Helland calls a "*virtual communitas*, a virtual space where interaction and sacredness ebb and flow in a continual state of transition" (207).

The initial enthusiasm for this kind of new spiritual space—liberated from the fetters of both institutional orthodoxies and the personal marks of gender, race, class, and other identifiers that the Internet allows us to erase—has abated somewhat in recent years. While it is true that Internet communication is impressively limited in its ability to represent personal status, and that Internet users now have staggeringly abundant resources for exploring their religious options, the vision of a completely democratic, nonhierarchical online spiritual utopia usurping the place of traditional religion remains largely unrealized. The Pew Internet and American Life Project cited above shows consistently that people who go to the Internet for religious purposes are also religious offline, with half attending weekly worship services (Pew 2004, 5) and about a third identifying as Evangelical Christians. The most common online religious activities tracked by the Pew studies—reading news about religious issues, sending and receiving e-mail with spiritual content, and sending online greeting cards for religious holidays—are best viewed as supplements to traditional offline religion rather than experiments in virtual spiritual community (4).

Interestingly, the Pew study has also concluded that those who do not identify with a particular religious tradition but rather as "spiritual but not religious" are not significantly more likely than those who identify with a traditional religion to be heavy Internet users. "These findings do little to confirm previous speculations that the Internet holds special appeal for those spiritual seekers looking for alternatives to conventional religious practice" (11). Another way of putting this is to say that online religion can be just as traditional as its offline counterparts. Indeed, it can serve radically reactionary interests just as well as innovative ones. Patrick Maxwell refers to the "gentle souls who are surprised and shocked at how much Web-based religion is full-blooded, reactionary and militant. (These gentle souls might fail to realise while fundamentalist/conservative religionists reject 'modernism' and its values, they are usually quite content to make use of 'modernity' and its technological enablements in order to spread their convictions)" (2002, 345).

At the same time, when traditionally religious people go online, they do not remain in insular conversation with their co-religionists. In 2001, fully 50 percent of those who used the Internet for religious purposes looked for information about another faith (Pew 2001, 13). Of course, there can be many reasons for learning about another religion, ranging from a quick search for a fact about another culture, to honing one's proselytizing skills, to enhancing one's own spiritual life. But these findings suggest at least the potential for online interfaith encounters. The 2004 Pew study reported that 12 percent of the "online faithful" use the Internet to find information about traditions other than their own, in whole or in part "for their own spiritual growth" (Pew 2004, 7–8). And the number and accessibility of online-religion sites where religious conversation really is many-to-many suggest that online interfaith dialogue may indeed represent a genuinely new moment in interfaith relations.

Finding Interfaith Dialogue Online

So where does online interfaith dialogue fit into this picture? Interest in interfaith relations is evident on the Internet in many settings: websites of particular religions engaged in apologetics toward others, like the evangelical Christian site, Answering Islam (http://www.answeringislam.org); the websites of interfaith organizations like the North American Interfaith Network (http://www.nain.org), the Council for a Parliament of the World's Religions (http://www.cpwr.org), the World Congress of Faiths (http://www.worldfaiths.org), and the Pluralism Project at Harvard University (http://www.pluralism.org); the websites of interfaith activist groups like The Interfaith Alliance (http://www.interfaithalliance.org), the Center for Global Ethics (http://astro.temple.edu/~dialogue/geth.htm), and the

Amnesty International Interfaith Network (http://www.amnestyusa.org/interfaith/); and finally in interfaith discussion groups on sites like Beliefnet (http://www.beliefnet.com), Religion Depot (http://www.edepot.com/religion.html), and the religion discussion groups hosted by Yahoo!, MSN, and other commercial sites.

In the loosest sense, interfaith dialogue could be seen to be occurring at all of these sites; interfaith activity on the Internet thus crosses the boundaries of religion-online and online-religion. Indeed, to the extent that when a Christian clicks onto the home page of the Council on American-Islamic Relations—clearly a religion-online site—to find out what the holiday of Ramadan commemorates, she is engaging in a kind of interfaith exploration, one that may well advance her understanding of and sensitivity to Muslim neighbors. But in keeping with the definition of dialogue offered in chapter one, I prefer to focus here on more fully conversational activities, in which two or more people of different religious affiliations consciously engage one another for purposes of greater understanding. For that reason, the interfaith encounters explored in this chapter are better understood as online-religion in Helland's sense, involving the potential for many-to-many communication, personal contributions, and feedback. A search for these kinds of encounters draws us to a more limited set of Internet locations: sites at which actual discussions are hosted by a neutral entity, or those at which affiliates of one religion post statements regarding other religions, to which responses can be made and, at the hosts' discretion, posted.

Four questions about online dialogue invite analysis: First, who participates? Are online interfaith dialoguers the same people who go to local interfaith council meetings? Are they as overwhelmingly Christian as the general online population? And if a third of them are Evangelical, as the 2004 Pew study reports (5), does the exclusivism that at least officially characterizes Evangelical approaches to non-Christians also dominate their online discussions of religious difference? Second, how does online dialogue differ from traditional interreligious encounters, and does it seem to be delivering on its promise of greater religious convergence and cooperation? Third, how might this mode of interfaith dialogue challenge established scholarly models of understanding religious diversity? Do the types hold in cyberspace? And finally, how does the overt commercialism of the Internet generally and some sites specifically shape the development of American understandings of religious difference? Does it matter that many interfaith encounters are occurring in commercial space, with links to products for sale?

For a close-up look at this kind of online encounter, consider two very different sites representing distinct modes of encounter: Answering Islam, a Christian site defined as "a Christian-Muslim Dialog," and Beliefnet, a for-profit multifaith religion site. With Internet sites, it is of course impossible to draw geographical boundaries around an American interfaith dialogue. The Answering Islam site is based in England, but gets lots of American attention as evidenced by contributors, books reviewed, and mentions on U.S.-based websites. In addition, donations to support "the ministry of Answering Islam" are directed to a post office box in Houston, Texas. These are both well established websites, at least in Internet terms; Answering Islam was launched in 1999, Beliefnet in early 2000. They are also both large sites, with multiple and extensive links. A million unique users visit Beliefnet in a typical month (Fadner 2004), while Answering Islam, though much less frequented, still claims thousands of hits each day. Interfaith issues are prominent on both sites, but are handled in distinctly different ways, reflecting the complexity of online interfaith encounters. Beliefnet represents one end of the spectrum of approaches to religious difference, Answering Islam the other.

Answeringislam.org: Dialogue or Polemic?

Since September 11, 2001, discussions of Islam have become a prominent feature of online religion, and spirited exchanges between Christians and Muslims represent one potent form of online interfaith dialogue. The increasing reliance of Muslims on the Internet as a source of news, information, and activism is well documented (Lawrence 2002; Bunt 2003); at the same time, Christians in the United States and elsewhere have turned to the Internet for information about Islam and, in places like AnsweringIslam.org, to clarify the relationship between the two religions.

The name of this site itself suggests a dialogue already in progress. From the Christian perspective of this site, Islam is both a question and a challenge that needs to be "answered." The attractive home page of

Answering Islam is dominated by two scriptural quotes, one from the Qur'an and one from the Gospel of John: "Let there be no compulsion in religion; Truth stands out clear from error" and "You shall know the truth; and the truth shall set you free!" These two statements fade in and out of each other repeatedly, and tell us something about the kind of "dialogue" featured on the site. In both scripture quotes the word "truth" appears capitalized and in red. Here, then, is an approach to interfaith relations that aims to arrive at a single *truth* on given religious issues—the divinity of Christ, the prophecy of Mohammed, the meaning of *jihad*, etc. Links from the home page then take the visitor to a series of articles by Christian writers on Islam or comparisons of Muslim and Christian doctrines. Topics include "The Qur'an," "Women in Islam," "Why They Converted," "Under Islamic Rule," and "Who Is God?" Each article attempts to show the errors of Islam and the superiority of Christianity. The article on Mohammed, for instance, consists of an attack on the legitimacy of Mohammed's prophecy in light of biblical revelation.

The articles are mostly of anonymous authorship, and when authors' names do appear, no institutional affiliation or credentials are included. The "About Us" link defends this anonymity with the assertion that the arguments should stand on their own merit, not on the academic or religious credentials of their authors, and that critics of Islam are often made the objects of death threats, so that anonymity is necessary for personal safety. The authors do reveal that "we are Evangelical Christians and agree without reservation with the statements of faith as given, for example, by the World Evangelical Alliance and the Lausanne Committee for World Evangelization" (http://answering-islam.org.uk/about.html).

It is easy to conclude, then, that this is not so much a dialogue site as a forum for anti-Muslim polemics. But this may be too hasty. There is no mission statement on the home page, but at the very bottom of the page there is a link to "site policies," where the visitor learns more about the authors' understanding of dialogue. In a true dialogue, the authors assert, "every party should have the opportunity for an undisrupted presentation of their own faith. . . . Understanding any religion needs a concentrated effort and it is not helpful to jump back and forth between pro and contra. Let the reader read in a concentrated way about the Christian view and come to a good understanding. Then he may go to the Muslim views on the issue which he will have no problem locating from the links refered (*sic*) to below" (http://www.anweringislam.org/policy.html). Acknowledging that Answering Islam "is not a dialog in the sense that Muslims have an equal say or equal influence on the content or presentation on the site," the authors nonetheless defend that "the site is highly interactive" through opportunities to e-mail responses to particular authors, suggestions for corrections, and critique of content to the website creators, and through links to Muslim responses to their critiques of Islam.

This, surely, is one coherent version of interfaith dialogue, though clearly not the most prominent. In many forms of online interreligious encounter, the model is interpersonal, the conversation focused on the participants—their commonalities, differences, areas of misunderstanding, and the like. The form and content of Answering Islam suggest an alternative model of interfaith dialogue in which the focus is an extrapersonal *Truth*—understood to be singular and to reside within one and not the other religious tradition. This is made clear on the "About Us" page: "We want that Muslims come to faith because they become convinced of the truth of the Gospel through the soundness of the material we present, and we want our Christian brothers and sisters to develop their convictions about their own faith and about Islam for the same reasons: Because it is true" (http://answering-islam.org.uk/about.html). Eagerness to get at the truth is also evident in the site's frequent call for readers to send in corrections to any errors of fact they may find on Answering Islam pages.

And if truth is the object, logic and reasoning are presented as the means of getting to it, as indicated elsewhere on the same page: "We do not want Christians (or anyone else) to believe what we write is correct just because we claim to be evangelical, or because we can tout some academic titles to the names of our authors, but because the arguments are biblical, well documented, and logically sound." The impression left by such language is that getting at the "truth" of one religion or another is a straightforward matter of getting one's facts straight. In adopting this language, the creators of Answering Islam keep alive an understanding of religious truth typically rejected by contemporary philosophers of religion—the Enlightenment notion that if ideas are aired in a fair and open forum and subjected to rigors of logic, clear and unassailable truth will emerge to which all right-minded people will be induced to submit.

In the approach to interfaith relations represented on Answering Islam, the explicit goal of dialogue is the conversion of the religious other, rather than mutual enrichment and appreciation. The authors of and visitors to this site may well be genuinely seeking to clarify and enhance their understanding of Islam, but they make no effort to hide their conviction that such understanding is of value only insofar as it advances Christian evangelical activity among Muslims. In this regard, Answering Islam reflects a view of religious others consistent with that of such Christian groups as the Southern Baptist Convention and the World Evangelical Fellowship. As noted in chapter one, however, we should not mark clear and passionate commitment to one's own faith and a desire to share that faith with others as disqualifiers to authentic interfaith dialogue. Indeed such passion is often the source of the most exciting and effective dialogue. Too often, interfaith enthusiasts dismiss the efforts of dogmatically committed people of (usually Christian) faith on the assumption that anyone who believes anything *that* strongly must be closed to the enriching possibilities of conversation with a religious other.

Rather than on content, then, it is perhaps wiser to judge the legitimacy of Answering Islam as a dialogue site on the basis of its structure and process, that is, the space it does or doesn't make available for the give-and-take of authentic speech, real listening, and informed response. On that basis, it is difficult to recognize Answering Islam as a legitimate space for online interfaith dialogue. For its own claims notwithstanding, this site makes very little room for Muslim voices and, more importantly, shows no evidence of "hearing" those voices that are raised. The majority of topics are presented with no Muslim perspective, and where references to material produced by Muslims are included, the links are often not viable. Those that do speak for Islam are typically professional polemicists like Jamal Badawi and Shabir Ally, who speak out of similar advocacy contexts, or Muslim individuals who have posted responses to Answering Islam's polemics. The result, of course, is that very polarized views are presented, often ill-informed and/or inarticulate, and rarely nuanced. In weeks of studying the site, I found no instance of a positive response to a Muslim statement, or of any Christian perspective being modified in return.

Finally, it should be noted that those who do remain devoted to Islam after reading the materials on the Answering Islam website are threatened

with eternal damnation (http://www.answeringislam.org/strengthened
.html). It seems clear, then, that no other is actually heard in this "dialogue," which is probably better understood as an exercise in defense and
reinforcement of religious identity rather than real interfaith encounter.
The significance of this site lies in what its popularity tells us remains a
strong current in American conceptions of religious difference; intolerance is alive and well in the postmodern space of the Internet.

Beliefnet.com: Multifaith, Multipurpose Dialogue Site

If Answering Islam's "dialogue" label is a misnomer, there is little doubt
that Beliefnet.com offers the real thing. The second-largest religion site
on the web (behind Gospelcom.net), Beliefnet has been widely touted in
the popular press as a smart blend of spiritual exploration and commercial savvy (Long 2000; Kaiser 2001; Fonda 2000). Visitors to Beliefnet can
find, in addition to numerous multifaith discussion groups and message
boards, online "prayer circles" and memorials, guided meditations,
columns and weblogs by leading religion writers, celebrity spirituality features, and a huge array of educational information about a wide variety of
religions. One of its most popular features, the one that has drawn many
people to the site for the first time, is the Belief-O-Matic quiz, which offers
to tell you, based on your answers to a short set of questions, what religious tradition your worldview best matches.

After declaring bankruptcy in early 2002 and emerging from it before
the end of that year, Beliefnet has remained profitable, thanks to a new
infusion of venture capital and a larger roster of sponsors, including, over
the past several years, eDiets, Liberty University, the Hallmark Channel,
and Netflix. Beliefnet has also launched its own "premium" products and
services, including books, e-books, and wireless delivery of Beliefnet content to mobile phones. Recently, perhaps in response to the success of
eHarmony, one of its former sponsors, Beliefnet also entered the competitive online dating industry with Soulmatch, a $25-a-month service that
connects singles with those who share their spiritual perspectives.

As "a multi-faith e-community designed to help you meet your own
religious and spiritual needs," Beliefnet creates a decidedly different online environment from that of Answering Islam. In a sense, one is engaged

in interfaith dialogue the minute one enters the site. Every page offers multiple religious options, whether it is for daily inspiration, prayer circles, discussion groups or jokes. A list of the seven items comprising the "new features" appearing on the home page for October 14, 2004, is a good snapshot of the breadth of Beliefnet's offerings: (1) Readers' inspiring stories on the theme of "My pet is a blessing"; (2) a poll on "do you believe in the devil?"; (3) prayer postings for actor Christopher Reeve (who had died three days earlier); (4) a scholarly article, "Does Evolution Have a Higher Purpose?"; (5) an inspirational account of "an angelic caregiver"; (6) a video of weekly "Dharma Talks" with the Dalai Lama; and (7) a letter from Ralph Reed, founder of the Christian Coalition, responding to a Beliefnet article critical of President Bush's Faith-Based Initiative.

In policy terms as well, the site is committed to even-handed treatment of all religious comers, as indicated in its Statement of Principles:

1. Beliefnet hopes to help people meet their own religious, spiritual and moral needs by providing information, inspiration, community, stimulation and products.
2. Beliefnet will be respectful of the wide range of religions and spiritual approaches.
3. Beliefnet will not exclusively promote one particular religion or belief system.

The site's Rules of Conduct further clarify this orientation by explicitly banning proselytizing in any discussion forum.

More subtly, the "ritual" space of the site also prompts interfaith reflection. For instance, on September 22, 2002, under "celebrations," a Buddhist refuge-taking ceremony was honored alongside a Lutheran First Communion. Intentionally or not, the juxtaposition of these two events on a single screen stimulates for the observer a kind of comparative reflection on initiation rites, in which neither is presented as normative.

Interfaith discussion occurs in a wide range of Beliefnet discussion groups, as participants with different religious affiliations weigh in on a given topic. For an analysis of more sustained, intentional interfaith conversation, I selected three open forum discussion groups: "interfaith dialogue," "religious tolerance," and "proselytizing," as well as the "interfaith dialogue" dialogue group, which is open to registered participants only.

The "Interfaith Dialogue" dialogue group is the largest of these forums, containing conversations on a wide range of topics from Paganism and Christianity, to science and religion, to interfaith relationships. New topics are added every day.

Beliefnet Participants

To get a profile of who participates in Beliefnet's interfaith conversations, I compiled data from the personal profiles of each participant in these four discussions over a three-month period in 2002 and a four-month period in 2004.[3] This sample comprised 507 different participants, 386 of whom identified a religious affiliation. This composite both affirms and challenges established models of offline interfaith work. Compare the profile of Beliefnet's dialogue participants with that of the American population (figure 1). While Christians are the largest group both nationally and in these online dialogues, correspondence between the nation's and Beliefnet's religious demographics breaks down after that. Buddhists, for instance, make up less than 1 percent of the United States population, but accounted for 7 percent of those dialoging on Beliefnet. Also notable in these samples was the significant presence (12 percent) of those who identify with more than one religious tradition. Identifying as multifaith is facilitated by Beliefnet's participant profile mechanism, which allows one to select multiple religious categories, as opposed to the more traditional survey method of checking a single box. This is one interesting example of the ways in which the structure of this ostensibly neutral site can make subtle normative moves: it's okay, this profiling system tells us, to be both Jewish and Buddhist, or Catholic and Pagan. Indeed, a number of participants seem to choose the "select all" option in identifying their religious affiliation, which may be a tongue-in-cheek gesture intended to challenge the significance of such labels, but also reflects quite accurately the growing eclecticism of American religious identity.

Perhaps the most significant way in which the profile of Beliefnet participants differs from the at-large population is the large representation of Pagans. Having established a strong presence on the Internet long before many traditional religious groups knew what the Internet was, many Pagans are accustomed to using the Internet for networking, resource sharing, and online religious activity. At a site like Beliefnet, where their

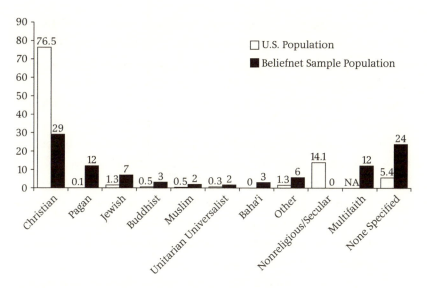

FIGURE 1 Religious Affiliation of Online Dialogue Participants and U.S. Population (percentiles)

Beliefnet sample = 507
Source: U.S. religious affiliation data based on American Religious Identity Survey 2001 (available at http://www.gc.cuny.edu/studies/key_findings.htm)

religion is represented in exactly the same form and in the same places as Christianity, Judaism, Islam, Hinduism, and other "world religions," Pagans, as Bruce Lawrence has said, become "equivalent, without being equal" (Lawrence 2001, 238). And while Paganism's emergence into the mainstream of American religious consciousness is itself noteworthy, it is especially so in the context of interfaith dialogue, which, because conceptually defined by religious institutions, has not heretofore been easily accessible to the decentralized and decidedly anti-institutional Pagan community. When Pagans have been part of major interfaith events, like the 1993 World's Parliament of Religions in Chicago, their participation has been highly contested, prompting the withdrawal, in that instance, of the Eastern Orthodox member of the organizing Host Committee. The dramatic growth in size and mainstream acceptance of Pagans, which their large Internet presence has no doubt facilitated, is demonstrated in the very different role of Pagans at the 2004 World's Parliament in Barcelona, where there were numerous Pagan-based sessions and a Pagan was elected to the Parliament's Board of Trustees.

It is also important to note the relative gender equity of Beliefnet. Of those who reported their sex (about 80 percent of participants), 51 percent were male and 49 percent female. This is in sharp contrast with the overwhelming male dominance of offline interfaith dialogue, as seen in everything from the photos of interfaith gatherings to the roster of participants at interfaith conferences.[4] Young people, too, who would rarely have access to formal interfaith encounters, are impressively represented online; the average age of the Beliefnet participants in this sample was 37, and teenagers alone made up 17 percent of the sample group. This is an interesting counterpoint to the finding of the 2004 Pew study of the "online faithful," which found that those who use the web for religious purposes are more likely to be between the ages of 50 and 64 than the overall Internet population (Pew 2004, 5).

Statistics do not fully capture the inclusiveness of these conversations, though. Some of the most active participants in these dialogues are people it would be difficult to imagine speaking up at an interfaith council meeting or attending an interfaith conference. Let one example suffice: "Themarirev," the user name of one participant in several discussions, is a disabled man who has spent much of his life homeless, now lives on $600 a month, and identifies his occupation as "clergy," referring participants to his web-based ministry. His religious identity is eclectic; he draws on the wisdom of many spiritual traditions, east and west, and resists the institutionalization of religious ideas. Themarirev has been an active participant in Beliefnet discussions, and has initiated sustained and probing conversations on a range of issues, from the wealth of churches to the nature of God. While he would likely decline to participate in traditional offline interfaith structures, none of which are likely to seek out people like him in any case, it is clear that this online community has been enriched by his contributions.

It is important, though, not to overestimate the inclusiveness of Beliefnet's interfaith dialogue. The early enthusiasm for the anarchic equality of Internet presences has given way to more realistic appraisals of cyberspace as characterized by the same systems of privilege, hierarchy, and exclusion as the "real world" (Eisenstein 1998). The most obvious form this exclusion takes is the most fundamental: for all of the global imagery of the Internet, huge segments of the world—mostly poor and

rural—have no access to the conversation. But there are more subtle hierarchies as well. As a text-based medium, Internet dialogues inevitably privilege the skilled writer. Those whose sentences don't parse properly are
frequently accused (usually very politely on Beliefnet) of presenting unclear
ideas, and often drop out of the conversation. It is possible that these participants would have fared better, and had their ideas "heard" more successfully, in face-to-face encounters. And while Beliefnet has clearly gone to
great lengths to be as inclusive and affirming of religious diversity as possible, there are, perhaps inevitably, gaps in its inclusivity. A member of an
African Traditional Religion noted in one post, for instance, that there was
no entry for her religion on Beliefnet's encyclopedic religions board. Still,
the structure and self-definition of Beliefnet make it at least open to a kind
of inclusiveness in dialogue that is so far unheard of offline.

Beliefnet Dialogues

The content of the interfaith exchanges on Beliefnet can be organized
under four headings: (1) false starts (threads of conversation initiated by
one participant that either get no response or that get diverted to other,
nondialogical topics); (2) information exchange (participants from one religion explaining something about their tradition to those of another
faith); (3) expressions of personal spirituality (statements of what individuals believe, based on their own experiences); and (4) real dialogue (back-
and-forth exchanges in which participants interact with each other's
posts). This is no different from what goes on in traditional interfaith encounters, though the informality and lack of structure of these dialogues
makes perhaps for more false starts, and the established use of the Internet for the proclamation of personal manifestos likely contributes to the
prevalence of personal belief statements. Still, the real dialogue observable on Beliefnet, in which participants come to an understanding of another religious perspective that they did not previously have, is impressive.

In one exchange in the Interfaith Dialogue discussion group, for instance, a Christian woman acknowledges that a conservative Jewish
woman has corrected her "media-distorted" view of Zionism. In another
conversation, a Wiccan, two Christians (one of whom was a sixty-year-old
Jehovah's Witness grandmother from New Orleans), and a member of
the Baha'i community discussed the notion of the Trinity. In addition to

finding interesting similarities (and differences) in all their triune notions of divinity, one of the Christians expressed gratitude to the Baha'i
for an explanation of the relation between God and Christ that he felt
both clarified and challenged the traditional Christian conception of the
Trinity. Surely this is an instance of the kind of enrichment and transformation that champions of dialogue have long promoted.

At the same time, academic and institutionally affiliated dialogues have
worked out many helpful guidelines for dialogue that are critical to its
success—not comparing the ideals of one religion with the lived practice of
another, bracketing assumptions about other traditions, openness to self-
criticism, etc. These are sometimes fumbled in online exchanges. The ones
that sustain themselves, though, seem to figure them out as they go. Perhaps the most difficult challenge faced by Beliefnet participants is that of
sticking with the dialogue when it becomes difficult. In one exchange on the
topic of "enlightenment" in the Interfaith Dialogue Group in the summer of
2003, for instance, one Christian participant, "arielmessenger," posted re-
peated long attacks on the nontheistic Buddhist notion of enlightenment,
with extended quotes from scientific studies that he believed debunked
Buddhist claims. In two different threads of this dialogue, arielmessenger
was chided by several others for violating Beliefnet rules of conduct pertaining to proselytizing and "dumping," or posting sequences of overly long
messages. Interesting developments followed in both conversations. In the
first, arielmessenger opted to leave the discussion with the following post:
"Look, we can go on and on with you all trying your best to defame my beliefs because you don't want to hear any criticism of the traditional and
seemingly politically correct Enlightenment belief system, Buddhism, but
God and science prove you wrong in my book and always will. So, not finding anything new to add to this discussion I am dropping out all together as
now you know what enlightenment means to me, something different than
what it means to most of you" (arielmessenger, July 12, 2003). But another
participant took him to task for this: "This dialogue is a learning experience for everyone involved. If you storm off now in frustration, thinking
you're wasting your time on unschooled and close-minded heathens, then
you've learned nothing—and that's a real shame. There is much more yet to
be discovered in this world, and if you think you've learned it all, then
you've completely missed the point (of life)" (aibrean000, July 12, 2003).

On the other thread, there were similar objections to arielmessenger's posts, and one participant scolded the entire group for the increasing bitterness of the discussion's tone: "I won't participate if you can't all be adults. Seriously. I don't need more crap than I've already got ☺. . . . Heck, I took part in discussing the hot topics of Evil, Satan, Murder, Horror, etc. I saw less hysteria and hatefulness while dealing with those difficult topics than I saw between Christians and Buddhists in dealing with Enlightenment. Be nice or go away. That goes for all of you" (solitaryworshipper, July 4, 2003). By the end of that day, when solitaryworshipper announced that she was leaving the discussion because "this group stinks," another participant, who had been quite critical of arielmessenger's anti-Buddhist posts, offers this response to solitaryworshipper:

> An online dialogue group is a lot like watching TV. You have control over what you read and what you ignore. But we're not here to entertain you. If we're disappointing you that we're not "enlightened," then you might consider starting your own group and only inviting people worthy of you. Yes, emotions run high on this kind of topic. Religious tolerance isn't easy—and the discussion of it isn't for sissies. . . . The bottom line, though, is that we really don't need a lecture from you about the quality of our discussions— participate if you want—I certainly welcome hearing your ideas, or don't let the door hit you on the backside on the way out—but keep your stinkbombs to yourself. (nightngle, July 4, 2003)

Following this post, what looked like a fast-disintegrating conversation made a remarkable turn. Nightngle offered her own (Buddhist) experience of working toward enlightenment, which was followed by similar posts, with suggestions for further reading, by others. And while arielmessenger did not return, solitaryworshipper, who had only hours before announced her departure, posted a thank-you to the participants for getting back on track, and an apology to nightngle for being "preachy." The dialogue group went on very productively for two more weeks, concluding with this post from solitaryworshipper: "Thank you all. I learned a great deal—not only about myself but also about enlightenment and human-beings-in-general. I am amazed at the tolerance and intelligence I encountered in this dialogue group. Peace to all. May the world continue to evolve. Bless the human-race. I am certain that we will mange to survive, no matter how horrible we CAN be at times. . . . I feel like we'll be OK. Good luck to you all" (solitaryworshipper, July 20, 2003). What are we to make of the blissful end to this bitter dialogue?

Among other things, it demonstrates that successful interfaith dialogue can be maintained in the absence of formal structures and agendas, guided only by an opening question and some basic rules of conduct. In this case, a critical level of commitment to the conversation and to each other coalesced over the course of the three-week dialogue, so that it could sustain the group through rough patches. In fact, it appears in this case that the quality of the discussion and people's engagement in it increased following the outbursts of a few participants. The spirited exchanges that gave the conversation an interpersonal texture seemed to add to its richness for participants. It's possible, then, that what is gained in these informally structured online dialogues is insight not only into another religious point of view, but also into the arts of interpersonal relating and self-knowledge.

Interfaith exchanges on Beliefnet run the gamut from bitter arguments to irenic mutual affirmation—sometimes, as just noted, in a single "conversation." The diversity of these exchanges is related not only to the neutrality of the site itself, but to the diversity of the people who enter it and the range of their intentions. As Steve Waldman, Beliefnet's founder and editor-in-chief, has said, "it's really a mix of people who want to learn more about their own faith and those who want to learn about others. People who want to argue about controversial subjects versus people who really want spiritual nourishment in a more serene and directly helpful way" (Voice of America 2004). Unlike Answering Islam, Beliefnet offers the space and the structural neutrality to accommodate an impressively wide sample of this mix, and the users of the site have proven to be quite adept at finding the places in Beliefnet that best fit their needs.

Exclusivism, Inclusivism, and Pluralism Online

While widely criticized for everything from christocentrism to philosophical incoherence, the academic model of exclusivism, inclusivism, and pluralism described in chapter one nonetheless continues to dominate intellectual efforts to make sense of religious diversity. It is important to ask, therefore, whether this model holds up to the new realities of online interfaith encounters. Are exclusivists, inclusivists, and pluralists to be found in cyberspace, or are these ideal types that exist only in scholars' formulations and in the official exchanges of religious leaders that are often informed by such typologies? If these types are represented in on-line exchanges, in what proportions? And do any new varieties emerge?

While Answering Islam and Beliefnet are only samples of the ways in which people of different religions are coming together on the Internet, they offer ample evidence that the kinds of thinking about religious difference that have been developing offline over the past several generations are still operative in this new context. Not surprisingly, exclusivists—those who hold that salvation is to be had only through a single religious path and that all other religions are devoid of spiritual significance—are well represented in the postings of the editors of Answering Islam. For these Christians, who employ an either/or model of religious truth-seeking, it is precisely the *otherness* of the religious (in this case Muslim) other that puts him or her in spiritual jeopardy. Ultimate religious reality—God—is understood to be single, unitary, and particular, so efforts to find cognates of that reality outside the Christian symbol system are, by definition, doomed. One of Answering Islam's first articles, "The Only True God," makes the exclusivist position clear at the outset, insisting plainly that "the Bible, both in the Old Testament and the New Testament, makes it clear that Christ's death is the only way for man's salvation" and that "[t]here is no salvation except that which is offered by God—Father, Son and Holy Spirit—the only true and living God" (http://www.injil.org/only _true_god.html).

Exclusivist voices can also be heard on Beliefnet, though they are less prominent in the site's explicitly interfaith discussions than in other, explicitly Christian discussions. While many use Beliefnet to engage those with religious views and experiences very different from their own, others can use it as a single-religion site, where they "meet" only those who share their faith commitments and thus where exclusivist views are likely to go unchallenged.

That exclusivists are a small minority in Beliefnet's explicitly inter-faith exchanges is partly explained by the perceived irrelevance or even danger of sites like Beliefnet to committed participants of traditional religions. The website Warriors of Christ.com, for instance, warns visitors in a "Beleifnet.com Q&A" that Beliefnet promotes "the unification of all religions," including many that worship idols and therefore "should not be accepted or tolerated" (Christian Computer Connection 2002). Once in the Beliefnet site, too, exclusivists are often made to feel unwelcome. Consider this post from a participant in a thread called "Can We Afford to Tolerate Intolerance?" who laments lack of diversity in the dialogue:

> I am in a sense disappointed that we didn't get to see any dogmatic believers joining us here, declaring that "yes, all those OTHER dogmatic beliefs that encourage divisiveness and hatred are wrong . . . but MINE is different because it's TRUE!" Perhaps laying the cards on the table and making clear that we know what they are all about makes even them, shameless as they are, too embarrassed to profess such nonsense here. Perhaps we should be working towards a world in which such people are too embarrassed to profess such nonsense anywhere at any time. (maltheist, August 28, 2002)

The arrogant, superior, and imperialist attitudes critics find implicit in academic pluralist theologies emerge fully formed in this statement, valuably affirming those critiques.

On the other hand, inclusivists—those who accept that truth can be found in other religions, but is only complete in their own—are well represented in Beliefnet conversations. This suggests that an inclusivist view is no barrier to genuine interfaith interest and appreciation. Here is one Buddhist voice:

> My acceptance of people following other paths than my own rests not on whether I think they are right, but on the fact that they are using their path effectively to become better people. Where I see that, I might still regard that path as in some way limited or even based on illusion. But I have to respect that path for being ethical and having methods that work for people who wish to progress toward sainthood. Their paths might not get them as far as the Buddha's path when followed to its limit; but let me face it, I doubt

whether I can do better in this lifetime either. (alfredson, August
30, 2002)

And one Catholic:

> As a Catholic, I believe that there is only one God, who is the Holy
> Trinity, Father, Son, and Holy Spirit. That is the nature of God; he is
> nothing else. However, I also believe that you do not have to ac-
> knowledge his nature to worship him. So, the Hindu who worships
> Ganesh truthfully is partly experiencing God. The Wiccan worship-
> ping the Goddess is partly experiencing the one God. . . . If a person
> follows their religion with their heart, believing that it is true, and
> follows the basic beliefs found in most religions . . . then they can
> be saved by the power of Christ. (JRJ26, July 19, 2004)

Karl Rahner himself couldn't have expressed the inclusivist position more
clearly than this eighteen-year-old college student. Inclusivists from a variety of religions seem to be at home on Beliefnet, where both tolerance
and traditional religious affiliation are widely affirmed.

Pluralists—those who believe that no single religious system has priv-
ileged access to truth and salvation—are, not surprisingly, the loudest
voices on Beliefnet. Consider these:

> In my humble opinion, all paths are equally valid. No one religion
> has the one and only lock on the Truth. (callalily, August 11, 2002)

> In my humble opinion, having a grasp on the "whole truth" (what-
> ever that "truth" might be) is impossible for any individual or
> human group simply because of our limited and fallible nature as
> human beings. To take an analogy from everyday life, I think that
> we have about as much chance of [knowing] what might (or might
> not) be going on in higher realms as my little cat, Emmie, has of
> understanding where cat food REALLY comes from—nor would any
> amount of sitting her down and patiently explaining grocery stores,
> national distribution networks, and currency accomplish that goal.
> Such things, and even the method of communicating them, are
> simply beyond her abilities. . . . All she knows is that when she's
> hungry she scratches at the pantry door and meows in a certain

tone—performs her little ritual, as it were, and food magically appears in her bowl. Thus perhaps, the Gods who love us smile upon our efforts, and grant us our daily bowl of Tender Vittles. (crowdog66, August 13, 2002)

The pluralists on Beliefnet, like their academic counterparts described in chapter one, can be sorted into two types, convergent and nonconvergent. Convergent pluralists are those who believe that there is one divine reality toward which all religions are oriented, and that all religious traditions share a common essence, their differences the product of historically determined cultural variety. Convergent pluralists often use the metaphors of multiple paths up a single mountain, or of single truths expressed in many languages, to understand diversity. Nonconvergent pluralists resist this common essence language and insist on at the least the possibility that the religions are incommensurately different, with no common transcendent referent. For nonconvergent pluralists, the language of difference predominates, and the goal of dialogue is understood to be that of increased understanding, not the discovery of universals.

Here are two examples of convergent pluralist voices on Beliefnet:

As the world grows smaller and we recognize that so many of our perceived differences are but different symbols for the same core beliefs, a common spiritual language will be possible. Language is but a symbol for a symbol and many of us are saying the same thing but using different symbols to do so. This alone is what creates perceived differences. The desires of the human existence are innate and the only difference is the method of fulfillment. (broscotty, November 2, 2004)

I think that enlightenment . . . can be achieved through many different paths. . . . Different faiths are like different paths up the same mountain. We all take different route, but in the end, we are all on the same peak. (MissElphaba, June 30, 2003)

Compare those with the following non-convergent expressions, in which different paths are acknowledged as legitimate, but for different reasons:

I absolutely disagree that we're all going to the same "place" or spiritual goal. I think that idea trivializes religion and makes it all seem like so much skim milk. There is great richness and diversity in the human spirit, and many different ways to express that spirit (nightngle, June 30, 2003)

And why is sameness such a grand thing? To think that sameness is the only way we can all get along, is to shortchange humankind. Conversely, to assume that we will all get along if we are the same religiously, is to ascribe more restraint to humanity than I believe will ever be possible. . . . Same is bland, flavorless. I can think of no worse torment than to live in a world of such sameness. Give me spice, and if it brings conflict, then we don't need to take away the spice; we need to grow up. (ChicagoHeathen, November 3, 2004)

It is interesting to note that ChicagoHeathen's rejection of sameness is echoed in that same discussion by an exclusivist Christian voice: "The ideology . . . that all beliefs are the same is on the rise. I intend to fight and disagree with it till the JESUS comes or I die. So no sameness for me" (samuelbb7, November 3, 2004). This exchange illustrates the interesting complexity and the strange alliances that interfaith dialogue generates—sometimes the left and the right meet by pulling farthest from the center.

As these examples suggest, the by-now traditional classification of attitudes toward religious difference are clearly alive and well online. Exclusivists, inclusivists, and pluralists are all using the Internet to express themselves and to engage others, though exclusivists seem (as in the offline world) to be the least active—and the least welcomed—dialogue participants. But online dialogue also raises challenges to this typology by airing the views of so many whose conception of religious difference does not fit neatly into these categories. Those who go online to make contact with religious others are often, as noted above, seekers of religious truth unaffiliated with any particular religious community, or identified with several religious identities simultaneously. Because of their tenuous or non-existent institutional affiliations, such people do not typically find a place in offline dialogue structures. Yet if current analyses of American religion are right, they may be more reflective of lived American spirituality than those sitting around the conference tables at church- and synagogue-based interfaith councils. And the thoughtfulness, depth, and passion of many Beliefnet exchanges suggest that these unaffiliated people of faith are doing some of the most intense and fruitful dialoguing in America today.

Democratizing, Personalizing (and McDonaldizing?) Dialogue

If we take Beliefnet, rather than Answering Islam, as the dominant model of online interfaith activity, we can find several important ways in which the online setting advances the project of dialogue. First, it goes far, though not all the way, to leveling the field for dialogue participants. The de-absolutizing nature of the web radically relativizes religious positions in a process Tom Beaudoin has called "electronic leveling" (1998, 56). The absence of orthodox filters, the fluidity of web representations that subtly undercut the notion of timeless religious truths, and the fact that all religious perspectives and groups are equally accessible in roughly the same form combine to "make cyberspace hostile to the hegemony of religious institutions" (56). This is good news for the marginalized dialogue participant who is young, or poor, or comes from a minority tradition or who is not institutionally affiliated, as well as for the Christian participant who wants to strip off the privilege of demographics and architecture.

It can also be argued that the online format facilitates the process of dialogue. Most obviously, it collapses the physical space that distances one group from another. At Beliefnet, one need not go to India or even across town to someone else's church basement to encounter the religious other. It may also help circumnavigate the institutional resistance some would-be dialogue participants face. One's pastor may refer one to the Warriors of Christ's admonitions about Beliefnet, but in the privacy of one's own home computer, such admonitions can be ignored anonymously and with impunity. In the exchanges themselves, participants may find that the posting system affords the time to carefully craft and edit responses, and that the anonymity of the Internet masks the outward religious and cultural marks of dress, accent, and the like that might stimulate bias and prejudice.

On the other hand, aren't the veil, the turban, the yarmulke, the bindi part of what draws people to interfaith dialogue? Such marks of difference, invisible in Internet dialogues, are part of the precious particularity of religious identity that is sometimes jeopardized online. Feminist analysis of online religion has raised the problem of virtual disembodiment, and how it has "functioned to deny the social, material fact that bodies are different and that this difference indeed counts, as well as to obscure the fact that not every body gets to be included in this supposedly neutral, universal utopia of disembodied minds" (Underwood 2000, 280). The shedding of bodies can be linked with Beliefnet's subtle and not-so-subtle pressure to shed religious particularity in order to partake of the religious smorgasbord. The very structure of Beliefnet, in which participants are offered a vast menu of religious options from which to choose (and from which an unlimited number may be selected as self-designators when setting up a personal profile), privileges a very particular view of religious identity as fluid and syncretic, one that is not hospitable to those whose view is characterized more by permanence, particularity, and commitment. Lynn Schofield Clark's characterization of the "Protestantization" of research in religion and media (2002) could aptly be applied to Beliefnet as well. A particular set of cultural values whose roots can be traced to the Protestant Reformation—individualism, freedom, pluralism, tolerance, democracy, and intellectual inquiry—are certainly normative on this site, as established by official rules of conduct, site layout, and the dynamics of interfaith conversations.

One participates in dialogue on Beliefnet as an individual, and the religious identity one represents there can be as eclectic as one chooses, and can change as often as one logs on. It is thus perhaps not surprising that the focus in Beliefnet's interfaith work is on personal spirituality rather than on social transformation. There is little evidence that the connections made here, while very personally enriching and transformative, lead directly to any practical interfaith work in the communities of the participants. It may be that the kind of soft pluralism fostered by this and other dialogue forums is not after all the best sustenance for committed social action, though it may be deeply personally enriching.

Beliefnet's multifaith site also offers a striking illustration of the problem of many pluralist approaches to interfaith dialogue: their failure to actually see the other *as other*. And it is here that Beliefnet's commercial status becomes critical to consider. Pluralism's inability to reckon with real religious difference, to include the exclusivist as fully as the multifaith seeker, is increasingly linked with problems of a culturally flattening globalization, what Robert Schreiter has called a "global hyperculture"

(Shreiter 1997) and what George Ritzer has more quotably called "Mc-Donaldization." Pluralism, it has been suggested, "is an ideology especially congruent with the global system that threatens to overtake distinctive local cultures" (Tilley 1999, 11). In other words, for all its embracing of tolerance and diversity, pluralism in fact often functions as a religion of its own, a syncretic, ahistorical, and distinctively western worldview with its own truth claims, intolerances, and conversionary thrust.

And if there is in fact such a religion growing in America today, surely Beliefnet is one of its largest churches. Its diversity-affirming structure must be seen not only as an endorsement of pluralist models of dialogue but also as savvy marketing. The smorgasbord model of religion, in which we can each heap our plates with bite-sized pieces of the world's religious offerings, does not in fact correlate with most of the world's, or even the country's, religious sensibilities. But it does appeal to a segment of the Internet market that is a critical commercial target (Lawrence 2001, 247).

Of course, the blending of commercial and spiritual interests is nothing new to religion in the United States. American religions have been deeply involved in commercial culture for centuries, and many religions have developed great skill in commercial self-promotion (Moore 1994). Scholars of American religion have long used the marketplace model to describe Americans' individualistic, voluntaristic, and sycretistic approach to religious affiliation, but it is new, I believe, as a model for interfaith dialogue. On Beliefnet, where your religious activity literally has commercial sponsors, banner ads stream across your dialogue threads, and your religious options have been crafted by market strategists, the marketplace metaphor threatens to collapse into literal description. Sacred space (which for many Beliefnet is) becomes commercial space, prayer an act of consumption, and the range of products available, colorfully displayed and apparently infinite in variety, may in fact be the attractive packaging of a generic mass-marketed McFaith, in which an "other" can no longer be found.

Internet Interfaith Encounters and American Spirituality

Both Answering Islam and Beliefnet exploit the power and structure of the Internet to advance particular strategies regarding religious pluralism. On

Answering Islam, a very narrow kind of exclusivism is promoted by the Internet's power to link massive amounts of data, by the intellectual leveling of website design that puts the statements of religious apologists on the same footing as those of academics, and by the digital anonymity that allows aggressive proselytizing to go unchecked by the standards of etiquette that might operate in face-to-face encounters. On Beliefnet, an eclectic and "Protestant" style of pluralism is served by a mission statement and rules of conduct that prioritize tolerance and discourage proselytizing, by prominently featuring critical and comparative analyses of religious ideas and practices, by representing all religions with formal parity, and by defining religious identity in terms that are personal, voluntaristic, and non-institutional. For all its promise of bringing people together across religious and cultural divides, then, the Internet is also an effective means of reinforcing those lines. Another way of putting this is to note that in spite of the richness of their internal conversations, visitors to Beliefnet are doing very little dialoguing with those who visit Answering Islam, and vice versa.

Together these two sites give us important insight into recent trends in American spirituality, trends at once reflected in and intensified by computer mediation. In the conclusion to their 2004 study of American religion online, the Pew researchers note that American religion is becoming "more personally expressive and individually oriented" (Pew 2004, 20); even if traditional religious affiliation is maintained, Americans are increasingly using extra-institutional resources to craft a spirituality that fits their personal needs. The Internet facilitates this tendency dramatically. Whereas offline I might opt to supplement my denominational practice with a yoga class or an interfaith council meeting, on the Internet I can finely customize my religious activity not only by the websites I choose to visit, but by the resources I select on those websites, from specific discussion topics to e-mail lists to jokes. And, of course, I can leave the site for another, or turn the computer off entirely, any time I choose. The same exit option exists in face-to-face religious communities, of course, but the anonymity and asynchronous nature of the Internet might tend to reduce the sense of obligation and commitment at the same time that it encourages the ongoing quest for the perfectly personalized spiritual home. In this regard, it is possible that the Internet may do as much to isolate people with different religious views as it does to bring them together.

But these are abstract ruminations. Online interfaith encounters are happening to real people, who have their own ideas about what these conversations mean, and are the only ones who know how they are affected by them. At the end of my study of Beliefnet, I invited participants in the Interfaith Dialogue discussion group to reflect on what their online exchanges had meant to them. In many cases, the most powerful outcome of these exchanges was not a changed view of the religious other, but insights into self:

> The thing that interacting on b-net has caused me to see in myself, over and over again, is how deep my conditioning and opinions do run.
>
> I think we all believe, to one extent or another, that the way we see the world is the "right" way. In my deepest heart, where I don't want to look, I know how true that is of me. I find myself "judging the judger" all the time. The truth is I *want* to have compassion and show tolerance for everyone because I know how inextricably connected we are, right down to the very air we breath! But in my head I still so very much react to what *I perceive* as intolerance and/or narrow-mindedness in others, which is obviously just my own self righteousness kicking in.
>
> For me, the very best thing about interacting with people of different faiths and beliefs is that it gives us so many opportunities to see one heck of a lot about ourselves. (wonderment, October 28, 2004)

Another participant, runegurl, has a similar view:

> i think it depends entirely upon the people having the dialogue.
> all too often, it isn't actually a dialogue, it's a monologue—one person preaching at another about matters spiritual or religious, and usually from a one-true-path perspective.
> but *dialogue*—actually talking to someone else about their path, their gods (or lack thereof), and how that all comes together in their life and makes it better ... that is the stuff of great conversation,

and yes, it can bring great change to one's life. speaking with someone who clearly has intelligent spirituality going on in their life is,
for me, a real treat, and gives me much to think about in my own
spiritual life. (runegurl October 28, 2004)

It was a Jewish Pagan woman whose response captured the best of what I
observed in interfaith dialogue online:

> I find these kinds of dialogues invaluable, on a number of levels.
>
> Much of what I gain is information, of course. From a practical
> standpoint, I see areas in my knowledge about my own "religion"
> that are weak or lacking and I have to take action. People ask ques-
> tions that I can't answer, so I head to books. Also, people are shar-
> ing information about their religion and spiritual practices, and I'm
> often times curious for more details. Again, I'm gaining knowledge.
>
> Sometimes, even over the internet, I feel blessed to be in
> someone's spiritual presence, even if we belong to different reli-
> gions or are traveling different paths. I see others expressing spiri-
> tual traits that I feel lacking in; finding and talking with those
> people, learning about their experiences inspires, encourages and
> (again) informs my own experience.
>
> I think the key is this: What does someone *expect* out of In-
> terfaith dialogue? In the truest sense of the word dialogue, I *ex-
> pect* to be informed; I expect to be changed; I expect to be blessed.
>
> And I usually am. (jewitch, October 30, 2004)

These are compelling words, and they convince me that for all its tenden-
cies to commodification, unruliness, and self-indulgence, the Internet
will indeed be a legitimate and important venue for twenty-first-century
interfaith encounter.

Conclusion

This tour of several sites of interfaith encounter affirms that the pluralist impulse is alive and well in the United States, despite the twin threats of fundamentalism and the homogenizing commodification of culture. For every gesture of religious intolerance that so captures media attention, we can find countless instances of individuals and groups stepping across religious lines with curiosity and open hearts. And although evidence of recent trends in American spirituality toward highly personal, flexible, therapeutic, and theologically thin approaches to religion can be found in these engagements, they are also reason to take a second look at such characterizations.

I began this project with four sets of questions about interfaith work: Who does it? What motivates them? What happens in the encounters? and What theology sustains them? While several clear patterns have emerged, it is clear that these questions need to be complicated considerably. After exploring four different kinds of interfaith exchanges, as well as the analyses of interfaith relations offered by philosophers and theologians, I have come to appreciate the difference context makes in these border-crossing encounters. It seems to matter, for instance, whether participants are individuals or institutions, whether they are part of a minority or majority culture, and whether exchanges are face-to-face or virtual, in public or private space. Each context involves different structures of accountability, levels of investment, and unique conditions that foster or inhibit genuine dialogical encounter.

Participants and Motivations

This study generally supports the hypothesis that interfaith exchanges will be most sought by individuals with a pluralist theological perspective and by religious groups identifiable as liberal or progressive. Whether it is an individual initiative to join an online dialogue or denominational affiliation with a community interfaith group, most interfaith programs are dominated by those who affirm that there are multiple, equally valid routes to spiritual fulfillment, who are disposed toward openness and tolerance on social issues, and who support liberal political causes. But there are important countercurrents in this pattern. As seen most clearly in the political coalitions analyzed in chapter two, there are conditions under which the most politically conservative and the most theologically exclusivist people of faith are prompted to do the work of interfaith dialogue. The achievement of a particular social aim—a Bible curriculum in the public schools, intensified political support for the state of Israel—is one motivator that can move such groups to engage one another. There are also personal reasons, as seen in the interfaith relationships detailed in chapter four, that make it important for those of one tradition to come to understand and appreciate that of another. At the communal level, too, such projects can prove beneficial, as with the Muslim community of greater Milwaukee, where interfaith collaboration is an important tool for maintaining and improving relations with the wider community. When these motivators are strong enough, these cases suggest, even those whose theology and wider worldview disdain the kind of relativism and counter-culturalism often associated with interfaith dialogue can be inspired to join, or even initiate, an interfaith program.

In none of these cases were the individuals or groups intrinsically motivated to engage with those of other religions; interfaith exploration in these instances is a means to another end—a good marriage, adoption of a particular national policy, a secure place in a community. But that is not to say that, once engaged in interfaith relationships, theological exclusivists and political conservatives are unskilled at the work of interfaith exchange. Indeed, as those who defend orthodox theology as a foundation for interfaith dialogue have argued, it is often those who are least open to relativizing their worldviews that are the most interesting interfaith interlocutors, especially when as individuals or institutions, they have a real stake in the outcome of the interreligious venture. It is one of the great challenges of the interfaith movement to find more and better incentives for those who might be religiously and socially conservative—whether they are white Evangelicals, Muslim immigrants, or black Pentecostals—to come into these programs, which all too often appear wholly irrelevant to their interests.

Different kinds of interfaith encounters draw different kinds of participants. One comes to an online encounter, for instance, as an unfettered individual, attached to no institution and without any markers of identity beyond those one chooses to reveal. Interfaith encounters in the context of marriage and family are also obviously individual, though the presence of extended family and religious and ethnic communities often loom large in the background. By contrast, it is hard to participate in a community-based interfaith group without congregational, or, in Milwaukee's case, denominational, sponsorship. There are important consequences to these structural differences. On the one hand, encounters among individuals have the advantage of being open to anyone, including the religiously unaffiliated or those affiliated with religions that do not yet have secure enough status in a community to be welcomed at the interfaith table. For this reason, the dialogues I listened to among family members and Internet discussion group participants involved the deepest personal engagement and the most searching spiritual explorations. I was routinely awed by the openness, courage, intelligence, and spiritual insight of the people I met and observed in these contexts. On the other hand, when interfaith participation is a matter of informal individual initiative, there is usually little impact beyond individual personal enrichment. It is unlikely that such encounters will do much to change interfaith relations at the structural level. For these kinds of encounters there is also little in the way of structure and guidelines to lean on, no moderator and no rules to keep the dialogue on track, and no shared task on which to focus energy and attention. For this reason, individual encounters often involve considerable wheel-spinning and get caught in frequent cul de sacs. They also, at least in the case of online exchanges, involve minimal accountability; one can log off as soon as the conversation takes a difficult turn and look for a more congenial conversation else-where. In a marriage or life partnership, of course, there is a much higher degree of accountability; while things that a partner may say or do about religion can profoundly trouble an interfaith relationship, the bonds of love and shared history are usually strong enough to hold partners to-gether to keep facing the issues anew.

On the other hand, interfaith work that is built around formal reli-gious communities usually has the benefit of by-laws, agendas, and ongo-ing institutional longevity. While these encounters are typically less diverse, and often less spirited, they also slowly and quietly accomplish some of the most important work there is to be done in any society—bringing diverse constituencies together to achieve a common good, whether that is a reduction in community violence, sheltering the home-less, or passing a piece of legislation. I was struck in my observation of this kind of interfaith exchange—whether in community interfaith coun-cils or in national public policy coalitions—at how little genuine interreli-gious dialogue actually occurred. In most of these cases, *acting* as an interfaith entity is more important than exploring what it might *mean* to be an interfaith entity; there is simply too much to be done. In fact, in some cases, as in the Evangelical-Jewish coalition for Israel, too much the-ological discussion might actually jeopardize what is in reality quite a fragile partnership. At the same time, such projects often make possible interfaith exchanges that would not otherwise have occurred. Conversa-tions before and after official meetings, online exchanges on a coalition website—these are occasions at which deeper individual interests in in-terfaith questions can be pursued in an established atmosphere of trust. This kind of encounter can also spur interesting reflection within the par-ticipating communities themselves; simply choosing to come to the table with religious others can prompt a religious group to reflect on questions of identity and priority that might not otherwise have come up.

No one sustains an interest in interfaith work, I have learned, without a genuine self-interest. The richest online conversations, the most suc-cessful community programs, the most truly interfaith activist coalitions were all those in which participants could clearly identify a real purpose—relevant to their own lives—for engaging in such collaboration. Interfaith marriages, of course, are the distilled illustration of this principle. Abstract

theorizing about religious difference has no place in most interfaith relationships. Deep and sustained interfaith dialogue is sustained in these
homes by existential demand—the need to develop ways of integrating
authentically different religious identities into something like a family.
The more programmatic, intentional interfaith encounters now established in communities and on websites across the country must articulate
similar existential relevance if they are to realize their potential of engaging the imagination and energies of those outside the already committed
pluralist camp.

Where's the Dialogue?

I came to this project with a deep interest in the theology of interfaith
relations—how those of one religious worldview make sense *religiously* of
those of another faith tradition. The questions involved in that theology—
What counts as religious truth and how can we know it? Is there one ultimate spiritual destination or many? Who can be saved and by what
power? Are such religious categories transferable across religious lines?
How do we reconcile particularity with universality, religious identity with
a commitment to pluralism?—have absorbed philosophers and theologians for over a century and have generated a distinct branch of philosophical theology. These are the questions I brought with me to my
investigation of real world interfaith encounters. Throughout the course
of the project, however, I found them remarkably irrelevant, even disori-
enting, in the effort to understand real peoples' experience of religious
others. I rarely heard any of these questions raised by participants, and
they often looked blankly at me when I raised them.

This incongruity is attributable at least in part to the fact that for
most people philosophical questions are not the stuff of everyday conversation. But in specifically interfaith contexts, in which individuals have
intentionally engaged with religious others, it seemed especially perplexing. This may be further evidence that we are moving, as sociologist Robert
Wuthnow has speculated, into a post-theological age in American religion
(2005, 99–100), a time when religious "preference" is not so much a matter of commitment to creedal formulas but rather of finding the right personal and cultural "fit." If he is right that the purpose of religion for many

Americans has shifted from a path to eternal life to personally fulfilling experience (194), then it makes sense that questions of conflicting truth claims would simply not arise in encounters with others whose spiritual path differs from our own. If individual existential satisfaction is the perceived goal, on what basis would judgments across religious lines occur? Wuthnow's hypothesis is strengthened by his finding that even Christian exclusivists seem loathe to pass judgment—at least in terms of truth claims—on their non-Christian neighbors; a full 54 percent of the exclusivists in his study expressed the belief that all major religions contain some truth about God (191).[1] This suggests that in reality a pluralist theology may not be the impediment to conservative groups' involvement in interfaith work that many in the movement have assumed it to be. Increasing those groups' participation may instead be a matter of creating a more diverse culture within the various encounter sites and demonstrating more effectively the personal and practical relevance of such work.

It is clear, however, that in spite of this general reticence to directly engage questions of conflicting religious worldviews, some sites were more conducive than others to genuine interfaith encounter. Not surprisingly, the intimacy of home and family provides a safe environment—and the luxury of time over the life of a partnership—for exploring the similarities, differences, and provocative cross-questioning that are the life of interfaith dialogue. The profound responsibility of building a relationship and a family provides one of the most powerful incentives to understand and take in a religious other and to reflect on the implications of religious difference for one's own identity.

Though not as sustained, and lacking the relationship commitment of marriages, online interfaith encounters are also, I came to see, legitimate venues for increasing interfaith understanding. The strength of these encounters was the passion of the participants' interest, and the open and exploratory spirit that seems to characterize those who people Internet communities. The relative anonymity of online presences, their complete freedom from institutional religious control, and the formal qualities of sites like Beliefnet that present religious traditions and identities with absolute equivalence go far in bringing in religious minorities and establishing the level playing field that is so elusive in places like local interfaith councils, where Christian dominance is still very much in evidence. But Internet encounters have their own dialogical limitations, most notably the lack of accountability to one another and to the dialogue that is sometimes the only thing that keeps difficult encounters alive. In addition, the communication of Internet space and its replication of individualistic, consumer-oriented models of spirituality risk trivializing all spiritual pursuits, including those of interfaith dialogue, which can too easily devolve into shopping excursions for attractive new religious possessions.

The most stunted sites of interfaith encounter that I explored here were those built around single social or political issues. While it is clearly beneficial to interfaith enterprises to have a common purpose beyond a generic desire for mutual understanding, these coalitions seem to make very little room for actual interreligious exchange. Political work is by habit if not by nature profoundly oppositional—we work for the adoption of one position over another or the election of one candidate over another, and ambiguity is no help to the cause. This pattern is not one into which interfaith dialogue can easily be woven. In the interfaith initiatives in public policy that I observed, the alliances between those of different religions were almost completely strategic, and the specific cause so important that participants were unlikely to risk the difficulties and possible rifts that might result from deeper exchanges. But in the way that such groups link their national purpose with interfaith solidarity, a vital element in the American interfaith movement is preserved—the premise that religious diversity is a national resource rather than a problem.

As places of encounter where those of one religious affiliation can truly engage those of another, community interfaith organizations were the most ambiguous, and the most surprising to me. On the one hand, these groups are defined by their interfaith status; being with those of another religion is neither an accident of love nor a means to another end but their reason for existing. It was perplexing to me, then, to see how little conversation about religion was to be heard in their gatherings. In some cases lack of clarity about the group's identity and mission contributed to this situation, but it was also a by-product of the great success of the groups in harnessing the energies of the various religious communities for the community good. What often begins with little more than an impulse to collaborate can generate so many programs—and community needs are so boundless—that actually talking about religious difference simply falls to the bottom of the agenda. It was clear, though, that participants in community interfaith groups maintained a strong commitment to learning more about each other and reflecting more deeply on religious matters, as evidenced by the parallel and spin-off dialogue groups linked to these organizations, and by the fact that interfaith council members are such regulars at dialogue-oriented events in the community. More than anything, the relative reticence on matters of religion in the interfaith organizations I observed bears witness to the fact that genuine dialogue is hard to do, and requires carefully established settings and guidelines, as well as commitments of time and the courage to take risks.

Emerging Interfaith Sites

The places I looked for interfaith encounters are the obvious ones. But as the intersections of American religion and culture continue to shift, it will be important to shift our gaze to more unlikely sites. I have been gathering snapshots of these possibilities throughout this project: Tonen O'Connor spoke at length about her encounters with Christian and Jewish clergy in her work in the Milwaukee prison system serving as a chaplain to Buddhist inmates. At a medium-security prison in California, inmates have established a "holy ground" in the exercise yard, where Christians and non-Christians can gather to worship (Thompson 2004). A recent report by the Pluralism Project describes the increasingly interfaith quality of the more than forty airport chapels in the United States. In these settings, Christians will find themselves praying in a religiously neutral space alongside Jews, Muslims, and those of countless other religious traditions shared by Americans and those who pass though. In response to discrimination charges by non-Christians, the Air Force Academy in Colorado Springs, Colorado, announced in 2005 a series of measures to enhance understanding of and respect for religious diversity. In the corporate world, the Ford Motor Company established the Ford Interfaith Network in 2000 to "assist the company in becoming a worldwide corporate leader in promoting religious tolerance, corporate integrity, and human dignity." Its activities, which include conventional diversity training opportunities as well as larger scale interfaith programming, are founded "out of love for human beings and all of creation," as well as on the belief that "diversity is a competitive advantage in a global economy."

All of these settings—corporations, the military, airports, prisons—may be identified as communities of circumstance, where—sometimes for only a very short time, sometimes over years—diverse people are brought together and must negotiate their differences. As the boundaries between secular and sacred continue to erode in this society, it is likely that such places will increase in their religious significance. And because they are places of religious heterogeneity, that significance will likely be defined in increasingly interfaith terms. It will be especially interesting to track the development of interfaith activity in the commercial sector of American life. Health clubs already offer yoga, Chai-Bo, and Gospel aerobics; can interfaith fitness programs be far behind? Will malls establish interfaith shoppers' retreats for spiritual renewal on the go? Such possibilities offer interesting new material for reflection on the de-privatization of American religion.

In addition to these communities of circumstance, there are also a growing number of intentional interfaith sites in American society. The Interfaith Center at the Presidio in San Francisco has reclaimed part of a decommissioned army base and transformed it into a center for interfaith networking and spiritual practice. Unlike other community-based interfaith groups, the Interfaith Center is an organization not of congregations or denominations, but of already established interfaith groups that it links in a supportive network. It organizes interfaith festivals and smaller events, links the local community with international interfaith initiatives like the World's Parliament of Religions, sponsors the interfaith chapel at San Francisco International Airport, and hosts religious and cultural events at the historic Main Post Chapel on the old army base. On the other side of the country, the New York Metro Mass Choir, founded and led by David Brown, unites people of diverse religions, ethnicities, social classes, and sexualities into one of the largest interfaith gospel choirs in the country, one that aims to create through music a "spiritual common ground." Brown's inspiration for the choir, which he formed in 2001, has a distinctly pluralist ring: "I was always taught that there was only one right way to believe in God, but I always knew there was something wrong about believing I was the only one who was right" (quoted in Heyn, 2003).

While they do not share a common theology, choir members enact the premise that the most successful interfaith work has a pragmatic, social service focus. Together, they have built a house with Habitat for Humanity, spent time with seriously ill children at a Ronald McDonald House, and donated musical mobiles for infants at New York's Foundling Hospital. Ventures like the Metro Mass Choir and the Interfaith Center at the Presidio demonstrate the growing appeal of "interfaith" as an organizational descriptor, and suggest that the absence of religious boundaries is an increasingly important component of many Americans' spirituality.

Finally, I suspect that some of the most interesting new interfaith encounters will be among young people, whose religious lives remain largely opaque to most observers. Although sociologist Christian Smith's study (2005) drew attention to an extremely high level of religious illiteracy among American youth, teens and twenty-somethings also consistently rank as the most religiously tolerant age cohort. Even if they are not deeply invested in the belief systems of organized religions, they are deeply interested in personal spiritual experience, as evidenced by their high levels of participation in campus religious activities, their prominence in alternative spirituality movements, their high rate of participation in online forums like Beliefnet, and in the themes of the popular culture products they produce and consume. For this generation, the shift toward eclectic, individualized, and protean religious identity is not so much a conscious choice or dramatic rejection of an inherited system. Indeed, many of them whose parents made that decisive break from structural religion may never have had a close-up view of any other kind of religiosity. In an unprecedented way, commercial culture is also part of the mix from which this generation will assemble its religious identity. Americans between the ages of fifteen and twenty-five have lived their whole lives in the context of megachurches with Broadway production values, and popular music, films, and television programs that are also purveyors of religious ideas and images, many of which are non-Christian. In this context, interreligious exploration requires no formal initiative but becomes a natural complement to other modes of spiritual gathering. Among young Americans, then, "interfaith" is an increasingly plausible religious identity, although, as suggested by the interfaith children discussed in chapter four, one that is not without its own problems. It will also fall to this generation to reckon with the full impact of the collision of commercial and religious culture. The homogenizing force of popular culture is a constant threat to pluralism of all sorts. Those for whom the lines between religion and other cultural forms are already blurry will be the ones to discover whether or not interfaith exploration can be a place of resistance to that force, or be devoured by it.

The interfaith encounters of this generation will look very different from the covered dish gatherings in church basements and high-level denominational strategizing that have characterized the movement until now. Precisely what shape those encounters will take remains to be seen, but if current trends are any indicator, individual and denominational resistance to interfaith collaboration, at least for certain clearly defined purposes, is likely to decline. If, as has been reported, even young Evangelical Christians who are content within their single tradition are eclectic in their practice, attending multiple churches to take advantage of diverse religious programming (Banerjee 2005), one of the most formidable barriers to interfaith bridge-building may be eroding. To the degree to which all religious identity comes to be seen as an assemblage of available options, inhibitions to meeting and talking with those who have made a different assemblage are likely to be lessened.

Holding a Place for Pluralism

I met no one in the course of this study whose religious identity changed as a result of encountering those of another faith. Nor did any group I observed show any signs of moving toward or advocating a single syncretistic religious worldview; almost all were at pains to firmly disavow such a concept. Indeed, one of the wonderful paradoxes I have found in this project is the way in which interfaith sites—whether they are online, in the home, or in local or national settings—are among the places in the United States where religious identity is most deeply nurtured. Encountering another requires us to encounter ourselves, to make conscious the beliefs, values, practices, prejudices, fears, and hopes that define our religious lives. For everyone I spoke with in the course of this project, that process is one of the great rewards of interfaith work.

In drawing individuals and institutions into relationship with others, in what they are accomplishing and in what they have not yet been able to do, interfaith projects call attention to the layered quality of American religious diversity. They help us to see, of course, the spectacular variety of religious traditions present in our communities and in our nation, as they bring Christians, Jews, Muslims, Hindus, Buddhists, Sikhs, Pagans, and others into conversation. But more subtly, they also expose the internal diversity of each of these traditions. In Chico, California, one Catholic church participates in the interfaith organization, another does not. In Milwaukee, the Interfaith Conference has more Christian groups than any other, and yet the largest churches in the area are not involved at all. A Muslim woman in an online discussion reports how well she and her non-Muslim partner have come to terms with their religious difference, but expresses intense regret that as a consequence of her marriage, her family has disowned her. The Jewish community wrestles with the complexity of its alliances with different Christian groups, some of which are its partners in social justice work, others that support its commitment to Israel. In the interfaith groups I got to know, participants often noted that they felt closer to those of other religions in the interfaith group than they did to many members of their own religious communities. The divisions within these communities, interfaith connections help us to see, are indeed deep and wide, and present the most difficult dialogue challenges.

Even more subtly, interfaith encounters help illuminate a pluralism at the level of individual religious identity. Historian Catherine Albanese reminds us that Americans have always lived in a "culture of religious combining," but that today we are more bold and self-aware in putting together our "creole" spirituality. In this setting, she suggests, "purists are everyday fewer and rarer (Perhaps this is why sometimes they seem to be louder and more strident?)," and "the 'other' seems to beckon with the promise of better and more coherent spiritual goods" (2000, 20). Interfaith encounters are an important locus for this combining, and help us to see that combining is indeed not syncretism. The people I met in interfaith settings did not develop new, hyphenated religious identities. Instead, they reported finding deep affinities with those of other traditions, learning ideas and sharing in rituals that brought new insight into their own traditions, and forging relationships that made crystal clear to them how arbitrary and false are the lines that divide one group from another. Interfaith encounters, in other words, can at their best make pluralism at all levels a lived, conscious, and deeply satisfying reality.

It is worth attending, then, to the lessons from these encounters as we plod through what is coming to feel like our interminable culture war. They are relatively simple: (1) Be quiet and listen. (2) Find a point of connection, but not too many—allow the other to remain other. (3) Enter deeply into your own religious identity, with all its difficulties and ambiguities. (4) Don't just talk; find something to do. These are the rules that seem naturally to evolve in the most successful interfaith ventures, whatever by-laws or mission statements they are working from. They would also seem to be a good point of departure for trying to engage someone whose bumper stickers yell at ours, or whose state is a different color, even if we check the same religious identity box. In their simple symbolic act of holding a place in American society—whether it is in an extended family, in a specific community, or online—where deepest differences are not an impediment but a resource for doing the work that binds us together, interfaith encounters are an important model.

Some of the organizations and activities that pass as "interfaith" in America today in truth involve next to no interreligious exchange, and require of participants no significant confrontation with religious difference; in many cases the interfaith label appears to serve simply as a legitimating label for projects that might not otherwise draw public support. More often, though, I found these encounters to be driven by genuine interest and sometimes profound religious insight. In the questions they raise and the blunders they survive, in their consistent spirit of generosity and openness, in the new relationships they engender, and in their incredible religious inventiveness, these and countless other interfaith encounters may be giving us a glimpse of a future for American religion in which we finally get pluralism right. At the very least, they are marking out a space where such a thing might someday occur.

NOTES

INTRODUCTION

1. These communities are vividly detailed in Diana Eck's *A New Religious America* (2001).

CHAPTER 1   THEORIES OF RELIGIOUS DIFFERENCE

1. The fullest history of the 1893 Parliament is found in Marcus Braybrooke's *Pilgrimage of Hope: One Hundred Years of Global Interfaith Dialogue* (1992), 5–42.

2. I offer a much fuller description, analysis, and assessment of these positions in "Reckoning with Religious Difference: Models of Interreligious Moral Dialogue," in *Explorations in Global Ethics*, ed. Sumner B. Twiss and Bruce Grelle (Boulder, CO: Westview Press, 1998): 73–117.

3. While both may express narrow conceptions of who can be saved, it is important to distinguish the theological position of exclusivism from the broader socio-religious phenomenon of fundamentalism, in Christianity and other religions. See McCarthy 1998, 82–85.

4. While "religious pluralism" is often used to refer to the fact of religious diversity globally or in a given society, "pluralism" is generally now used by scholars to refer to a specific intellectual response to that diversity—some form of positive affirmation of its value. For a fuller discussion of terminology, see the introduction to William R. Hutchison's *Religious Pluralism in America: The Contentious History of a Founding Ideal* (New Haven: Yale University Press, 2003), 1–10.

5. Another summary of this criticism of pluralism is found in Terrence Tilly, "'Christianity and the World Religions,' A Recent Vatican Document." *Theological Studies* 60:2 (June 1999): 318–38.

6. Another analysis of the paradoxical role of religion in a globalized world is offered by Gregory Melleuish (2005), who argues that globalization has produced both a liberal Western Christianity that is indistinguishable from secularism, and subcultures of Christians, Muslims, and others becoming more determined in the defense of their own orthodoxies.

7. Orbis Books, through its "Faith Meets Faith" series, is one of the major publishers in the field of interfaith dialogue, and its titles reflect this contentiousness. The most complete (at that time) exposition of the theology of pluralism came out in the essays collected in *The Myth of Christian Uniqueness* (1987), edited by John

Hick and Paul Knitter. In 1990, another volume in the series, *Christian Uniqueness Reconsidered: The Myth of a Pluralistic Theology of Religions*, edited by Gavin D'-Costa, firmly established the oppositional structure of the conversation.

8. Paul Knitter (1995) has developed a full theology of religious pluralism built on the foundations of liberation theology, insisting that shared participation in the common "soteriological" thrust of the world's religions to liberate the oppressed is the best premise for interfaith understanding.

9. Knitter summarizes this comparative theological approach to dialogue in *Introducing Theologies of Religions* (Maryknoll, NY: Orbis Books, 2002), 202–215. The growing popularity and academic legitimacy of this approach is suggested by the fact that the American Academy of Religion, the leading professional organization for religion scholars, established "comparative theology" as a program unit in 2006.

10. For accounts of women in interfaith dialogue, see O'Neill 1990, King 1998, and Mollenkott 1988. For one assessment of what women's experience brings to theologies of pluralism see McCarthy 1996.

11. "Double Belonging" was the theme, for instance, of a session at the 2001 Annual Meeting of the Society for Buddhist Christian Studies in Denver, Colorado.

12. See for instance the essays in Cornille 2002.

CHAPTER 2   STRANGE BEDFELLOWS

1. On Slate.com, readers can take a quiz to determine where they fall on the red state-blue state continuum; questions include what movies one might add to a video collection, and whether or not it is ever appropriate for women to wear white pantyhose (Kornblut 2004).

2. There has been a recent spate of television dramas that some might classify as religious, due to their explorations of paranormal spiritual experience. Ecstatic visions, visitations by angels, and spells all seem to draw large audiences, but shows with these themes very rarely depict anyone going to church, or referencing positive identification with a particular religion. The kind of exotic, eclectic spirituality dramatized on television is easy to reconcile, it seems to me, with most theories of secularization.

3. There are also factors that might contribute to *under*-reporting of religious observance, including the de-centralized nature of certain religions, like Wicca, which lacks a denominational structure capable of tracking religious participation.

4. As a professor of both religious studies and women's studies, I am especially sensitive to the historical tendency of feminism to embrace diversity in matters of ethnicity, sexuality, and class, but to give very little attention to religious diversity. This tendency is understandable, of course, in light of institutional religious complicity in many forms of women's oppression and the ongoing opposition of many religious groups to women's reproductive and sexual freedom, but seems to me also to represent a largely missed opportunity for powerful and enriching alliances.

5. The civil rights movement was itself an interfaith effort, drawing on a powerful Christian base and extensive Jewish support. See Wald (2003, 123–124) for a

discussion of the role of religious communities in the passing of the Civil Rights Act of 1964.

6. Based on the 2001 ARIS survey, it is reasonable to conclude that there are now more Pagans in the United States than there are Quakers, Baha'is, or Sikhs (Ontario Consultants on Religious Tolerance 2005).

7. As of December 2003.

8. One group promoting the complete abolition of public schools on religious grounds is The Alliance for the Separation of School and State (http://www.honestedu .org/index.php). This California-based organization led by a conservative Christian educator but with Jewish and Muslim endorsements, demonstrates the strategic value of interfaith participation. While the rationale the group offers for "liberating" schools from all government control is solidly fundamentalist Christian, endorsements from members of other traditions and inclusion of articles on, for example, how public schools require observant Muslims to violate religious precepts like modest dress and sex segregation, promote an image of the group as a broad, non-sectarian coalition based on a common educational vision. The Alliance's call for Christian (and other) families to remove their children from public schools has been promoted by such prominent Christian leaders as James Dobson (Cutrer 2002).

9. While somewhat dated, the essays in Rhys H. Williams's collection, *Culture Wars in American Politics: Critical Reviews of a Popular Myth* (New York: Walter de Gruyter, 1997), offer in-depth analyses of the complexities of left and right in American politics and the ambiguous role of religion in shaping those categories.

CHAPTER 3   WHEN THE OTHER IS NEIGHBOR

1. Groups were selected among those with an Internet presence that met the following criteria: identification with a particular local community (as opposed to a national or international focus); explicit identification as "interfaith," with evidence of involvement of at least two different religious groups (as opposed to an ecumenical Christian membership); and availability of a mission or vision statement for the organization. Selected groups represented all regions of the country: northeast (3), east (5), south (2), midwest (6), west (5), southwest (3), and northwest (1).

2. Diana Eck's *A New Religious America: How a 'Christian' Nation Has Become the World's Most Religiously Diverse Nation* devotes a chapter to American Hindus that richly details these activities (2001, 80–141).

3. An ironic consequence of this merger is that Milwaukee, like Chico, now has no overarching ecumenical Christian organization. In Milwaukee many Christian churches participate in the statewide Council of Churches, but in Chico the transformation from a Council of Churches to an Interfaith council has meant an awkward persistence of some of the functions of an ecumenical organization—pulpit exchanges, joint Good Friday services, etc.—under the auspices of the interfaith organization.

CHAPTER 4   INTIMATE OTHERS

1. For this chapter, references to "interfaith" data in historical context include cross-denominational (Catholic-Protestant) Christian partnering, since these, along with Jewish-Christian marriages, were the focus of most conversations about intermarriage prior to recent decades. My analysis of contemporary inter-faith families refers only to partners who come from entirely different religions, although it is interesting to note that for some conservative Christian groups, other Christian denominations like Roman Catholicism and Mormonism are per-sistently seen as "non-Christian."

2. See for instance, Silvia Barack Fishman's review of American media treatments of Jewish-Christian marriages (2004, 122–123).

3. Both of these studies measure Jewish identity by religion only, not "born Jews," a category used in some other surveys that includes those with one Jewish parent and raised in a non-Jewish home. The intermarriage rate for Jews is obviously much higher when all those who identify as Jewish in any way are included.

4. See, for example, John Paul II's Encyclical Letter *Redemptoris Missio* (1990), and the Sacred Congregation for the Doctrine of the Faith's "Declaration on the Unic-ity and Salvific Universality of Jesus Christ and the Church" (2000).

5. See for instance the personal accounts offered in interfaith guidebooks like Rosenbaum and Rosenbaum 1994, Hawxhurst 1998, and the detailed portraits provided in Glaser 1997. All of these report only on Jewish-Christian partnerships.

6. In total, seventy-one people are represented in this sample, thirty-two Christians, fourteen Jews, eight Muslims, six Buddhists, six Pagans, four Hindus, and one Baha'i. The names of interview subjects have been changed; Internet discussion participants are identified with their online user name.

7. The significance of constructive communication as a strong predictor of marital satisfaction among interfaith couples is supported by recent research. See Hughes and Dickson (2005).

8. All online postings are from Beliefnet.Com's "Interfaith Families" discussion group, 2000–2005.

9. See for instance, the anecdotes reported in Hawxhurst 1998, 2–3.

10. Robert C. Fuller (2005) makes a similar point in his defense of the eclecticism of "unchurched" Americans more generally. See especially pp. 153–174.

CHAPTER 5   MEETING THE OTHER IN CYBERSPACE

1. Margaret Wertheim's 1999 book, *The Pearly Gates of Cyberspace*, offers a fascinat-ing example of this position. She argues that cyberspaces offers us a return, after centuries of the modern conception of space as purely physical, to a medieval no-tion that there exists another spiritual realm in which our souls might dwell, a realm that lures with promises of cyber-gnosis, cyber-immortality, and cyber-utopia. Wertheim's analysis takes seriously the limits of cyberspace as soul-space, as well as its promise. In particular, she notes the "cyber-selfishness" that lets online participants get "the payoffs of a religion without getting bogged

down in reciprocal responsibilities" (282). She also acknowledges the "not insignificant inequalities"—of gender, race, and class—that characterize many cyberspace communities today (299).

2. This view seems to have been shared, at least in 2001, by religion surfers, 62 percent of whom were reported to believe that the availability of material on the Internet encourages religious tolerance (Pew 2001, 3).

CONCLUSION

1. Exclusivists are here defined by Wuthnow as those who agree with the statement that "Christianity is the best way to understand God," and disagree with the statement, "All major religions, such as Christianity, Hinduism, Buddhism, and Islam, are equally good ways of knowing about God" (2005, 190).

BIBLIOGRAPHY

Albanese, Catherine. 2000. "The Culture of Religious Combining: Reflections for the New American Millennium." *Cross Currents* 50:1–2 (spring/summer):16–22.

American Religious Identification Survey. 2001. The Graduate Center, City University of New York, http://www.gc.cuny.edu/faculty/ research_briefs/aris/aris_index .htm.

Ariarajah, S. Wesley. 2003. "Religious Diversity and Interfaith Relations in a Global Age." Paper presented at the International Conference on Religion and Globalization, Chiang Mai, Thailand, July 27–August 2, 2003. http://isrc.payap.ac.th/document/speeches/speech01.pdf.

Arrington, Leonard J. and Davis Bitton. 1992. *The Mormon Experience: A History of the Latter-day Saints.* Chicago and Urbana: University of Illinois Press.

Associated Press. 2005. "Jews Condemn Southern Baptist Effort." *CNN.Com* (September 29). http://www.cnn.com/2005/US/09/29/southern.baptists.ap/.

———. 2003. "Interfaith Families Seek Holiday Balance." *Ashville Citizen-Times Online* (July 29). http:cgi.citizentimes.com/cgi-bin/story/faith/24379.

Azumah, John. 2002. "The Integrity of Interfaith Dialogue." *Islam and Christian-Muslim Relations* 13, 3:269–280.

Banerjee, Neela. 2005. "Going to Church to Find a Faith That Fits." *New York Times* (December 30):18.

The Barna Group. 2001. "More Americans Are Seeking Net-Based Faith Experiences." The Barna Update. http://www.barna.org/FlexPage.aspx?Page=BarnaUpdate &BarnaUpdateID=90.

Barrows, John Henry, ed. 1893. *The World's Parliament of Religions.* Chicago: Parliament Publishing Company.

Beaudoin, Tom. 1998. *Virtual Faith: The Irreverent Spiritual Quest of Generation X.* San Francisco: Jossey-Bass.

Bellah, Robert N. et al. 1986. *Habits of the Heart: Individualism and Commitment in American Life.* Berkeley: University of California Press.

Berger, Peter L., Ed. 1999. *The Desecularization of the World: Resurgent Religion and World Politics.* Washington, D.C.: Ethics and Public Policy Center and Grand Rapids, MI: W. B. Eerdmans Pub. Co.

Bible Literacy Project. 2005a. "Scholars Agree: New Breakthrough Public School Bible Textbook Bridges the Cultural Divide." http://www.bibleliteracy.org/Site/PressRoom/index.htm

———. 2005b. "Bible Literacy Report: What Do American Teens Need to Know and What Do They Know?" Fairfax, VA: Bible Literacy Project.

Brasher, Brenda E. 2001. *Give Me that Online Religion*. San Francisco: Jossey-Bass.

Braybrooke, Marcus. 1992. *Pilgrimage of Hope: One Hundred Years of Global Interfaith Dialogue*. New York: Crossroad.

Brock, Rita Nakashima. 2002. "The Fiction of Church and State Separation: A Proposal for Greater Freedom of Religion." *Journal of the American Academy of Religion*. 70: 4 (December):855–861.

Brown, Jessica. 2002. "Keeping the Faith: What Role Does Religion Play in Your Child's Life?" Child.com. http://www.child.com/moms_dads/parenthood_issues/keeping_faith.jsp?page=1.

Bunt, Gary R. 2003. *Islam in the Digital Age: E-jihad, Online Fatwas and Cyber Islamic Environments*. London: Pluto Press.

Caplan, Jeremy. 2004. "Om-Shalomers Come of Age." *Forward* (January 16). http://www.forward.com/issues/2004/04.01.16/living1.html.

Carlson, Jeffrey. 2003. "Dual Belonging/Personal Journeys: Responses." *Buddhist-Christian Studies*. 23:77–83.

Casanova, José. 1994. *Public Religions in the Modern World*. Chicago: The University of Chicago Press.

Chafets, Zev. 2005. "The Rabbi Who Loved Evangelicals (and Vice Versa)." *New York Times* (July 24). http://select.nytimes.com/gst/abstract.html?res=F60F17F93D58 0C778EDDAE0894DD404482.

Cherry, Conrad, ed. 1998. *God's New Israel: Religious Interpretations of American Destiny*. Chapel Hill: University of North Carolina Press.

Christian Computer Connection. 2002. "Beliefnet.com Q & A." *Warriors of Christ*. http://www.warriorsofchrist.com/editorials/beliefnetq&a.shtml.

Clark, Lynn Schofield. 2002. "Overview: The 'Protestantization' of Research into Media, Religion, and Culture." In *Practicing Religion in the Age of the Media*. Ed. Stewart M. Hoover and Lynn Schofield Clark. New York: Columbia University Press.

Clooney, Francis X. 2003. "Theology, Dialogue, and Religious Others: Some Recent Books in the Theology of Religions and Related Fields." *Religious Studies Review*. 29:4 (October):319–327.

———. 2002. "God for Us: Multiple Religious Identities as a Human and Divine Prospect." In *Many Mansions? Multiple Religious Belonging and Christian Identity*. Ed. Catherine Cornille. Maryknoll, NY: Orbis Books.

Cobb, J. 1998. *Cybergrace: The Search for God in Cyberspace*. New York: Crown Books.

Committees for Monastic Interreligious Dialogue. 2005. "What is MID?" http://www.monasticdialog.com/mid.php?id=14.

Common Dreams Progressive Newswire. 2005. "Limbaugh's Religious Hate Talk Blasphemes Religion, Interfaith Alliance President Says." (April 28). http://www.commondreams.org/news2005/0428–19.htm.

Cornille, Catherine, Ed. 2002. *Many Mansions? Multiple Religious Belonging and Christian Identity*. Maryknoll, NY: Orbis Books.

Cutrer, Corrie. 2002. "'Get Our Kids Out:' Dobson Says Pro-Gay School Curriculum Has Gone Too Far." *Christianity Today* (August 5):15–16.

Davidson, James D. and Widman, Tracy. 2002. "The Effect of Group Size on Interfaith Marriage Among Catholics." *Journal for the Scientific Study of Religion* 41:3 (September):397–404.

Davidson, James D. 1998. "Interfaith Marriage." *Commonweal* (September 11):12–13.

Davis, Derek H. 2004. "Explaining the Complexities of Religion and State in the United States." In *Democracy and Religion: Free Exercise and Diverse Visions*. Ed. David W. Odell-Scott. Kent, OH: Kent State University Press.

D'Costa, Gavin. 2000. *The Meeting of Religions and the Trinity*. Maryknoll, NY: Orbis Books.

Deane, Claudia and Darryl Fears. 2006. "Negative Perception of Islam Increasing: Poll Numbers in U.S. Higher Than in 2001." *Washington Post* (March 9). http://www.washingtonpost.com/wp-dyn/content/article/2006/03/08/AR2006030802221.html.

Depuis, Jacques. 2002. *Christianity and the Religions: From Confrontation to Dialogue*. Maryknoll, NY: Orbis Books.

Duin, Julia. 2003. "Zionism Meeting Brands 'Road Map' as Heresy." *Washington Times* (May 18). http://www.washtimes.com/national/20030518–114058–5626r.htm.

Durusau, Patrick. 1998. *High Places in Cyberspace: A Guide to Biblical and Religious Studies, Classics, and Archaeological Resources on the Internet*. Atlanta: Scholars Press.

Eck, Diana L. 2001. *A New Religious America: How a "Christian Country" Has Become the World's Most Religiously Diverse Nation*. New York: HarperCollins.

———, and the President and Fellows of Harvard College. 2005. "The Pluralism Project: Mission." http://www.plurlaism.org/about/mission.php.

Eckstein, Yechiel. N.d. "Walking Together." CBN.Com. http://www.cbn.com/spirituallife/biblestudyandtheology/jewishroots/yechiel_eckstein.asp.

Edelheit, Joseph A. 2005. "*The Passion of the Christ* and Congregational Interfaith Relations." *Shofar: An Interdisciplinary Journal of Jewish Studies* 23:3 (Spring):109–113.

Eisenstein, Zillah. 1998. *Global Obscenities: Patriarchy, Capitalism, and the Lure of Cyberfantasy*. New York: New York University Press.

Fadner, Ross. 2004. "Getting Religion: Faith Goes Online, Advertisers Find Attractive Demo." *Media Daily News*. April 9. http://www.mediapostcom/dtls_dsp_news.cfm?newsID=245987&newsDate=04/09/2004.

First Amendment Center. 1999. "The Bible in Public Schools: A First Amendment Guide." Nashville, TN: First Amendment Center.

Fishman, Silvia Barack. 2004. *Double or Nothing? Jewish Families and Mixed Marriage*. Waltham, MA: Brandeis University Press.

Fonda, Daren. 2000. "Online Believer." *Time* 156:24 (December 11):24, 86.

Ford Motor Company. 2003. "On the Team: Valuing Diversity." Ford Motor Company Website. http://www.mycareer.ford.com/ONTHETEAM.ASP?CID=15.

Foxman, Abraham. 2002. "Why Evangelical Support for Israel is a Good Thing." ADL.org. http://www.adl.org/Israel/evangelical.asp.

Fredericks, James L. 1999. *Faith Among Faiths: Christian Theology and Non-Christian Religions*. New York: Paulist Press.

Glaser, Gabrielle. 1997. Strangers to the Tribe: Portraits of Interfaith Marriage. Boston: Houghton Mifflin.

Goldstein, Isaac. 2005. "Growing Up as an Interfaith Person." *CSEE* Connections (Newsletter of the Council for Spiritual and Ethical Education) (September):1, 4, 6.

GreenFaith. 2005. "About GreenFaith." http://www.greenfaith.org/core-values.html.

Grelle, Bruce. 2005. "Defining and Promoting the Study of Religion in British and American Schools." *Religion & Education* 32:1 (Spring):23–41.

Griffiths, Paul J. 2001. *Problems of Religious Diversity*. Malden, MA: Blackwell Publishing.

Guttman, Nathan. 2005. "Getting Tight with the Bible Belt." *Haaretz*. (February 16). http://www.haaretzdaily.com/hasen/pages/ShArt.jhtml?itemNo=540774.

Hammond, Phillip E. 1992. *Religion and Personal Autonomy: The Third Disestablishment in America*. Columbia: University of South Carolina Press.

Harris, Grove. 2005. "Pagan Involvement in the Interfaith Movement: Exclusions, Dualities, and Contributions." *Crosscurrents* (Spring): 66–76.

Hawxhurst, Joan C. 1998. *The Interfaith Family Guidebook: Practical Advice for Jewish and Christian Partners*. Kalamazoo, MI: Dovetail Publishing.

Haynes, Charles C. and Oliver Thomas. 2002. *Finding Common Ground: A Guide to Religious Liberty in the Public Schools*. Nashville, TN: First Amendment Center.

———. 2006. "Playing Politics with the Bible: Coming to a School Near You?" (April 16) First Amendment Center. http://www.firstamendmentcenter.org/commentary .aspx?id=16762.

Heim, S. Mark. 1995. *Salvations: Truth and Difference in Religion*. Maryknoll, NY: Orbis Books.

Held, Tom. 2005. "State's poverty rate rises fastest in nation." *Milwaukee Journal Sentinel* (August 31). http://www.jsonline.com/news/state/aug05/351964.asp.

Helland, Christopher. 2002. "Surfing for Salvation." *Religion*. 32:293–302.

———. 2000. "Online-Religion/Religion-Online and Virtual Communitas." In *Religion on the Internet: Research Prospects and Promises*. Ed. Jeffrey K. Hadden and Douglas E. Cowan. New York: JAI.

Heyn, Dalma. 2003. "Sing Hallelujah." *O, The Oprah Magazine* (December): 220.

Hick, John. 1993. *Disputed Questions in the Theology and Philosophy of Religion*. New Haven: Yale University Press.

———. 1989. *An Interpretation of Religion*. New Haven: Yale University Press.

———. 1984. "Religious Pluralism." In *The World's Religious Traditions*. Ed. Frank Whaling. New York: Crossroad.

———. 1981. "On Grading Religions." *Religious Studies* 17:451–467.

——— and Paul F. Knitter, eds. 1987. *The Myth of Christian Uniqueness: Toward a Pluralistic Theology of Religions*. Maryknoll, NY: Orbis Books.

Hoover, Stewart M. and Lynn Schofield Clark, eds. 2002. *Practicing Religion in the Age of the Media: Explorations in Media, Religion, and Culture*. New York: Columbia University Press.

Hopkins, Dwight. 2001. "The Religion of Globalization." In *Religions/Globalizations: Theories and Cases.* Ed. Dwight N. Hopkins, Lois Ann Lorentzen, Eduardo Mendieta, and David Batstone. Durham and London: Duke University Press.

Huff, Peter A. 2000. "The Challenge of Fundamentalism for Interreligious Dialogue." *Cross Currents* (spring-summer):94–102.

Hughes, Patrick C. and Fran C. Dickson. 2005. "Communication, Marital Satisfaction, and Religious Orientation in Interfaith Families." *Journal of Family Communication* 5:1 (January):25–41.

Hunter, James Davison. 1991. *Culture Wars: The Struggle to Define America.* New York: Basic Books.

Hutchison, William R. 2003. *Religious Pluralism in America: The Contentious History of a Founding Ideal.* New Haven: Yale University Press.

———. 1999. "Diversity and the Pluralist Ideal." In *Perspectives on American Religion and Culture.* Ed. Peter W. Williams. Malden, MA: Blackwell Publishers.

Iannaccone, Laurence R. "Religious Practice: A Human Capital Approach." *Journal for the Scientific Study of Religion* 29:3 (September):297–314.

Ingram, Paul O. 2001. "'Fruit Salad Can Be Delicious': The Practice of Buddhist–Christian Dialogue." *Cross Currents* (winter 2000–2001):541–549.

The Interfaith Alliance. 2005. "About The Interfaith Alliance" http://www.interfaithalliance.org/site/pp.asp?c=8dJIIWMCE&b=120694.

Interfaith Council for Environmental Stewardship. 1999. "Cornwall Declaration on Environmental Stewardship." http://www.stewards.net/CornwallDeclaration.html.

Interfaith Worker Justice. N.d. "About Us." http://www.iwj.org/aboutus/aboutus.html.

International Fellowship of Christians and Jews. 2004. "Who We Are." http://www.ifcj.org/site/PageServer?pagename=whoweare.

Jewish Outreach Institute, N.d. "Survey of the American Rabbinate." http://www.joi.org/library/research/rabbis.html.

Kaiser, Laura Fisher. 2001. "Searching for Faith." *Yahoo! Internet Life.* 7:12, 98–100.

Kaplan, Esther. 2005. "The Christian Right and the Jewish Left." *Jewish Currents* (July-August). http://www.jewishcurrents.org/2005-july-kaplan.htm.

King, Sallie. 1998. "A Global Ethic in the Light of Comparative Religious Ethics." In *Explorations on Global Ethics: Comparative Religious Ethics and Interreligious Dialogue.* Ed. Sumner B. Twiss and Bruce Grelle. Boulder, CO: Westview Press.

King, Ursula. 1998. "Feminism: The Missing Dimension in the Dialogue of Religions." In *Pluralism and Religions: The Theological and Political Dimensions.* Ed. John May. London: Cassell Academic.

Knitter, Paul F. 2002. *Introducing Theologies of Religions.* Maryknoll, NY: Orbis Books.

———. 1995. *One Earth, Many Religions: Multifaith Dialogue and Global Responsibility.* Maryknoll, NY: Orbis Books.

Kornblum, Janet. 2004. "New Online Dating Service is for Those Who Have Faith." *USA Today.com* (26 May). http://globalfactiva.com/en/arch/display.asp.

Kornblut, Anne E. 2004. "Red or Blue: Which Are You?" *Slate* (July 14). http://slate.msn.com/id/2103764/.

Kosmin, Barry A. and Seymour P. Lachman. 1993. *One Nation Under God: Religion in Contemporary American Society*. New York: Harmony Books.

Kress, Michael. 2005. "Today's Orthodox Judaism." *MyJewishLearning.Com*. http://www.myjewishlearning.com/history_community/Jewish_World_Today/Denominations/OrthodoxJudaism.htm.

Lampman, Jane. 2004. "Mixing Prophesy and Politics." *Christian Science Monitor* (July 7). http://www.csmonitor.com/2004/0707/p15s01-lire.html.

Lawrence, Bruce B. 2002. "Allah On-Line: The Practice of Global Islam in the Information Age." In *Practicing Religion in the Age of the Media*. Ed. Stewart M. Hoover and Lynn Schofield Clark. New York: Columbia University Press.

———. 2001. "God On Line: Locating the Pagan/Asian Soul of America in Cyberspace." In *Religion and Cultural Studies*. Ed. Susan L. Mizruchi. Princeton: Princeton University Press.

Lefevere, Patricia. 2003. "Sharing Wisdom, Prayer." *National Catholic Reporter* (November 11):10, 12.

Lehrer, Evelyn L. 1998. "Religious Intermarriage in the United States: Determinants and Trends." *Social Science Research* 27:245–263.

Liberty News Forum. 2005. "Good News or Bad News?" http://www.libertynewsforum.com.

Lippy, Charles H. 1999. "Pluralism and American Religious Life in the Late Twentieth Century." In *Perspectives on American Religion and Culture*. Ed. Peter W. Williams. New York: Blackwell.

Long, Marion. 2000. "True Believers: Beliefnet Preaches the E-Business of Religion." *Interactive Week*, 7:49: 98–100.

Margolis, Robin. 2003. "The Horse's Mouth: Ask the Adult Children How to Raise Interfaith Kids." *InterfaithFamily.com*. 63 (June). http://www.interfaithfamily.com/site/apps/nl/content2.asp?c+ekLSKMLIrG&B=297382.

Marks, Alexandra. 1999. "New Creed: Love Thy Neighbor's Religion." *Christian Science Monitor* 91:98 (April 14), 3.

Maxwell, Patrick. 2002. "Virtual Religion in Context." *Religion* 32:343–354.

McCarthy, Kate. 1998. "Reckoning with Religious Difference: Models of Interreligious Moral Dialogue." In *Explorations in Global Ethics: Comparative Religious Ethics and Interreligious Dialogue*. Ed. Sumner B. Twiss and Bruce Grelle. Boulder, CO: Westview Press.

———. 1996. "Women's Experience as a Hermeneutical Key to a Christian Theology of Religions." *Studies in Interreligious Dialogue* 6:2:163–173.

McClain, Ellen Jaffe. 1995. *Embracing the Stranger: Intermarriage and the Future of the American Jewish Community*. New York: Basic Books.

Melleuish, Gregory. 2005. "Globalized Religions for a Globalized World." *Policy* 21:2 (winter):16–18.

Mollenkott, Virginia Ramey, ed. *Women of Faith in Dialogue*. New York: Crossroad, 1988.

Moore, R. Laurence. 2003. *Touchdown Jesus: The Mixing of Secular and Sacred in American History*. Louisville, KY: Westminster John Knox Press.

———. 1994. *Selling God: American Religion in the Marketplace of Culture*. New York: Oxford University Press.

National Council of Churches, Committee on Regional and Local Ecumenism. 1980. "Survey of Interfaith/Inter-religious Councils in the United States." http://www.nain.org/library/councils.htm.

National Council on Bible Curriculum in Public Schools. N.d. *The Bible in History and Literature: A Comparison of Two Public School Curricula*. Greensboro, NC: National Council on Bible Curriculum in Public Schools.

National Religious Partnership for the Environment. 2005. "Partners in Stewardship." http://www.nrpe.org/index.html.

Network of Spiritual Progressives. 2006. "Network of Spiritual Progressives: A Project of the Tikkun Community." http://www.spiritualprogressives.org.

O'Leary, Stephen D. 1996. "Cyberspace as Sacred Space: Communicating Religion on Computer Networks." *Journal of the American Academy of Religion*, 59:4:781–808.

O'Neill, Maura. 1990. *Women Speaking, Women Listening*. Maryknoll, NY: Orbis Books.

Ontario Consultants on Religious Tolerance. 2005. "Comparing U.S. Religious Beliefs with Other 'Christian' Countries." *ReligiousTolerance.org*. http://www.religioustolerance.org/rel_comp.htm.

———. 2004. "How Many Wiccans Are There?" *ReligiousTolerance.org*. http://www.religioustolerance.org/wic_nbr3.htm.

Panikkar, Raimundo. 1981. *The Unknown Christ of Hinduism*. Maryknoll, NY: Orbis Books.

Patel, Eboo. 2005. "Inclusiveness and Justice: The Pitfalls and Possibilities of Interfaith Work." *Crosscurrents* (spring): 17–21.

Pedersen, Kusumita. 2004. "The Interfaith Movement: An Incomplete Assessment." *Journal of Ecumenical Studies* 41:1 (winter): 74–94.

Pew Forum on Religion & Public Life. 2003. "Religion and Politics: Contention and Consensus." http://pewforum.org/docs/print.php?DocID=26.

Pew Internet and American Life Project. 2005. "Digital Divisions: There are clear differences among those with broadband connections, dial-up connections, and no connections at all to the Internet." http://www.pewinternet.org/PPF/r/165/report_display.asp.

———. 2004. "Faith Online: 64% of wired Americans have used the Internet for spiritual or religious purposes." http://www.pewinternet.org/PPF/r/126/report_display.asp.

———. 2001. "CyberFaith: How Americans Pursue Religion Online." http://www.pewinternet.org/PPF/r/53/report_display.asp.

Pew Research Center for the People and the Press. 2002. "Among Wealthy Nations . . . U.S. Stands Alone in Its Embrace of Religion." http://people-press.org/reports/display.php3?ReportID=167.

Plaskow, Judith. 1990. *Standing Again at Sinai: Judaism from a Feminist Perspective*. New York: Harper Collins.

Pluralism Project. 2006. "Resources by Tradition: Interfaith." The President and Fellows of Harvard College and Diana L. Eck, *The Pluralism Project*. http://www.pluralism.org/resources/tradition/index.php.

——. 2005. "Statistics By Tradition." The President and Fellows of Harvard College and Diana L. Eck, *The Pluralism Project*. http://www.pluralism.org/resources/statistics/tradition.php#Paganism.

Porterfield, Amanda. 2001. *The Transformation of American Religion: The Story of a Late-Twentieth-Century Awakening*. New York: Oxford University Press.

Race, Alan. 1983. *Christians and Religious Pluralism: Patterns in the Christian Theology Religions*. Maryknoll, NY: Orbis Books.

——. 2001. *Interfaith Encounter*. London: SCM Press.

Roof, Wade Clark. 1999. *Spiritual Marketplace: Baby Boomers and the Remaking of American Religion*. Princeton, NJ: Princeton University Press.

——. 1993. *A Generation of Seekers: The Spiritual Journeys of the Baby Boom Generation*. New York: HarperCollins Publishers.

Rose, Anne C. 2001. *Beloved Strangers: Interfaith Families in Nineteenth Century America*. Cambridge: Harvard University Press.

Rosenbaum, Mary Heléne and Stanley Ned Rosenbaum. 1994. *Celebrating Our Differences: Living Two Faiths in One Marriage*. Shippensburg, PA: Ragged Edge Press.

Schippe, Cullen and Chuck Stetson. 2005. *The Bible and Its Influence*. New York and Fairfax: Bible Literacy Project Publishing.

Schrag, Carl. 2005. "American Jews and Evangelical Christians: Anatomy of a Changing Relationship." *Jewish Political Studies Review* 17:1–2 (spring). http://www.jcpa.org/cjc/cjc-schrag-s05.htm.

Schreiter, Robert. 1997. *The New Catholicity: Theology Between the Global and the Local*. Maryknoll, NY: Orbis Books.

Schwöbel, Christoph. 1990. Particularity, Universality, and the Religions." In *Christian Uniqueness Reconsidered: The Myth of a Pluralistic Theology of Religions*. Ed. Gavin D'Costa. Maryknoll, NY: Orbis Books.

Sherkat, Darren E. 2004. "Religious Intermarriage in the United States: Trends, Patterns, Predictors." *Social Science Research* 33:4 (December):606–625.

Shulevitz, Judith. 2000. "Racism, Schmacism: Opposing Intermarriage." *Slate* (May 1). http://slate.com/id/1005219.

Smith, Christian. 2005. *Soul Searching: The Religious and Spiritual Lives of American Teenagers*. New York: Oxford University Press.

Smith, Wilfred Cantwell. 1991 [1962]. *The Meaning and End of Religion*. Minneapolis: Fortress Press.

Stark, Rodney, and Roger Finke. 2000. *Acts of Faith: Explaining the Human Side of Religion*. Berkeley: University of California Press.

Surin, Kenneth. 1990. "A 'Politics of Speech:' Religious Pluralism in the Age of the McDonalds Hamburger." In *Christian Uniqueness Reconsidered: The Myth of a Pluralistic Theology of Religions*. Ed. Gavin D'Costa. Maryknoll, NY: Orbis Books.

Swearer, Donald K. 2003. "Religious Identity and Globalization: Would Jesus, Buddha, and Mohammed Drive an SUV?" Paper presented at the International Conference on Religion and Globalization, Chiang Mai, Thailand, July 27–August 2, 2003. http://isrc.payap.ac.th/document/speeches/speech07.pdf.

Swidler, Leonard. 1983. "The Dialogue Decalogue: Ground Rules for Interreligious Dialogue." *Journal of Ecumenical Studies* 20:1–4 (winter).

Takim, Liyakateli. 2004. "From Conversion to Conversation: Interfaith Dialogue in Post 9–11 America." *Muslim World* 94:3 (July):343–356.

Third International Christian Zionist Congress. 1996. "Proclamation of the 3rd International Christian Zionist Congress." http://christianactionforisrael.org/congress.html.

Thompson, Don. 2004. "Religious Study May Cut Prison Violence." *Sacramento Bee.* Religionheadlines.org. http://www.religionheadlines.org/heads_040513.php.

Tikkun magazine. 2005. "Spiritual Activism Conference." http://www.tikkun.org/community/spiritual_activism_conference/main-page.html

Tilley, Terrence W. 1999. " 'Christianity and the World Religions,' a Recent Vatican Document." *Theological Studies.* 60:2:318–338.

Troeltsch, Ernst. 1923. "The Place of Christianity Among the World Religions." *In Christian Thought: Its History and Application.* Translated by various hands and edited with an introduction by Baron F. von Hugel. London: University of London Press, Ltd.

Underwood, Meredith. 2000. "Lost in Cyberspace? Gender, Difference, and the Internet 'Utopia' " In *Religion and Popular Culture in America.* Ed. Bruce David Forbes and Jeffrey H. Mahan. Berkeley: University of California Press.

U.S. Newswire. 2005. "Interfaith Organizations Call on Congress to Form Ethical Commission for Reconstruction of Gulf-Coast Region." (September 23). http://releases.usnewswire.com/GetRelease.asp?id=53927.

Voice of America Press Releases and Documents. 2004. " 'Beliefnet' Offers On-line Alternative for Spiritual Growth." http://global.factiva.com/en/arch/display/.asp

Wald, Kenneth D. 2003. *Religion and Politics in the United States*, 4th Ed. Lanham, MD: Rowan and Littlefield.

Walsh, Andrew. 2005. "Presbyterians Divest the Jews." *Religion in the News* 8:2 (fall):18–21.

Weber, Sheila. 2005. Personal interview with author. November 4.

Wentz, Richard E. 1998. *The Culture of Religious Pluralism.* Boulder, CO: Westview Press.

Wertheim, Margaret. 1999. *The Pearly Gates of Cyberspace: A History of Space from Dante to the Internet.* New York: W.W. Norton & Company.

Williams, Rhys H., Ed. 1997. *Culture Wars in American Politics: Critical Reviews of a Popular Myth.* New York: William de Gruyter.

Wuthnow, Robert. 2005. *America and the Challenges of Religious Diversity.* Princeton, NJ: Princeton University Press.

———. 1998. *After Heaven: Spirituality in America Since the 1950s.* Berkeley: University of California Press.

———. 1988. *The Restructuring of American Religion: Society and Faith Since World War II.* Princeton, NJ: Princeton University Press.

Zalesky, Jeffrey P. 1997. *The Soul of Cyberspace.* San Francisco: HarperEdge.

INDEX

ABOUT THE AUTHOR

KATE McCARTHY is an associate professor of Religious Studies and coordinator of the Women's Studies Program at California State University, Chico.